IN THE FAMILY WAY

Only a generation or two ago, illegitimacy was one of the most shameful things that could happen in a family. Today, babies' parents are as likely to be unmarried as married. This revolution in public opinion makes it easy to forget what it was like to give birth, or be born, out of wedlock in the years between the First World War and the dawn of the permissive age. *In the Family Way* tells secrets kept for entire lifetimes; in it we hear long-silent voices from the workhouse, the Magdalene Laundry, and the distant mother-and-baby home. Anonymous childhoods are recalled, spent in the care of Dr Barnardo or a child migration scheme halfway across the world. There are sorrowful stories — but also stories of hope, of triumph and the everyday strength of the human spirit.

JANE ROBINSON

◆

IN THE FAMILY WAY

Illegitimacy Between the Great War
and the Swinging Sixties

Complete and Unabridged

CHARNWOOD
Leicester

First published in Great Britain in 2015 by
Viking
Penguin Books Ltd
London

First Charnwood Edition
published 2016
by arrangement with
Penguin Books Ltd
The Penguin Group
London

The moral right of the author has been asserted

For full details of the Notes, Bibliography and Index,
please refer to the standard print edition of this title
published by Viking, Penguin Books Ltd.

A catalogue record for this book is available
from the British Library.

ISBN 978–1–4448–2708–8

Published by
F. A. Thorpe (Publishing)
Anstey, Leicestershire

Set by Words & Graphics Ltd.
Anstey, Leicestershire
Printed and bound in Great Britain by
T. J. International Ltd., Padstow, Cornwall

This book is printed on acid-free paper

For Sue, and in memory of Helen

Contents

List of Illustrations xi

Acknowledgements........................xv

Introduction............................xix

1. Filius Nullius: Illegitimacy before
   the Great War...............................1

2. Little Bastards: The Meaning of
   Illegitimacy 40

3. The Woman Who Did: Unmarried
   Mothers....................................68

4. Pater Nullius: Unmarried Fathers 100

5. Black Lamb of the Black Sheep:
   Moral and Legal Judgement 131

6. All the Way to Blackpool: Sex,
   Pregnancy and Birth-control.............161

7. Ungentle Birth: The Confinement.......192

8. Love-child: The First Six Weeks 222

9. Odd One Out: Growing Up Without
   Birth-parents..............................253

10. Lost Innocents: Child Migration 281

11. Mummy's Little Secret: Staying
    Together..................................303

12. Bad Blood: Attitudes to Single Parents ..332

13. Shame and Pride: Reflections...........350

List of Illustrations

Section One

1. 'Able Bodied Inmates' at a Leeds workhouse in the 1920s *(Medical Illustration Services, Leeds Teaching Hospitals NHS Trust)*
2 & 3. Foundlings were left at Coram's Hospital with distinctive tokens to identify their origins *(Foundling Museum)*
4. Captain Thomas Coram, who established the Foundling Hospital in London in 1739 *(Coram in the care of the Foundling Museum)*
5. The grandeur of Coram's Hospital and its illustrious patrons made his charity fashionable *(Coram in the care of the Foundling Museum)*
6. At the Babies' Castle, a Barnardo's home in Kent, it is time for a non-negotiable nap, October 1935 *(Getty Images)*
7. Saying prayers at the Babies' Castle, March 1963 *(Getty Images)*
8. A magazine appeal for Dr Barnardo's homes, 1930s *(Advertising Archives)*
9. Barnardo's boys in Stepney being trained as wheelwrights *(Bridgeman Art Library)*
10. Chastened single mothers sew church embroideries at the Horbury House of Mercy in Wakefield *(Mary Evans Picture Library)*
11. Success stories like Tom Bertram's were publicized to prove that illegitimate and disadvantaged

xi

children were not inherently corrupt *(From If?, a Dr Barnardo's Homes pamphlet,* 1911)

12. Maud was inspired by the suffragettes in exercising her right not to marry the father of her children *(Private collection)*

13. A birth-control nurse outside one of Marie Stopes's mobile clinics in the 1920s *(Wellcome Institute)*

Section Two

14. A cautionary tale is told in the Christmas edition of *Lucky Star,* 1936 *(Colindale Newspaper Library)*

15. *The Deliverer* reported the Salvation Army's mission to rescue unmarried mothers and their illegitimate children between 1889 and 1993 *(Salvation Army)*

16 & 17. Feeding-time was part of a strict routine at Salvation Army mother-and-baby homes (Salvation Army)

18. Children set off on SS *Oronsay* en route for Fairbridge Farm School, Molong, Australia, 1938 *(Molong Historical Society)*

19. 'Future landowners' in Canada photographed by Barnardo's in 1912 *(Mary Evans Picture Library)*

20. A plan of Fairbridge Village in Pinjarra, Australia *(www. pinjarrabibleschool.com)*

21. Clearing the ground at Pinjarra in order to expand the Fairbridge Village *(State Library of Western Australia, the Battye Library 4648B/5)*

22. Good Shepherd Magdalene Asylum looms over the Co. Cork countryside *(Tarquin Blake)*

23. A memorial to deceased single mothers — or

'Penitents' — from the Mecklenburg Street Asylum in Dublin *(Magdalenlaundries.com)*

24. The unwelcoming door of Gloucester St. Magdalene Asylum in Dublin, where Samantha's mother, Margaret, spent thirty-five years of her life (John Fitzpatrick)

25. Mealtime in the nursery at Sean Ross Abbey, Co. Tipperary, in the mid-1950s *(Brian Lockier/ Adoptionrightsalliance.com)*

26. An empty cradle in a convent wall ready to receive modern foundlings in Poland *(www.d-.naszemiasto.pl)*

27. A Health Education Council poster of a 'pregnant' father *(Poster by Alan Brooking © Gift of the American Friends of the V&A)*

Acknowledgements

When I first thought of writing *In the Family Way* my worry was that I might not find enough material. I could do the history bit: that only needed some judicious research. But at the core of the book in my mind's eye was a narrative of other people's secrets; untold stories of masquerade and in many cases, of shame. Naturally, these are very private matters, shared only — if at all — with those we trust implicitly.

Miraculously, it turned out that all I had to do was ask. A short paragraph in a few different magazines and newsletters asking for experiences of the stigma of illegitimacy brought in scores of responses (the editor and readers of *Saga Magazine* were particularly magnificent). So did an email to everyone I knew, to be forwarded to everyone they knew, requesting help. Visitors to my website, blog and Twitter account came up trumps; each time I gave a talk and was asked about work in progress, I appealed for contributions. In the end I had well over 100 secret histories in my possession. I could not offer much in return: just my determination to tell other people what it was *really* like to be or to bear an illegitimate child during the cloyingly polite years between the Great War and the so-called Swinging Sixties. That, and the promise of confidentiality.

My promise means that even though some

people didn't mind my using their real names, I rarely did so and have made a decision not to acknowledge contributors individually. That feels mean, but it avoids confusion and the possibility of distress. I hope they appreciate why I have come to that decision, and realize that it doesn't diminish my sense of obligation and gratitude. It was not easy for most of them to revisit what happened, and few of our interviews passed without tears (of happiness and relief, as well as sorrow or regret). Thank you, all of you, for the privilege you have given me.

On a more practical note, for permission to quote from material in their custody I am indebted to Barnardo's and the Liverpool University Library Special Collections; the British Library Oral History Collection; the *Foundling Voices* project at the Foundling Museum, London; Faber and Faber Ltd; Steve Humphries of Testament Films; the Imperial War Museum; Herbert Kretzmer; the Trustees of the Mass Observation Archive, University of Sussex (material reproduced with permission of Curtis Brown Group Ltd London on their behalf); the Museum of London Oral History Collection; Major Kevin Pooley and staff at the Salvation Army International Heritage Centre; the Principal and Fellows of Somerville College, Oxford; Elizabeth Roberts; Christine Wilkinson of the Elizabeth Roberts Archive, Centre for North-West Regional Studies, Lancaster University; and the 'Their History' website.

I found valuable background material at the Bodleian Library; Cambridge University Library; East Midlands Oral History Archive; the East

Sussex Record Office; the UK Data Service (particularly Dennis Marsden's study on fatherless families); the library at the Wellcome Collection; and the Women's Library at the London School of Economics, which houses the archive of the National Council for the Unmarried Mother and her Child.

As ever, I owe much to my agent, Véronique Baxter; to my editor, Eleo Gordon, who is beyond compare, and to my friends who always seem to know when I need rescuing from reclusion. This was never supposed to be a book about my own family, but I realize now that on several levels it is just that, and I am grateful to my cousins, my sister, my husband and my children. I love them all dearly, and am so proud to think that they belong to me, and I to them.

While every effort has been made to contact copyright holders, the publishers would be pleased to hear from any not here acknowledged.

Introduction

*I sometimes think we're close in this family but
I realize it's because we don't talk about
anything.*

The year 2013 was a momentous one. If Philip
Larkin is to be believed, it marked the half-
centenary of sex. In his poem 'Annus Mirabilis',
he reckons that 1963 is when it all began (too
late for him, unfortunately), between the lifting
of the ban on *Lady Chatterley's Lover* and the
Beatles' first album. I can't say I remember any
particular festivities surrounding the anniversary,
but I do live in the provinces, where there is
sometimes a bit of a time-lag.

In some ways, this book commemorates that
jubilee. It is not a celebration of the discovery of
sex, because that isn't what Larkin meant. He
was really writing about the arrival of the
permissive age, when we were allowed to *talk*
about sex frankly for the first time. *In the Family
Way* breaks the silence which surrounded
illegitimacy, one of the most potent of sexual
taboos. It centres on the first-hand experiences
of unmarried parents and their children in an era
when no one talked about them except with
crude humour, disgust or derision. In fact no
one talked about them so successfully that even
now, fifty years and more from Larkin's year of

marvels, their stories are stigmatized by guilt and shame.

I was a child in the 1960s, a student in the late seventies and early eighties, and have been a working mother since 1990. That means I am a daughter of Larkin's permissive age, and therefore of the generation which is not supposed to care if people had children, or were born, out of wedlock. When I mentioned the subject of this book to a young friend in his early twenties, he simply shrugged his shoulders and asked 'And?' He and his contemporaries can have no idea how dark a secret illegitimacy was, and what was the cost of keeping it hidden away. The concept of illegitimacy hardly exists any more, either in law or in our daily lives. The parents of babies born now, in the second decade of the twenty-first century, are more likely to be unmarried than married.

While this moral latitude is broadly welcomed, it does beg a few questions. Why did most of my interviewees insist on anonymity? Why did some of them tell me things they had not yet dared to tell their closest family? Given our comparative liberality as a society, why are we so ignorant of what illegitimacy really meant such a short time ago? Those of us born during the 1960s and afterwards accept it largely without demur, but in our rush to do so, have not yet had time to understand its legacy. The ability to talk freely about things that matter must surely be the greatest gift of the permissive age, but the stigma surrounding illegitimacy was so intense, so lingering, that the subject is still concealed by shadows.

Perhaps our collective passion for family history will eventually rescue illegitimacy from its embarrassed obscurity. Tracing our ancestry is the fastest-growing hobby in the UK and North America. When the 1911 census went online in Britain there were 1.2 million hits an hour on the first day alone. So feverish was the public appetite for first-hand family history that the site crashed. Television screens and news-stands are full of programmes and magazines attracting masses of enthusiasts. Genealogy websites teem with subscribers engaged in finding out where they came from, and imagining the lives of their forebears. A recent newspaper article attributed this popularity boom to the need for a strong sense of self in what some would have us believe is a broken society; a society where the family unit has been irreparably fragmented: 'the crux of it is a need to feel rooted and connected'. No doubt that is true, but I think it also has to do with a widespread fascination with the social history of ordinary people, people who belong to us and with whom we can identify.

No family history is complete, however, without the acknowledgement of illegitimacy. Writing this book has taught me that in many cases, making such an acknowledgement requires both courage and forbearance. Family life can still be governed by silences, and things — people — we do not care to discuss. Few of us have a family tree without unexplained gaps here and there; a cupboard devoid of skeletons; a genealogy that has not been redacted in some way. Family history is full of illusions.

Many of the people I met in the course of my research found it hard to express what happened to them, and how they were treated. Secrecy is a difficult habit to break, after all. Despite that, *In the Family Way* turns out to be less a story of victims or outrage than of coping with difficult circumstances, and the everyday strength of the human spirit. One gentleman I interviewed even said he was proud to have been born on the wrong side of the blanket and brought up in care; it meant he could start his own dynasty on his own terms, unfettered by the past. That, he said, was a rare privilege. Others spoke of the special closeness that can exist between single parents and their children, or the triumphant discovery of new relationships. It's not all bad.

The hushed whispers surrounding illegitimacy in the past offend me as an historian, because they have resulted in censorship. On a more personal level, given the amount of emotional upheaval, I can't help feeling it to be unbelievably unfair that those involved have been denied a voice on the grounds of public decency. If the stigma of illegitimacy still so potent among older generations were demystified a little, we would learn more about ourselves and our society; about our strengths as well as our weaknesses. This is what I have tried to do: hand over the stage to those mothers, fathers and children who have traditionally been regarded only as associate members of the family or as outcasts. It is a credit to them that as well as being about sorrow, this is a book about hope, forgiveness, and finally telling the truth.

Those who have contributed their experiences to *In the Family Way* have been extraordinarily generous. Most were happy to help on condition that they be given pseudonyms. It is therefore a good idea to assume that all names have been changed, even though a few people asked me to keep their own. I have used first names only, unless quoting from an already published source. Occasionally, for various reasons, two people have the same name; to avoid any risk of confusion in these cases I have simply added the initials 'A' or 'B'.

1

Filius Nullius:
Illegitimacy before the Great War

Great inconveniences have been found to arise from single women pregnant with children likely to be born bastards.

Doesn't everyone think at some time during childhood that they have somehow been landed with the wrong family? I remember the moment clearly. I was six, sitting on my bed, having just been grounded by my father for riding a new bicycle too near the main road. I was struggling to understand how my parents could be so unfair. Then it came to me: they did not realize who I was. There had obviously been a calamitous mix-up at the maternity hospital, and while some king and queen somewhere were bringing up an ordinary child as their own, I — the rightful princess — was stuck here in Yorkshire with a confiscated bike and no tea.

For a while I rather liked the romantically tragic idea of being with unnatural parents, and often used to ask whether or not I had been adopted. Eventually, to keep me quiet, my mother Helen told me the story of her marriage to my father.

Helen was a student at the London School of Economics, which was evacuated *en masse* to

Cambridge during the war. She had a nice boyfriend called Rob. At the same time my father, Neil, had been sent to the university town from his native Glasgow to complete his military training before a two-year posting to India. Beryl was his girlfriend. One summer's day in 1945, Helen and Rob went punting. So did Neil and Beryl, and as the two couples slid past each other in opposite directions, my parents' eyes met, and briefly locked. Two weeks later they became engaged.

Neil's posting was imminent, so they decided to marry as quickly as possible. They needed the permission of Helen's father to do so, since at twenty she was legally still a child. Persuading him that such a hasty marriage was a good idea would take time, however, which they did not have. So they forged a letter and went ahead with the ceremony, within a month of meeting. That, said my mother, meant that technically I was quite possibly illegitimate, even though I was born fourteen years after the event. To me, this was almost as good as being adopted.

I am embarrassed by my ignorance about illegitimacy and adoption, young as I was. No one told me; my own family, though well-intentioned, was complicit in the sort of denial we shall hear about over and over again in this book. They knew the truth about my cousin Sue, for instance, but kept silent.

Sue is beautiful, articulate, witty and kind. She is one of the least judgemental people one could meet. Her house is welcoming, full of light and colour; she lives for the day, makes the most of

2

things, and to me, is a bit of a hero.

She is also illegitimate.

Sue was born in 1949, well before illegitimacy lost its toxic implication in the real world. Then, any child born out of wedlock was called a bastard. Not a mistake, nor even misbegotten, but a bastard. Her mother, Paula, already had a daughter, born after a shotgun wedding to a wealthy farmer's son when Paula was eighteen. The marriage soon ended in divorce. Then Paula met Arthur. He was a teacher, remembered by the family as gorgeously handsome. Paula was intelligent and cultured; she had been a model, and now worked as a cashier at a fashionable seaside pavilion, where she loved to dance. They made a pretty couple. A year later, another girl was born, and a year after that, Sue.

Just before Sue's first birthday, Arthur's elderly father unburdened himself of a secret. It was Arthur's secret, really. He and Paula had been together for three years now, and all this time he had been married to somebody else. Looking back from our own permissive age, it is difficult to see why this should have mattered too much, since they had not attempted to marry each other. Bigamy wasn't involved. Yet the news appears to have had a seismic effect on the family: straight away the girls were bundled off to live with Arthur's parents, and when they couldn't cope, Sue was sent on to a succession of private foster-homes. It is at this point that the girls were separated. Sue did not even know she had sisters until more than forty years later.

What was it that really splintered the family

apart? A false sense of decorum, probably, and the simplistic hope that by removing the product of sin, the sin itself would disappear. So much unhappiness has sprung from the fear of what the neighbours might think. But during the buttoned-up 1950s, and before, what the neighbours thought could define who you were, and the sins of the fathers were constantly hacking at the door, eager to visit themselves on the next generation.

Sue's recollection of those foster-homes is confused. One of them, where she stayed for about eighteen months, was nice; when the money dried up to pay for it, however, she was sent to a cheaper establishment where the woman looking after her used to brand her with the bowl of a heated teaspoon. The next people were supposed to be interested in adopting Sue, but changed their minds. So, at five years and seven months old, she ended up in a Church of England children's home.

The next chapter in Sue's life is almost Dickensian in its awfulness.

Sue's memories of the home are as lucent as lantern-slides, but unconnected. A boy sweeps down the banister towards her, and asks whether she is happy. She answers guilelessly. 'Too bad,' he replies, 'because you're going to be here for the rest of your life.' She steals another child's birthday cards and pretends they are hers. At Easter she is the only one with no chocolate eggs. When most of the inmates are treated to a cinema visit, Sue has to stay behind (she is only five and therefore too young to go). Instead, she is told to clean everyone's shoes. She is not used to school, since her various foster-parents rarely bothered to send her. All Sue will do is draw repeated pictures of a house with brave rows of flowers outside.

At the age of six-and-a-half, Sue was chosen by a middle-aged couple to be their adoptive child. If this were a fairy-tale, she would be whisked to that very house with the flowers, and grow up cherished and secure. It would be easy to trace her present generosity of spirit to her rescue in the nick of time from the curse of illegitimacy. Give me a child for his first seven years, say the Jesuits, and I shall give you the man. In reality, life was still extremely difficult for Sue. Her new parents had lost a daughter at the age of twelve; Sue was to be her substitute. This was not particularly unusual. Perfectly respectable women's magazines used to carry advertisements for infants wanted or (essentially) for sale, sometimes pathetically explaining that they were to take the place of drowned daughters, or sons who had been run over.

Sue's new mother was forty-three: my mother Helen's sister. Her father was fifty, and she had a ready-made and temporarily resentful sibling, understandably suspicious of the cuckoo in the nest. She smiles about it now: how terrified she was on the first night in her new home when she felt something slip into bed beside her in the dark, its breath hot and heavy on her neck. The poor child was used to being molested, and assumed this to be another episode in the bewildering and bleak adult world to which she

5

had been consigned. Too scared to move, she lay shuddering all night, until with a warm, wet lick and a grunt, her companion revealed himself to be the resident whippet. Whippo went on to become one of Sue's closest friends.

For the first eighteen months, Sue was 'on approval'. Miss Trump was a social worker in a leaden-grey suit who regularly came to visit, and Sue was well aware that she could be returned to the children's home at any time, either by Miss Trump or by her new parents. When she was eight, however, all the necessary papers were signed, and Sue formally became someone new.

She was an introverted child. Undoubtedly clever, she had neither the confidence nor the support to excel academically. Expectations of her were cripplingly low, as they were of most illegitimate children at the time. Questionable morality was considered heritable, and with it, intellectual weakness. A clever bastard was something else altogether. Sue was lonely — although members of her parents' family welcomed her with warmth — and unsure how to relate to other children. She was sometimes left out when her mother and father went to the pub or on other outings and felt puzzled and unwanted. By the time she reached her twenties, she was, as she puts it, 'a mess'. By then my uncle had died; my aunt had married again, selling up the home, and determined to forget her old life. Although they later became close, at this point Sue felt abandoned.

With graceful understatement Sue attributes her problems to flaws in her own character, to clashes of personality and to the stigma of being adopted, a fact my aunt pointed out to friends and acquaintances. She would not have been adopted were she not a bastard, however. It was from her illegitimacy that the problems stemmed — or rather, from the public revelation of her illegitimacy. In common with many people in this book, whether birth-mother, occasionally birth-father, or illegitimate child, she was cast as a victim. But the fact that she eventually refused this role is something else they have in common, as we shall see.

* * *

During the medieval period, marriage had little to do with the state. All that was required to make holy matrimony lawful was a formal priestly blessing. Illegitimacy, therefore, did not exist in a literal sense, and the Church looked more kindly than we might imagine on couples 'wed' without the 'lock', as long as they lived in faithfulness and love. It was not uncommon for betrothed men to try before they buy, to test whether or not their intended wife was fertile. Once she had become safely pregnant, they would marry. Different corners of the country dealt with this trial period in different ways. In parts of Wales courting couples were positively encouraged to indulge in 'bundling' by sharing a bed, and in Dorset, a groom was expected to 'prove' his bride before they wed. Yorkshire men and women had only to hold hands and leap cleanly over a broomstick wedged in a doorway to cement their relationship. They could get married properly later on, if a baby came; if not, they could just reverse the move over the broom (not easy) and the job would be done.

Christianity teaches forgiveness and charity. So whenever possible, 'unwanted' babies were embraced into close-knit families, sponsored by the feudal lord, passed on to someone who could bring them up usefully, or taken into the care of a local religious order. One of the benefactions of Richard ('Dick') Whittington, Mayor of London at the turn of the fifteenth century, was 'a newe chambyr with viii beddys for young wemen that had done a-mysse, in trust for a good mendement'. Such 'wemen' were not automatically assumed to be beyond redemption, and their children were gifts from God. This does not mean that bastardy was accepted without demur. Marriage was a sacrament, and fornication a sin. But the spirit could be credited for being willing, even if the flesh proved weak. 'Give me chastity, oh Lord,' said St Augustine, 'but not yet.' He knew what he was talking about: he had a bastard of his own.

Things changed in the sixteenth century. Parish registers were instituted, where bastards were officially recorded for the first time, set apart from their peers, and their status articulated.

More significant than this was the dissolution of the monasteries in the 1530s. Religious houses had traditionally offered alms and sanctuary to the homeless, including abandoned mothers and their children; now other arrangements would have to be made if the country were not to be overrun with costly and possibly dangerous social misfits. The answer, as it has been so often since, was to tether them with red-tape.

Lists were drawn up categorizing the poor. Three degrees of poverty were identified: the poor by impotency, the poor by casualty, and the thriftless poor. Each of these classifications was in turn subdivided into three. Top of the list of the impotent poor came 'the fatherless and poor man's child' (not necessarily bastards, more likely the children of beggars' widows). Then came the aged, blind and lame, and finally the chronically diseased. The poor by casualty comprised wounded soldiers, 'decayed' house-holders (those who had fallen on hard times), and the acutely ill. 'The rioter that consumeth all' headed the thriftless poor, with people of no fixed abode, and 'the idle person, as strumpets and others'.

Strictly speaking, a strumpet was a prostitute, but by association it became one of a pungent litany of terms referring to an unmarried mother, embracing lewd woman, fallen woman, she who had 'deviated from the paths of virtue', and bitch. These creatures were doubly culpable if they chose to bring fatherless children into the world (and it was deemed a choice, whatever the circumstances). By breeding irresponsibly, they diminished everyone's share of the parish purse. Being subsidized for doing so tempted other weak-willed women to try the same thing. They were the sponging single mums of their day.

In London, and gradually elsewhere, specific institutions were built to accommodate all these types. The impotent could go to 'hospitals' founded by charitable donation to feed, educate or nurse them according to their needs. The poor by casualty were cared for similarly, with medical hospitals like St Thomas's or St Bartholomew's available for the grievously sick. For the thriftless — those who were wilfully poor — somewhere desperate like Bridewell Prison was prescribed. They were the least deserving and the most expensive members of the parish. They must be punished.

This new fashion of categorizing the poor neatly designated the class distinctions of bastardy. Like Charles II, with his Fitzroys and Fitzcharleses, Henry VIII is said to have fathered at least six illegitimate children (including another Fitzroy), in a fine old tradition stretching from the love-child William the Conqueror, through Shakespeare's 'Bastard Plantagenets', then beyond the Tudors as far as George IV, and possibly further than that. The upper-class fashion of cheerfully producing lusty little offshoots for the family tree did not fall out of favour until the First World War, and the 'baton sinister', that heraldic device used discreetly to denote a bastard on his coat-of-arms, was almost a badge of pride.

The African explorer Sir Henry Morton Stanley was illegitimate; so were Lawrence of Arabia, the MP Ramsay MacDonald, who went on to become the UK's first Labour prime minister, and Sarah Bernhardt (although she *was* an actress). Writer H. G. Wells fathered a son by his lover Rebecca West, and then there was

Bertie, of course, King Edward the Caresser, with a silken string of mistresses and — allegedly — a number of unacknowledged bastards for souvenirs.

The Poor Law Act of 1576 obviously did not affect such people as kings and public figures; it dealt instead with

> Bastards begotten and born out of lawful matrimony (an offence against God's and Man's laws) the said bastards being now left to be kept at the charge of the Parish and in defrauding of the relief of impotent and aged true poor of the same Parish, and to the evil example and the encouragement of lewd life.

Building on the logic of that list of the poor, illegitimacy became an economic as well as a moral problem. After 1601, rates were levied on all parishioners to provide relief for the impoverished, and in the case of unwed mothers there is a sense that parishes resented having to pay the wages of sin themselves. The focus of that resentment spread from the feckless, lascivious women who bore children out of wedlock, to putative fathers, and inevitably to the children themselves. A mother accused of giving birth to a bastard could be ordered to repay the parish, although she rarely had the means to do so. It was a more profitable notion to pursue the natural father for financial support, but first the mother needed to know who he was (not always certain), then have the courage to name

11

him, before the parish could attempt to collar him and extract his money.

Meanwhile, to punish the mother and deter her or others from repeating her crime, penalties were stipulated. These varied according to the circumstances of the offence, the relative leniency of the parish authorities, and the perceived degree of evil intent. Repeat offenders were much more harshly treated than novices. The mildest of sentences was public penance, usually performed during 'churching', when a mother was blessed after childbirth. It was a ceremony of purification, and for unwed mothers especially, a timely opportunity to shrive the soul as well as the body. More shameful scourges included being clamped in the stocks or whipped, or having to parade the streets dressed all in white with a notice pinned to you, proclaiming your sin. Worst of all was committal (after 1610) to a house of correction for a year, with hard labour.

Fathers, if they could be identified satisfactorily and apprehended, were fined if they refused to pay maintenance; the financial responsibility for a bastard was theirs, but the moral culpability remained the mother's. That is not to say that men were not punished in other ways, if the local authorities saw fit. There is a record in Shropshire of an 'old, old, very old man', Thomas Par of Alderbury, ambitiously being arraigned in 1588 for refusing to maintain his bastard baby. He is said to have been 106 at the time.

The unfortunate child in the middle of all this

censure was commonly forgotten, or dismissed as an inconvenience. No one's son: that is the meaning of *filius nullius*, the legal term used historically to denote children born out of wedlock. According to the commentator William Blackstone, writing in 1766, even *filius nullius* was something of a misnomer, since in law bastards were not strictly children at all. Real children inherited their fathers' property; they passed down their fathers' name; they were supported by their fathers and supported them in return, when the time came. Bastards had no inherent claim to do any of these things. Well into the twentieth century it was popularly believed that they could not even go to heaven. They lived in a perpetual limbo, associate members of society only, with neither rights nor responsibilities of their own.

One of the first people to challenge this attitude was Thomas Coram (1668 — 1751). He was a retired sea captain who embarked on a mission to provide care for the street children of London. Many of them were discarded illegitimates, living and dying in appalling conditions, quite unprotected by parents or any other authority. Coram campaigned for seventeen years to raise funds for his Foundling Hospital, which opened 'for the Maintenance and Education of Exposed and Deserted Young Children' in 1739. The Coram charity still exists, although the hospital finally closed in 1954.

Thomas was a master of public relations. He attracted a Royal Charter from George II, allegedly the father of two bastards himself; one of the most fashionable artists of the day, the childless William Hogarth, was a founder governor, and similarly childless George Frederic Handel conducted and composed for the Foundling musicians. The first two children to be received into the hospital — of 117 received on the opening day — were given a unique honour. When they were baptized and re-named, as everyone was on admission, they were given the surname Coram. The philosophy behind a change of identity was simple. An anonymous start would mean a clean slate, a new life, and a future sustained by good will rather than victimization. No matter what their origins, the children were assumed to be innocent — not usually a term associated with bastardy.

Until the beginning of the nineteenth century, women allowed to leave their babies at Coram's were asked to include a little token with them, to identify them in the future, should some unexpected good fortune mean the child might be reclaimed. It could be a button, a bunch of ribbon, a cheap coin or a squashed thimble; each would be carefully attached to the child's record. Poignantly, most remain in the hospital's collections. Coram's was begged to take many more babies than it could maintain, especially when it was given a grant by the Government in 1759 on condition that it turned no one away. After that, consignments started arriving from all over the country, like sub-standard fruit to market; some were reported to be half-dead, sent to Coram's to avoid funeral expenses. No doubt others were dispatched in the genuine hope that their lives might be saved. Even so, the mortality rate of all the children at the hospital, in the early days, was said to be 66 per cent.

Though slightly higher than the national average, estimated at about 45 per cent, this was still better than most alternatives for illegitimate babies. At a similar establishment in Dublin, a forerunner of the notorious Magdalene asylums for fallen women, four out of every five babies died. The Magdalene asylums themselves were run more as houses of correction than refuges, and were later taken over by the Catholic Church. The first one opened in Whitechapel, London, in 1758, for unchaste women between the ages of fifteen and twenty. A second one appeared in London thirty years later, and another in Edinburgh in 1797, both with a wider age-range but the same unforgiving principles. They were penitentiaries, whose inmates were held to be solely responsible for their transgressions, and made to work in expiation, sometimes for the rest of their lives.

⋆　⋆　⋆

Magdalene asylums strike the same sort of terror in the public imagination now as workhouses, or poorhouses, used to do in Victorian times. The workhouse lurked menacingly in the background of Charles Dickens's most memorable novels; it featured in popular wood-engravings of doe-eyed, wan-faced children in rags, used as publicity for an ever-growing number of philanthropic enterprises; and in real life, the threat of ending up there was sinister enough to deter generations of young men and women from pre-marital sex. Right up until the 1930s, when the last ones closed, being sent to the workhouse was a palpable sort of hell: the sure consequence of doing wrong. At worst it meant separation from family members, complete denial of dignity, and too often in times of disease, a sentence of death.

At best, it offered sanctuary and a source of free medical care. Not all workhouses were terrible. It depended on the local Guardians in charge, and on the sense and sensibilities of any lady volunteers who could be mustered to visit and bring donations of food and clothes for residents. The main problem for unmarried mothers with regard to workhouses was a clause in the Poor Law Amendment Act of 1834, stating that they were not eligible for 'out-relief', or alms disbursed to help them in their own homes. So the choice was stark: if they could not maintain their own bastards, they must be committed to the workhouse with prostitutes, rogues, the senile, the insane, and all the other flotsam and jetsam of society.

Only their local workhouse — that is, the workhouse in their place of birth or settlement — was obliged to take them. When emergencies arose, other arrangements could be made, but there are shocking stories of abandoned mothers in labour far from home being forcibly carted to the next neighbourhood and dumped, as someone else's problem. Certain workhouses dressed them in a uniform to advertise their special sinfulness. In Bristol, for example, they were given a bright red gown. On the Isle of Wight they had coarse and scratchy yellow coats to wear, and were not allowed to eat 'solid' meat, only soup. Elsewhere they were fed gruel, not permitted to go to church and neglected to the extent that in Steyning in Sussex, local men used to climb through the windows and rape them — and so the cycle of pregnancy and punishment would begin all over again.

Outside the workhouses' forbidding walls, and despite Captain Coram's kind-hearted legacy, nineteenth-century city streets still teemed with unclaimed and unprotected bastards. Courts tried to galvanize their fathers into providing for them; now they could be imprisoned if they failed to maintain a child proven to be theirs. But proof was almost impossible. A mother's word was not enough; her evidence had somehow to be corroborated. Occasionally the putative father would admit to his misdemeanour. An iron worker called John Noble appears at Lincoln Petty Sessions in November 1853, accused of being the father of a bastard whose mother is applying for 'affiliation' or maintenance pay-ments. This sounds reasonable: he has only been married for three months, and that is to another woman. Besides, he has half a dozen other children 'in different parts of the country' so knows the ropes. He is already paying affiliation to their mothers, and pleads that while content to contribute to this most recent little Noble, he should not be expected to offer too much. He wants a discount for quantity. Nevertheless, he is

17

ordered to pay two shillings a week, which amounts to just below 10 per cent of his income. His new wife must have been thrilled.

Local parish records have been kept since 1538 but in July 1837, the state registration of births, deaths and marriages became compulsory in England and Wales (Scotland followed in 1855). That is when birth certificates were first issued, thus intensifying the shame attached to illegitimacy. Contrary to popular belief, a bastard's father was never officially entered as 'unknown', nor was the appropriate box left blank. The registrar simply drew a dash through it. *Filius nullius*. The only exception would be if the father came along with the mother to register the baby, and she gave her express permission for him to be acknowledged and his surname used. If he was not physically present, the child was obliged to take the mother's surname.

Five years later, in 1842, the ratio of illegitimate to legitimate live births was published for the first time. There were sixty-six per 1,000. The total number of live births that year was just over 517,000, which suggests about 34,000 bastards. They could not all be sent to Coram's or other such hospitals; they wouldn't fit into the workhouses, and there were too many for every straitened birth-family to take in themselves. It was clear that something more must be done. Not necessarily for the unmarried mother: despite the best literary endeavours of Charles Dickens, Elizabeth Gaskell, George Eliot, Wilkie Collins — all of whom wrote sympathetic novels involving illegitimacy — the

18

general attitude to her was that she had made her bed and must lie in it. (Besides, novelists themselves were not always as well-behaved as they should be in that department — hadn't George Eliot lived in sin? And wasn't Mary Braddon, author of the sensational *Lady Audley's Secret*, herself an unmarried mother?) Perhaps the child might be salvaged, however. A young doctor working in London in the 1860s certainly thought so. His name was Thomas Barnardo.

Barnardo was born in Dublin in 1845. He came to London in 1866 to study medicine, with the ambition of becoming a missionary in China, but was distracted. Treating cholera victims in the East End, he began to realize how overwhelming the problem of street-children had become — and how much worse it was likely to grow during the epidemic, when parents, married or not, were dying in their hundreds. He considered the problem not so much a consequence of sin, as a waste of spiritual resources. These children would grow up, if they managed to grow up at all, in ignorance of God, unable to serve Him, unless they were rescued and nurtured in a Christian environment. His radical philosophy was that 'character is better than ancestry, and personal conduct of more importance than the highest parentage'. His missionary focus shifted from the heathen inhabitants of China to the deserted children of the East End, and in 1867, at the age of twenty-two, he opened a 'ragged school' in a donkey stable in Stepney, where he offered a free

19

basic education to all comers.

Orphan Jim Jarvis was one of Thomas Barnardo's first pupils. He offered to show the doctor where his kind lived, huddled next to chimney stacks on steep and greasy rooftops. As soon as he saw them, Barnardo determined to open a home, his East End Juvenile Mission, where no destitute child would ever be refused admission. No destitute boy, rather; it was only when Barnardo married in 1873 that he was able to admit girls as residents, although beforehand they could attend a reading room if they liked.

The mission attracted financial and moral support right from the start, thanks largely to some deft marketing on the part of Thomas Barnardo, tapping into the sentimental and increasingly charitable spirit of the age. His first annual report (1868) revealed that one of his highest priorities was to associate these children with the 'poor by casualty' rather than the thriftless poor. He wrote about how the boys had formed a shoe-black brigade, to earn some money for their upkeep, and perhaps a little over. The girls were learning sewing as well as reading; there was a penny savings-bank at the mission, and a free library. These were children with aspirations to be useful members of society, willing to work their way towards respectability. 'Before' and 'after' photographs stare out from the pages of his brochures, sometimes with a few sentences about personal circumstances. Minnie and Dick are eighteen-week-old twins. 'They are unwanted children in every sense of the word. Their mother knows nothing of their father; she is a hard, callous, inhuman sort of girl . . . She seems to hate them.' They look, of course, adorable.

For all his sympathy and softness of heart, Dr Barnardo was not lily-livered in his approach to illegitimacy. His charity extended to the single mother: he would help her if he could, by taking her baby into his care and then perhaps finding it foster-parents. But if that same mother were to 'fall' again by getting herself into trouble a second time, his doors were closed. He was not in the business of condoning sin. Nor did he believe that the children of sin were entirely untainted. He considered himself a realist. It was possible for nurture to overcome nature, certainly, but sometimes that proved mightily difficult.

Behind the hearts-and-flowers publicity, the children's characters were carefully monitored, and predominant traits noted down, whether good or bad. Years later in the 1940s, continuing this clear-sighted approach, Barnardo's commissioned psychologists to test children's IQs. Of the 139 cases examined in the first eight months of testing, 14 were found to be 'certifiable' (i.e. with an IQ score below 70); 34 'dull' (71–85); 74 'normal' (86–115); 11 of 'technical and secondary school ability' (116 — 129); only four 'of university ability' (above 130), while one was 'untestable' and another 'too upset'. All these children were acknowledged to be emotionally disturbed 'or failing in one way or another'. Although this might have been representative of the general population, it did at least prove that rescuing a child from the gutter — either physically or metaphorically — did not confer magical powers of happiness, wisdom and success. There was nothing romantic about it. Dr Barnardo realized this, even if his comfortable and possibly complacent supporters did not. The important thing, in all matters, was to maximize potential.

The organization developed in the twentieth century to administer aid for unmarried mothers as well as for abandoned, largely illegitimate children, and we shall hear about the practicalities of life in a Barnardo's home in due course. It also supported child migration. In that inaugural annual report of 1868, Dr Barnardo stated that he cordially agreed with those who maintained that the only real solution to the problem of what to do with homeless children was to send them abroad, 'and that too upon a large scale'. The UK is the only country to have exported its young. In 1619, the Virginia Company took 100 'poor, unattended' waifs and strays from London as slaves, to labour on plantations in the North American colonies. The company was given the authority by London's City Council to imprison, punish or 'dispose' of any children who resisted. There was no reference to parents, nor any terms of employment; they were simply plucked from the streets and shipped away. More followed until the War of Independence in 1776. Then attention moved elsewhere, and from 1787 to 1868, convicted children were transported to Australia, just like adults, to serve the dual purpose of ridding the motherland of undesirables, and colonizing a new and conveniently distant addition to the British Empire.

Annie Macpherson's scheme was more benevolent. She was a Quaker who ran what she called a home of industry in Spitalfields for juvenile delinquents — then distastefully called 'street Arabs'. She also opened a farm school in the countryside outside London, to remove her Arabs from their criminal environment and train them for work on the land. As an ambitious extension of this, from 1870 onwards she conducted parties of children to Canada, helped by her two sisters and their families, and travelled with them to 'distributing homes' or depots in Quebec and Ontario. From there she would take small groups out into the backwoods to find them family homes where, it was hoped, they could live, work and be happy. Things did not always turn out that way, inevitably, but Annie was one of the angels in a business that has become tainted by accusations of cruelty and opportunism. About 14,000 children emigrated in her personal care, and for long after her death in 1904 she was talked about fondly as their little Scottish saint.

Maria Rye was a contemporary of Dr Barnardo and Annie Macpherson; she dealt in 'gutter children', also sending them to Canada, but this time furnished with adoption forms and indentures of employment. Her work was so well respected that she was given permission by the Board of Guardians to scoop up children from the overpopulated workhouses of London. Some suspicion was cast on her enterprise when a Catholic inspector from the Board reported after a trip to Canada in 1874 that she was contaminating the innocence of blameless orphans by keeping them in company with devious street Arabs; she was failing to train her charges properly before they went, or to arrange any supervision of their placements. Rye, who was an Evangelical, repudiated the criticism, ascribing it to bigotry. Nevertheless, the seeds of doubt were sown: emigration might not always be in a child's best interests. Sadly, those seeds lay dormant for almost a century, and it is only during the last fifty years or so that the awful truth has come to light. Emigration schemes helped thousands. They also damaged thousands, robbing them of childhood and denying them a history of their own.

* * *

The best-known agency working for the well-being of illegitimate children and their mothers back home in Great Britain was the Salvation Army. It was founded in the same place and at the same time as Dr Barnardo's and Annie Macpherson's missions: the East End of London in the 1860s. William and Catherine Booth were street-preachers first of all, setting up mission stations in the Whitechapel area, as outposts of evangelism. Converts were encouraged to plough their new-found faith into helping the poor and needy of their own neighbourhoods, and so the message spread. The movement adopted its familiar name in 1878, together with the concept of fighting the good fight for Jesu's sake.

An early recruit, Elizabeth Cottrill, took a particular interest in the girls and young women encountered by the Army, offering them shelter in her own home from 1881 to 1884 and, three years later, opening a dedicated building for them in Whitechapel. Some of them were pregnant, and in 1887 the first hospital for unmarried mothers was established in Hackney. Caring for unmarried mothers remained at the heart of the Salvation Army's social work programme from then on, until the last maternity home closed in 1981, exactly 100 years after Elizabeth Cottrill's mission began.

Like Dr Barnardo, the Booths tried not to be judgemental in offering aid to those who needed it. Second offenders could be admitted if there were room enough; sometimes women were given a third or even a fourth chance; maybe more. During the 1880s, the Army reckoned that about a quarter of London's fallen women were prostitutes; even they were not refused if their cases were deserving enough. Those in charge tried to administer rules of precedence based on the welfare of the unborn child, and the benefits that might accrue to the mother.

Applicants to early mother-and-baby homes were referred by a family member or someone in authority, or self-referred, and then formally interviewed. Detailed and evocative entries were made in a series of interview books, held in the organization's archive. One applicant is a distraught wife made pregnant by another man; she tried to asphyxiate herself with coal gas before her husband promised to stand by her, and suggested she go discreetly to the Sally Army for her confinement. Winifred is nineteen; the father of her baby is a gentleman called Sydjad, 'now in India'. Her family have tried to trace him, but he cannot be found. Sagria is a twenty-year-old coloured girl who finds herself with child after an Atlantic crossing. She does not know who is responsible, but thinks it might be a steward on the *Queen Mary*. Children of mixed heritage, like Winifred's and Sagria's, were particularly hard to cope with. The ingenuous matron of a Barnardo's home in Lancashire used to say how fond she was of 'little half-caste children', how she used to love her 'fuzzy-haired girls' and do her best to teach them to defend themselves from the rudeness of the outside world. It was an uphill struggle. For their birth-mothers, the sense of stigma was worse than usual, combining a dual disgrace.

A twenty-year-old widow faces similar heartache: she spent six months in a mental hospital after the birth of her first child (she has two), probably suffering from postnatal depression. The putative father of her third says he will support her and the baby, but only if she disposes of the first two in an orphanage or by adoption. What a terrible choice.

The stated intention of the Salvation Army's missionary work with unmarried mothers was to be inclusive. In an echo of the 1576 Poor Law, they categorized the women they aided into three classes: the fallen; young and pitiable women who have been betrayed and abandoned; and 'girls who rush headlong into vice' along with those damaged in other ways, like the 'mentally defective'. Their admission interviews prove that the Army practised what it preached, despite the unattractive aspects of doing so as far as the prospect of fund-raising might be concerned.

They help a 'quiet, respectable woman' who is charged with the murder of her first child. A prostitute, aged fourteen, is referred by the police; a sixteen-year-old, though 'very free with the soldiers', is allowed to stay, as is a thirty-three-year-old member of the Salvation Army who is a war widow. The putative father of her baby is her own brother-in-law, but her father-in-law has also 'had association with her'. This will be her third child. The Army welcomes someone who cannot read or write, is excitable, 'feeble-minded' and bad-tempered — but refuses a girl charged with attempted suicide: she has bitten a nurse's hand, accused a policeman of being responsible for her pregnancy, and threatened to kill the cook in another Salvation Army home. 'Under no circumstances is she to be admitted.'

Some of the applicants are almost gentle-women. A nurse probationer is impregnated by a guest in her mother's boarding-house. As soon as her mother realizes, she throws her daughter out (and presumably keeps the lodger). The girl now has nowhere else to go. Elizabeth is a Salvationist's daughter, 'a refined, well-educated girl'; her sponsor is none other than Major Olive Booth, granddaughter of the Sally Army's founder. Phoebe, the daughter of 'one of the leading tradesmen' in a nice market town, is pregnant by the married manager of the local gasworks. He, quite understandably, does not want his wife to know anything about it, and as the tradesman is similarly anxious to keep things quiet, Phoebe is packed off to the Salvation Army. No doubt she will reappear in due course with a respectable excuse for her absence, and no baby. This is a pattern that will be repeated again and again in the stories of those who have contributed to *In the Family Way*.

Unlike Barnardo's, the Sally Army never admitted babies on their own. There is a sad letter in the archives from a young mother in Bolton:

> I am writing to ask you if you could find room in your homes for Babys for my little girl she is a month old. And you see sir I am forced to get my living. I would pay whatever you charged me and find the little darling in clothes. I may not want you to have her for long as her father has promised to marry me when able . . .

The reply gently refuses this mother's plea. They might be able to take the baby if the mother comes too, but otherwise she must look for help elsewhere. 'God bless you.'

For dignity's sake, as well as to help raise funds, the Army encouraged mothers to contribute what they could when they entered the home, even if it was only a penny. To keep things business-like, rules and regulations were issued to the officers in charge of the homes, aimed at the smooth running of the household, and maintaining a kind but professional atmosphere at all times. These regulations were published from 1898. A glance at them reveals the Army's priorities, and how progressive was its attitude to illegitimacy.

It is clear from the interview books that no one is debarred because of religion or the lack of it, race, colour, or nationality. It does not matter if they have been or still are criminals, drunkards, or addicts of any sort. In the 1916 edition of *Orders and Regulations for Social Officers (Women)* this inclusive approach is stated explicitly, with the proviso that individuals must cooperate in their own moral and physical salvation with confidence, hope, belief in the possibility of their deliverance (in both senses of the word), with patience and with forgiveness. If they do not want to change, off they must go 'to suffer again'. The allusion to forgiveness on the part of the unmarried mother is highly significant: at some time during the first few decades of the Salvation Army's existence, the 'fallen woman' subtly evolved in the public imagination into the 'wronged woman'. Mid-nineteenth-century flibbertigibbets like William Makepeace Thackeray's Becky Sharp and Hetty Sorrel in George Eliot's *Adam Bede*, whose undisciplined sexuality was the instrument of their own (and others') downfall, were succeeded by more tragic heroines. Tess Durbeyfield for example, created in 1891: surely the perfect candidate, if only she had known about it, for the

29

bracing ministrations of the Sally Army.

All mothers must be encouraged to work, according to the *Orders and Regulations*, whether they need the money or not. This bestows a sense of pride and achievement. They must furnish details of the father, if he is known; the Army will help bring him to justice and obtain maintenance from him. He — or some other family member — must pay for his baby's funeral, if that sad occasion arises. No one should be constrained to convert to Salvationism, or even Christianity. If officers use compassion to encourage repentance and forgiveness, conversion should follow automatically. In the Army's statement books, in which residents' details were recorded at the time of leaving (usually no longer than six months after the birth), there is a space for 'professing conversion', which is often ticked.

Some of the girls — they were always called girls — were able to take their babies home with them, whether or not they were married by the time they left. Occasionally a snapshot flutters loose from a statement book, of a happy-looking baby, a beaming mother, and sometimes a proud father too, with a note of gratitude from the mother on the reverse. Other mothers were married while still in the home, so their babies could be registered in the father's name and no one need ever know the circumstances of the birth. Some babies died, of course, and the rest were sent to children's homes (Dr Barnardo's and others), to foster-parents, or adopted.

★　★　★

Dr Barnardo's and the Salvation Army might have been the bravest, but they were not the only agencies concerned with the well-being of illegitimate children and their mothers. As time went on, the attitude of the professional classes towards these disadvantaged members of society slowly developed from the blanket condemnation of earlier times into a more progressive and compassionate stance. The concept of the deserving poor gained credibility. Orphans were deserving; street-children were probably deserving, along with those workhouse inmates who were defeated by indigence rather than vice. Private charities and institutions emerged to help them all, with varying degrees of commitment and success. But what about those who neither sought nor wanted help?

Elizabeth was a true Cockney. All her mother's sisters had shotgun weddings. Elizabeth herself was conceived three months before her parents' marriage in 1912. She and her cousins used to boast about who was born closest to the wedding ceremony. The winner was a lad who arrived in just twelve hours. The shorter the period, the more impressively virile the father was supposed to be. Elizabeth remembered a game she and a friend used to play in their early teens, which involved stuffing cushions into their knickers to see what they would look like when 'in the family way'. They would sing a rude little ditty, too:

> It is only human nature after all
> When a boy gets a girl against a wall
> And puts his abomination

31

Into her accommodation
To increase the population
Of the coming generation.
It is only human nature after all.

Elizabeth's family was extravagantly improper, and by the sound of it, would have been bewildered at, or derisive of, any offer of charity. But the stigma of illegitimacy still remained for the majority of people less brazen than them, despite assurances from the Salvation Army and elsewhere that single mothers might be victims as much as villains. Those involved in social reform were often removed from the middle ground of public opinion. It is easy to be tolerant if you are a benefactor. But your tolerance does not necessarily alter the attitude of the recipient. As an increasing number of British families strove towards middle-class respectability, codes of acceptable behaviour among them grew if anything more rigid, and transgression more taboo. Being taboo implies an element of secrecy, or at the least, of glossing over unpleasant truths. Few truths were more unpleasant than illegitimacy, nestling like a worm at the core of so many precious family secrets.

It is hard to imagine any frank discussion of sex — let alone lust — in the drawing-rooms of a society that pantalooned its piano-legs. Children were brought up to be institutionally naive, with the result, according to a contemporary pamphlet, that by 1913 one child in every twenty-four was born illegitimate. The attitude of nurses and midwives towards single mothers (unless they were attached to a charity) was derisive. When the councillors of Queen Victoria's Jubilee Institute for Nurses requested their associate members to be more sensitive, especially to workhouse inmates sent to local hospitals for their confinement, they argued along the lines of the Sally Army that 'the rules which deprive unmarried women at the time of childbirth are uncharitable in principle and exceedingly harmful in practice'.

> How far the principle of punishing the offences of mothers (which are not condoned), by neglecting and injuring their unoffending children, can be reconciled with the dictates of humanity and the teaching of Christ, must be left to the conscience . . .

In reply, it was explained by a superintendent of nursing that while that theory was a fine one, in practice 'there might be some local feeling roused' if unmarried mothers were placed on exactly the same footing as the married ones. And that would never do.

This response smacks of the same sort of hypocrisy which taught in the Victorian and Edwardian eras that a lady should never ask her husband for sex, and never deny it to him; that brides must be virgins while their grooms are expected to have sown their wild oats. A thriving sub-culture of abortionists performed desperately dangerous and expensive operations on so-called 'floating kidneys'; the courts were full of cases of infanticide and baby-farming. The respectable science of eugenics preached about breeding pure children, possessed of the sort of moral and intellectual pedigree befitting the builders of an empire, while their mothers were denied higher education and the responsibilities of public office. Until 1929, astonishingly, girls had only to be twelve to marry legally, and boys fourteen. So ostensibly, the child of a married couple in their early teens, or of a fourteen-year-old boy and a wife twice his age, was perfectly acceptable, while the offspring of an independent, educated woman in her late twenties and living with the man who was to become her partner for life was a disgrace.

Maud was such a woman. She was born in 1887, and as the eldest of nine children was expected to stay at home and do her domestic duty by helping to look after her younger brothers and sisters. She was inconveniently curious, though; ambitious, and educated enough to be able to follow local and national news avidly. The suffragette movement was gathering pace, and Maud was captivated by the novel idea of a woman living life on her own terms. At the age of about sixteen she decided the time had come to leave home. She found herself various jobs as a parlour-maid (the only work for which she felt qualified) until meeting Fred, a young man whose wife had deserted him and left him with their baby.

By 1910, Maud and Fred were living in sin together, with no intention on Maud's part to marry. Maud mothered Fred's baby and they had two children of their own. Together they built up a prosperous business in which Maud was an equal partner in every way. Maud's family could not bring themselves to approve of poor Fred: when Maud used to visit them in her big, posh car and a fashionable hat, Fred had to wait outside. Their own children did not realize their illegitimacy until Maud died in 1982. The eldest was consumed with shame, but the youngest passed on proud memories of Maud to his own daughter, who cannot help but admire a woman whose acquired self-confidence and tenacity ensured a life of true equality. Society assumed that marriage was the only acceptable way to bring up children, yet Maud considered marriage to be a symbol of subjection; she felt more strongly about this than about the risk of stigmatizing the children as bastards. She lied to them, in the cause of truth and independence for herself. Who are we to judge? Only her own family could — and did — do that. In some ways Maud's decision may have been selfish, but it was made with conviction and integrity, and it worked for her.

From 1913 onwards, secrets like Maud's and Fred's might bring not only shame if they were revealed, but incarceration. That is when the Mental Deficiency Act was passed, with the euphemistic purpose of furthering and bettering provision 'for the care of Feeble-Minded and other Mentally Defective Persons'. According to the Act, women could be deemed moral imbeciles as well as mental ones, and sent to an appropriate institution: a lunatic asylum. Moral imbeciles were defined as 'persons who from an early age display some permanent mental defect coupled with strong vicious or criminal propensities'. This chillingly included unmarried mothers who could not support themselves and were pregnant with their second (or later) child. Repeat offenders, in other words, whom the workhouses did not want to subsidize, or whose families had had enough of them.

Under the terms of the Act, all it took for a moral imbecile to be committed if she was under twenty-one was a word from her parent or guardian. She did not even have to be medically diagnosed an imbecile. Her status as a young, abandoned and unmarried mother was enough. Those over twenty-one were in the treacherous hands of the Poor Law Guardians, who were often only too pleased to send them, with their babies, somewhere else.

The Act was not repealed until 1959. Some of those interned under its provision will be telling their stories later on, but it is important to note that tales from recent dementia wards and old people's homes about unmarried mothers lingering on as patients are often true. They were committed as young women, their children taken away, and then they were forgotten. They became institutionalized and so unable to cope in the world outside. A young single woman who used to be a nurse told me that when she was pregnant not so long ago, one of the old ladies in the home where she worked suddenly blossomed, delighted at the prospect of a baby. She thought it was wonderful that here was a girl, in almost the same circumstances in which she had been all those years before, who could look forward to love, support and congratulation instead of shame and a lifetime of loss.

Maud was not alone in her fight against the hypocrisies of the age. An outfit called 'The Legitimation League' was launched in 1894 by a group of professional people based in Leeds — women as well as men — whose aim was to establish a legitimate alternative to marriage. 'The principal fault of wedlock is 'the lock',' claimed its rather dramatic president; 'If you intend waiting till you can repeal the marriage laws the worms that have consumed the marrow of your bones will have sunk a thousand times beneath the mould of your graves.'

The League's proposed new partnership would involve a mutual announcement, some sort of registration process — and that would be that. Divorce would be just as simple: 'in a free country men and women should be at liberty to contract and dissolve any partnership they please'. Any children born of the union would belong equally to each parent, and be allowed to inherit without constraint. Thus would the concept of illegitimacy be removed at a stroke.

One of the League's first campaigns — only campaigns, in truth, for it did not last long — was in support of the notorious feminist Edith Lanchester (1871 — 1966). Her story transfixed London society in 1895. She was twenty-four, one of London University's first female gradu- ates, and had worked both as a teacher and a clerk to earn her own living. Her father was a prominent architect, who did not share his forceful daughter's 'advanced' opinions, and who panicked when Edith announced her intention to cohabit with her lover, James Sullivan. Mr Lanchester arranged for an eminent specialist in mental disease to interview and certify his daughter the day before Edith and James were due to move in together. With the help of this doctor, and Edith's two brothers, Mr Lanchester physically manhandled her off to the Priory, 'a house licensed for the reception of the insane', and committed her.

The League sprang into action, dispatching its secretary, a Leeds solicitor called Oswald Dawson (who was himself living in sin with 'Mrs' Dawson), to do what he could. His solution to the problem was imaginative: he made a random guess at which window in the Priory might be Edith's, then engaged a cornet-player to march about underneath, in the manner of a royal piper, tooting rousing tunes to raise her spirits.

Meanwhile James Sullivan got to work, and persuaded the Lunacy Commissioners to order Edith's discharge, whereupon she was immediately committed again by a different doctor (the family GP). It was only after Sullivan involved the Home Secretary and the Chief Commissioner of Police that Edith was freed permanently, and left to live her life as she chose. Her family washed its hands of her, and she and James lived together for fifty years, with their two illegitimate children.

The suffragette movement which inspired Maud and Edith was full of 'modern women' suspected of wanting to clatter down every social barrier they could. No doubt many of them cheered Miss Lanchester, but their voices were drowned out by the massed harrumphs of those who thought her immoral and wickedly self-indulgent. Modern women were not to be relied upon — and with good reason, as a correspondent to *The Times* pointed out: 'Sir — The decline in moral standards during the past 50 years has been coincident with the gradual emancipation of our women. Is it not time we asked ourselves how far it is consequent upon it?' If society could not trust its wives and mothers, then who on earth could it trust?

2

Little Bastards: The Meaning of Illegitimacy

Clear off. You haven't got a father.

It is important to realize, in this story of stigma and prejudice, that not every unmarried mother was ostracized before the advent of the permissive age; nor was every illegitimate child an outcast. Jennifer's experience proves this. In 1965 she lived in the village in which she was born, surrounded by her parents, her younger brother, a loving wider family and a close-knit working-class community. She had been having an affair with a prominent — and married — member of that community since she was about eighteen (she was now in her mid-twenties); they knew they shouldn't, she says, but found it impossible to stop.

When Jennifer fell pregnant, she didn't plan to keep the baby. She applied to social services for advice and was found a place at a mother-and-baby home run by an Anglican order of nuns some eighty miles away, on the understanding that the baby be adopted at six weeks. Jennifer managed to reconcile herself to this decision, though her own mother wanted to keep the child in the family.

We shall hear much more about life in

mother-and-baby homes later on; many of them sound austere at best and at worst, unbearable. But when Jennifer described hers to me, there were none of the usual tears; instead she smiled fondly at the memory of 'naughty' Sisters Angela and Alban, who were young, pretty and constantly up to some sort of mischief. On one occasion the pair of them hijacked a pram belonging to the home and used it to dispatch a particularly dreary statue of the Blessed Virgin Mary. Under cover of darkness they spirited Our Lady out of the building, loaded her into the pram, trundled her off the premises and across the road before catapulting her over the parapet of a bridge into the river below.

A fortnight after Jennifer arrived at the home her daughter was born, a month early. At first it was thought the baby might have a heart defect, which meant a future in foster-care, since 'imperfect' children were not offered for adoption. Jennifer decided to keep the child instead, encouraged by messages from neighbours in her village, one of which read simply, 'Bring that baby home.' Jennifer's family was overjoyed, especially when it was later discovered that the little girl was perfectly healthy after all.

The atmosphere in the home was kindly, almost conspiratorial. The nuns spent time with the residents, supporting them as best they could. One girl had twins while she was there; when she married their father soon afterwards the wedding took place from the mother-and-baby home at the church next door. The bride wore an opulent dress stitched by another resident who was a professional seamstress. Sister Superior used to borrow Jennifer's coveted winter coat when she had appointments outside the home, and Sister Angela became the godmother of Jennifer's baby. Jennifer felt sorry for Sisters Angela and Alban: they obviously loved children, yet would never be able to have any of their own. Photographs of the little community taken at the time of Jennifer's stay show radiant, well-fed babes dressed in elaborate infant finery belonging to the home, cradled in the arms of their birth-mothers, or a nun. Jennifer recalls weekly film-shows, frequent family visits, and friendships which still endure.

Six weeks after her daughter's birth, Jennifer brought her home. She was tentative about taking her out for walks in the pram at first, feeling guilty and expecting blame. When an aunt heard this she insisted on accompanying them: 'You're coming out with me.' It soon became clear that both mother and baby were welcome, and Jennifer's confidence grew. She and the baby's father secretly continued their relationship, though he never left his wife and other children and only after he had died, some twenty years later, did Jennifer feel able to marry someone else. The victim of this story should be the 'wronged' wife, who somehow accommodated decades of her husband's infidelity. But remarkably, she and Jennifer are reconciled and chat, when they happen to meet, about old times.

The baby grew up loved by her family and freely accepted by friends and neighbours. Jennifer still lives in the village, where her sitting-room is full of photographs of her daughter and grandchildren. The mother-and-baby home has been demolished now, and for many of its former residents, no doubt, the memory of it must bring to mind the most traumatic time of their lives. But Jennifer cannot be alone in recalling it as a humane and warm-hearted place; a place of love. Nor can it have been the only home to treat single mothers and their illegitimate children with good humour, dignity and respect.

Historically, however, the easiest way to talk about (if it must be talked about) and to deal with the problem of illegitimacy has been to treat those involved entirely without compassion. That is why the term 'bastard' still makes us flinch. It's a brutal word, abrasive and bitter. It offends us. Back in the days before political correctness, bastards were graded in terms of moral corruption, like slaves in terms of colour, and given a taxonomy to define them. Least offensive was the 'natural' illegitimate, born of parents who were free to marry at the time of the child's birth, but chose not to. 'Spurious' bastards had an acknowledged mother, but no known father, with the implication that this was because there were too many casual lovers for her to pinpoint a single one. 'Adulterines' were the product of one or two parents already married to someone else. It is obvious what 'incestuous' illegitimates were; 'sacrilegious' ones were the offspring of a mother, father, or both, constrained by holy orders. 'Abandoned' infants, like Moses or Oedipus or Ernest Worthing, were deemed to be

43

illegitimate because there was no proof to the contrary. There was no official classification for children born of rape; presumably they came into the 'spurious' category.

These legalistic terms might sound harsh to us, but not as cruel as the common names traditionally spat at illegitimate children. Base-born, whoreson, by-blow, child of the devil, chance-child: they were all bastards. Sometimes entries in parish registers were a little kinder, naming foundling (abandoned) children as 'merry-begot' or — more descriptively — 'lane-begot', 'friendless', and in one case, the baby 'raked-out-of-the-ashes'. But to the man on the street, this was fancy nonsense, even as late as the 1970s: 'I had an aunty that had a baby out of wedlock and they [sic] were called bastards. And they are still called bastards, not love childs [sic] like you would call them today. That's bull.'

The term 'bastard' is not in itself an insult; it originally meant the child of a pagan marriage — i.e. not recognized by the Church — and legally, simply meant one born out of wedlock. But centuries of moral and social discrimination infused the word with malice and shame, until it became the keenest weapon of insult available. A mass court-martial case caused a sensation in 1919 when seventeen Privates in the West Yorkshire Regiment refused to attend morning parade because their sergeant-major had called them bastards. 'The President of the Court . . . observed that, while a soldier would tolerate being called almost anything, he would not tolerate being called a bastard.' In 1952, a victim

44

was murdered merely because he called a belligerent but unknown man a bastard during an altercation; unhappily, it turned out he really *was*. A journalist reporting the incident in *The Times* could not bring himself to mention the word in print, coyly noting only that it was 'a name which inferred that he was of doubtful parentage'.

From the labelling of illegitimate children with cold-hearted epithets like these, it was only a short step to assigning them all with the same doomed characters. A bastard was essentially the bodily representation of its parents' (particularly its mother's) sin.

Bastards are as likely to be brave, and have shown themselves as brave, as others. True; but it is probable they will inherit the moral flabbiness, the uncontrollable impulse, the selfishness, and the lack of self-respect which usually characterises one or both of the parents of illegitimate children.

A lawyer wrote that in the 1890s, attempting to explain why all bastards were congenitally rotten. Outrageous, we splutter — but only thirty-odd years ago it was not an uncommon opinion that 'whether they be coloured or whatever they are', bastards are bad news. 'I honestly believe some of these people they were bred wrong and from them you breed a wrong one and you'll never breed a right one.'

My cousin Sue was dumped by her first boyfriend when she revealed her secret to him:

he told her she had 'bad blood'. One's moral heritage could never be expunged. Even if the law were changed, mused a Victorian commentator, it would make no difference: 'A bastard is a bastard, and to make him a legitimate one by abolishing all illegitimacy, leaves him a bastard still.'

Another name for illegitimate children in the period before the First World War was scapechild, or scapegrace — as in scapegoat, the animal invested or polluted by Hebrew high priests with everybody's sins, and then cast out into the wilderness and forgotten. It is not difficult to understand why. While researching this book, time and time again I came across lurid details of court cases involving the neglect or death of scapechildren at the hands of vengeful adults. Some of the saddest were about babies born out of wedlock to women whose husbands were away fighting. Private Thomas Pole was a distinguished soldier, with a medal to prove it, when he was sentenced to death (though later reprieved) for the murder of his wife's infant child.

> The baby, which was 11 months old, was born while Pole was serving in France. The day before he should have rejoined his regiment [in February 1918] ... he drowned the child in a dolly tub in the yard. On being arrested he said 'I ought to have drowned my wife as well, if I had done right, but I was sorry for her father and mother.'

There are several reports during both World Wars of frightened mothers murdering their own illegitimate babies, after desperately trying to find help by tramping streets in search of a mother-and-baby home willing to take them in. This was not just a wartime phenomenon. In the spring of 1921, seventeen-year-old Violet Buckle was charged with abandoning her 'baby darling'. She left him in a shop doorway, later explaining that she had lost her job and so could not afford to look after him. She had been seduced at fifteen by an army officer, and even though she served a 'Bastardy Order' on him, which was supposed to compel him to pay maintenance, he had never given her a penny. In what we might now consider to be a suspicious postscript to the story, a 'City man' present at the court proceedings stood up and offered to adopt the child, to find Violet a new job, and to buy her a railway season ticket so she could visit her son whenever she liked. The court agreed, and Violet was given a year's probation. In most of these cases there was a plea for mercy on behalf of the woman, in charitable recognition of her predicament, but it was not always heeded.

The pressure on lonely mothers to hide or deny their 'mistakes' throughout the span of this book meant, in extreme cases, that children were neglected, shut away, abandoned, dehumanized — or sold. Every baby is a potential commodity, even a bastard one. Especially a bastard one, in fact. During the First World War, when fatherless babies were in plentiful supply, unofficial cottage industries began to emerge, offering long-term care for such infants for a down-payment of perhaps £10 (equivalent to £500 today). In theory, they could be redeemed later, as though they had been left at the pawnbroker's. Walter and Lydia Elms were found to be running an establishment like this in Llanelli, Wales, in 1917. To increase turnover, they disposed of the children in their care one by one, accepting new ones to take their places. At their trial the prosecution alleged that one child was found in a parcel in a river, another was last seen being driven away in a car by an unknown woman; a third was kept in a large tin upstairs in the Elms' house, where it eventually suffocated, and yet another 'was at present in the workhouse with its back covered with bruises'.

David's first memory is of a children's home in about 1930 where he is living, aged three, with 'aunty'. Aunty runs the home as a private enterprise, and tells David she loves him dearly. But she beats him, and bizarrely insists on dressing him in a pair of girls' high-laced boots, which he pulls off whenever he can, to go barefoot instead. Sometimes she locks him in the cellar for two days at a time, with neither food nor water. One day she confesses that much as she loves him, on more than one occasion she has tried (without his knowledge) to sell him, by dressing him up in his best clothes and standing him in the front garden. Once, he was nearly bought and taken away, but the two men interested in having him argued with aunty so much that in the end, they gave up. Neither of them was prepared to give her enough money for the boy.

David went on to become a highly respected member of the local and national community: a citizen who stands up for natural justice. Like Sue, something in his spirit meant that he could overcome the blameless horror of his childhood, to love himself and other people. Lucy is the same: her unmarried mother gave birth to her at eighteen, in 1936. In order to get a job that paid enough for Lucy to be looked after, her mother tucked the baby under her arm and travelled to the other end of the country, where she became a parlour-maid, and Lucy was fostered. Three years later her mother married, and the husband adopted Lucy.

Lucy remembers a blissful childhood; no one ever mentioned her mother's indiscretion (Lucy herself knew nothing about it until she was about fourteen) and she felt loved and cherished. When her adoptive father came back from the war, however, things changed. He was without a scratch, but utterly exhausted. Lucy had been 'a sweet little five-year-old' when he had left; now she was on the brink of adolescence, emotional, and because he had forbidden her to go to grammar school, angry and frustrated. 'Of course we both were — I was looking forward to Dad coming back from the war, and it turned out to be a disaster. I think it must have been even worse for him, and I think he must have given up at some point.' The atmosphere at home became charged with tension and verbal abuse. Lucy became an outsider. At his lowest point her adoptive father even threatened to shoot her with his 12-bore, but decades later, she finds she can forgive him. There was no help available for families like hers, and she knows that her parents lost a baby boy shortly after the war in particularly tragic circumstances, which would have devastated even the happiest of couples.

★ ★ ★

In fact Lucy's mother would have been more likely to find support as a single mother had she remained just that. Once she married, it was assumed her husband would take care of her, just as it was assumed that any illegitimate child born to a married woman was her husband's by default. Then, as far as the outside world was concerned, the problem conveniently disappeared. As we shall see later on, agencies existed to help unmarried mothers or their children, even before the invention of the welfare state. Cousin Sue went to a Church of England home, some of which were lovely, others less so. David and Lucy found themselves in unregulated foster-care. Dr Barnardo's homes were operated under the promise that no child was ever turned away (although they were often passed on somewhere else); before him Thomas Coram, in the eighteenth century, freely accepted foundlings surrendered by their stricken mothers and gave them new names, new lives.

Often these agencies offered children a welcome sanctuary. Former residents can recall their carers with love, as well as gratitude. 'Sister Ethel had the firmest, safest hand hold I have ever felt ... She gave us a safe place in a dangerous world ... '; 'I loved every minute of my time; never, ever was I sad or unhappy, I made many friends'; 'if it wasn't for the home ... and the support and dedication from the staff I would not be the man I am today'.

The Salvation Army and Dr Barnardo's tried to help unmarried mothers as well as their children, either with grants of clothes and equipment, or with finding subsidized accommodation and childcare. The National Council for the Unmarried Mother and her Child was founded in 1918, giving material support and campaigning to change public attitudes towards these highly disadvantaged members of society. Limited help was available, therefore, for the minority who happened to live in the right area, knew where to look and had the courage to ask.

An alternative to giving up a baby was to absorb it into the family, like Jennifer's baby, fully acknowledged as its mother's child. This tended to happen most often at either end of the social spectrum: among the aristocracy and in working-class communities. Surnames with the prefix 'Fitz' are common in the UK and Ireland: Fitzgerald, Fitzwilliam, and so on. It is not a difficult code to crack. 'Fitz' comes directly from the French *fils*, or son, so Fitzroy for example means son of the king (or by extension, daughter). Of the thirteen illegitimate children of King Charles II, five were given the surname Fitzroy and one was a Fitzcharles. If you have a double-barrelled surname, it might not be because of the marriage of two proud and noble

51

scions in the past, but because somewhere perched in the family tree is a hybrid given two names instead of the more conventional one.

Few of the 'best' families in England — anywhere in Europe — would be without a bastard or two in each generation, more or less openly accepted by their fathers, as long as the mother had some distinction. The legions of sons and daughters of the gentry born to housemaids and the like were not so lucky. That was the difference: in working-class communities, the birth-father tended to disappear from the picture, if he and the mother were not already living together 'in sin'. An unmarried mother would bring her trouble home, if her own parents were willing to have her, and cope as best she could.

Jessie fell into this category. She was a mill-worker in Yorkshire, one of twelve children. Jessie was the quiet one of the family, who never liked going out much. She would rather stay in and do the housework, helping her mother, who always had a baby on the go. She was shy, and used to take a little Bible with her to the mill to read during breaks, so that she would not have to chat to people.

Jimmy was what Jessie called a man of the world; he worked in a part of the mill that Jessie and her friends had to pass through, mortifyingly, on their way to the lavatories. He used to catch her eye and make her blush. When an insistent friend persuaded Jessie to come with her to a local fairground one evening, she was reluctant, but finally agreed. Jimmy was there. They began seeing one another, and soon afterwards, it happened. Their son was born in 1913, when Jessie was nineteen. Jimmy was not interested. He did not even pay maintenance after Jessie reluctantly took him to court, and she doubts if he was ever sent to gaol.

Jessie told her parents about her pregnancy when it became impossible to hide the fact any longer. They 'minded a lot', she remembers economically, but did not send her away. The boy was born at home, and Jessie went back to work almost immediately, leaving him with her mother, who had another baby herself soon after Jessie's lad was born. Poor Jessie was so ashamed when her painful breasts leaked on to her pinafore at work that she used to have to hurry to the lavatory (past Jimmy again, presumably) and express the milk into the wash-hand basin.

She survived, though. In fact another illegitimate son was born in 1918; Jessie married in 1939, and went on to have nine much-loved grandchildren, and a little great-grandchild — who was illegitimate. And by then, that didn't matter.

When Nancy A wrote to me declaring her illegitimacy, she was at a loss to know what all the fuss was about. She was one of six children; her parents never married, nor ever had any ambition to do so. Yet Nancy remembers a home full of mutual respect and support, and is proud of her parents 'for hanging on in there' and keeping the family together.

Jessie's and Nancy's stories are unusual, in that they are not about secrets. In most of the cases I have come across involving illegitimacy from the First World War to the late 1960s, secrecy is at the heart of everything. In cousin Sue's case, it was the secrecy common to most adoptions, when birth-family and adoptive family are separated by a chasm of anonymity. But I have met children who were not allowed to acknowledge their mothers in public, lest they give the awful game away. They had to call them aunt, or by their Christian names instead, and most imagine it is because their mothers are ashamed of them. I have met parents who hide from their children the fact that they are not really married, or were not when the children were born.

Harold's mother, Lily, once accidentally took the same bus as Harold when he was on his way to school at the age of eleven. She whispered to him that he must not admit to being her son, causing an immediate sense of loss which lingers still, more than sixty years later. Although he grew up with her at home, by the time of her death she had managed to convince herself and others that he had never really happened. Yet she never quite got over her pregnancy, according to Harold. She went into labour at home, after a brief relationship with a man in the Canadian Air Force; that was the first her parents knew about the situation. Fortunately for Lily, once he had got over the shock, her father let her stay at home with the baby. Her sister Rose, strong, forceful and supportive, would not have had it any other way. Harold's birth-father was pursued in court for maintenance; Lily refused to change her name, and life went on much as before, except with a mysterious little boy in the house. For neighbours, friends, even members of the family, to ask questions would have been impolite. No doubt speculation filled the vacuum left by the absence of explanation.

Harold was not aware that children were supposed to have fathers as well as mothers until he was asked at school one day to construct a family tree. He was about ten, and had no idea where to start. He left his piece of paper blank, and was hauled up to the front of the class by his teacher to be asked why. When he couldn't articulate the reason, he was told to sit down. He was petrified of telling his mother about this incident, feeling it was somehow his fault.

Harold remembers Lily as an ultra-respectable and rather prim lady, always impeccably dressed, and she became a regular churchgoer. 'She was never a real person to herself,' he claims. That real person disappeared at Harold's birth. In mitigation of Lily, it should be mentioned that her own mother spent long periods in a mental hospital suffering from schizophrenia. When Harold was born it was still the custom in some circumstances to commit unmarried mothers to a similar institution for moral as well as mental instability; Lily must have been terrified that given her family history, if anyone found out about Harold, she might be shut away.

Harold left home — and the country — as soon as he could, and settled abroad. He kept in touch with his mother, however, and cared for her during her last illness. When she died, he realized that very few people in her life knew anything about him. 'My, she kept you under wraps!' said a surprised mourner when introduced to him. 'And to think I worked with her for thirty years!' Lily had succeeded in denying her son's existence. He was the stranger at her funeral.

At least Harold knew his own history. It was a secret he shared with his mother, along with the heavy responsibility of keeping it hidden. He even managed to trace his birth-father, but with neither the expectation nor hope of any reconciliation. He just needed to know where he had come from. Christopher, on the other hand, only realized he was illegitimate very recently, when his mother died. He was in his late sixties when the truth came out, via an old family friend. He finds it hard to understand why the secret could not be told during his mother's lifetime and is upset not so much by the fact of his illegitimacy as by his mother's silence, her masquerade. After all, it was his secret too. He has suffered throughout his life from a vague sort of disquietude about family relationships: wondering why his mother was so anxious he should leave home at eighteen, and why the man who turns out to have been his step-father rather than his natural one was so distant and difficult to get on with. He still feels the shock.

Em's story encapsulates the anger that so many victims of this secrecy feel. She was born in 1942, and felt 'different' all through her childhood. At the age of twelve her mother explained that she was illegitimate, but absolutely refused to tell Em anything whatsoever about her father.

Em was desperate to know. She tried asking the few relations she had, but the answer was always the same: 'Ask your mother,' and her mother never told. Even when her mother died at the age of eighty-seven, she refused to put Em's mind at rest. 'She said to me it was her secret — she would take it to her grave.'

When Em married, she was required to produce a birth certificate, and was deeply ashamed by her mother-in-law's disgust at the official lack of a father revealed by the document. At work, when people talked of their families, she would pretend she was an only child whose daddy had been killed in the war (which might well have been true). She is still embarrassed by the secret, and admits to having lied throughout her life to mask her illegitimacy.

Em resents the fact that this ineradicable stigma is her parents' only legacy to her. Even though we are supposed to be living in an enlightened age now, illegitimate people still confess that they are afraid to make close friends in case the ghastly truth is discovered; that they have a sense of not being good enough for legitimate friends and family; that they avoid situations when they might be asked to produce a birth certificate — applying for a passport, for example — even though this can cause real day-to-day difficulty. Such obfuscation makes them even more ashamed, and often angry. This is what an illegitimate friend told me:

'I am a product of post-war English morality and hypocrisy. Lovers' plans have always been, and continue to be, thwarted. Nowadays, though,

57

few people go to such lengths to disguise the simple facts of nature from their children. Through their denial of reality my parents deprived me of the opportunity to empathize with them. More importantly, my mother missed a chance to deepen our relationship at a time when I desperately needed it: in late 1969 I became pregnant with my first child by the man who would later become my first husband . . . [My parents' pretence] offered my wider family a spurious respectability that was utterly dishonest.'

Someone else I met was horrified at feeling sexual desire as a teenager, thinking that bastardy was something she might transmit to her own offspring, and it is true: illegitimacy does often run in families, as the excerpt above suggests. Many illegitimate people feel uneasy about having children in case their birth-fathers have conferred some secret genetic curse on them. Others feel lonely and lost. Helen was left on a doorstep when she was a baby in 1928 and despite fifty-six years of happy marriage, is still longing for a blood-brother or sister, so that she can find out who she is. She watches all those television programmes about families reuniting and wishes someone would turn up out of the blue with a hug and tears of joy, to claim her as their own.

* * *

The cult of secrecy surrounding illegitimate children is not solely a matter of saving face. It could be a safety mechanism, in communities which found it hard to forgive transgression. There is a heartbreaking account by an Irishman called Frank who was found to be 'illegitimately living with his grandparents' in Dublin and so taken to court (in the absence of a culpable parent), accused and sentenced to a childhood in care. In effect, he was convicted of his own illegitimacy. At the same sort of time, in the 1930s, Bridget was arrested in Dublin for begging on the streets at the age of two-and-a-half. She was officially described as 'discarded offspring' and, like Frank, sent to an industrial school — a sort of cross between a borstal and a children's home — until she reached the age of sixteen.

One would hope the notion of punishing a child for the sins of its fathers (and mothers) would be obsolete by now. It is difficult to imagine Frank's or Bridget's experience happening today, or any youngster being told to clear off, as the novelist Catherine Cookson was, because they 'haven't got no Da''. But it was not so long ago that Pat, born in 1934, was forbidden by her uncle to enter his house because of her illegitimacy. Maureen, who like Em was always aware of something not being quite right at home, only found out about her illegitimacy when a Christmas card she had sent to her mother's brother was returned with a note informing her that he did not correspond with bastards. She was a child; she did not even know what the word meant.

There are repeated stories of illegitimate people being turned down for posts in the

Foreign Office, the Metropolitan Police, holy orders, even nursing, and ascribing their lack of success to the lack of an identifiable father. The prohibition was rarely explicit, but often implied. In one case a woman applying to be a librarian was told on the revelation of her illegitimacy that her sort was not at *all* suitable, thank you very much. Other people felt handicapped by their illegitimacy in less concrete ways. Not knowing who they were undermined confidence. Kay was brought up in a rural community believing her grandparents to be her parents, and her birth-mother to be her sister — a very common pattern. She found out the truth when she went to school, where everyone seemed to know but her — again very common — and though her grandmother insisted that she was 'a child of love, and that makes you very special', Kay was shattered. Despite the reassurance, she knew that illegitimacy was considered shameful, and whenever anything went wrong in her life, she attributed it to a perverse kind of personal punishment.

Kay has never lost that sense of shame. It betrayed her when she was recommended for a commission while working at Bletchley Park, the Government code-breaking centre, during the war. The interview went well until the subject of her father came up. Who was he? Flustered after admitting that she didn't exactly know, she did not perform well in the rest of the interview and was rejected for officer's training. She was not given a specific reason, but is convinced it was because of her illegitimacy.

It is understandable, though not to be condoned, that some of the harshest retribution meted out to bastards for being bastards came from their own mothers. It took courage for Ella to reveal her history. 'Mum, bless her! Never failed to tell me about my unwanted birth, would not allow me any credit because of 'what and who you are'. I had many boyfriends (looking for love, no doubt). I was good-looking, tall and slim. I married in 1952 and had two daughters. I was insecure and an emotional wreck. I loved my mum, but she did not return this love. She never forgave me for being born.' Those born out of wedlock speak of feeling like 'the biggest mistake that ever happened'; incomplete, exiled, disgraced or inferior. It is like being born on 29 February: you feel ineffably different, and somehow cheated.

All that is the bad news. But positivity and pride have their places in this history, too. Freddie was born in 1942; like Em, he was never told anything about his father, but he made the decision in adulthood not to let the stigma of illegitimacy (though keenly felt) overshadow his life. Being a bastard made him resilient, independent, content to go his own way. He is a loving father, and proud of his role at the roots of a new and vigorous family tree. That refusal to be tainted by the past is something shared by the ten-year-old daughter of Peter and his partner, who never quite got round to getting married. The girl asked one day why they did not have any wedding photos. Peter took a deep breath, and told her. 'How would she take it? How would she react? She thought for a while and said with delight 'But that means I'm free!'' Ignorance can indeed be a sort of bliss: in the absence of hard facts, anything is possible.

Illegitimate children told nothing about their birth-fathers are free to imagine, or reinvent, all sorts of things. One person who contacted me even went so far as to sign herself, with a calligraphic flourish, 'your majestic bastardness'. She feels the perceived disadvantages of her birth confer solidarity with other oppressed peoples in the world, and takes courage in having survived society's collective prejudice. She also wants to reclaim the term 'bastard' and burnish it with pride.

Lesley was the illegitimate daughter of a seventeen-year-old girl and a married South African soldier in the King's African Rifles. She was always told her father had died in the war, but later found this not to be so. In fact he had stayed in touch with her mother; he was the 'Uncle Richard' with whom she vaguely remembered once having tea, and in a confusing and shifting world, he became her unknown hero.

This remained the case throughout Lesley's life. Her daughter Marianne — Richard's grandchild — did not share Lesley's feelings. Her sympathies tended towards Richard's betrayed wife, and Lesley's teenage mother. Nevertheless, when Lesley began to disappear into the haze of Alzheimer's, Marianne, terrified of flying, bravely offered to take her to visit South Africa, something Lesley had always longed to do. Marianne did some homework before they went, to discover where her grandfather had lived, worked and died. She wrote to the people living in his old house to ask if they might visit, but no one replied. She even contacted the cemetery where he was supposed to be buried, but frustratingly, there was no trace of his grave. It was as though he had never existed.

But this was all one to Mum. She was finally in South Africa, finally breathing the air breathed by her beloved dad. It was worth conquering my fear of flying to see Mum's delight in achieving this dream.

What matter if now she remembers nothing of it?

It is natural that some illegitimate children will try to find out as much about their near-mythical fathers as they can. They speak with pride of distinguished war records, reports of good character, even of their fathers' 'real' families. Anything positive they can unearth helps to eclipse the negativity involved in growing up illegitimate. Christopher is the gentleman now in his seventies who only discovered his illegitimacy after the death of his mother. When he started researching the identity of his father, Christopher was rather hoping for some heroics. A family friend said that before being sworn to secrecy, she had been told his father was a fighter-pilot, shot down in the war. A little poking about revealed something slightly less dashing: he was in fact a hairdresser on an RAF station.

Vivien's is a complicated story of truth and deceit, even more overwrought than Lesley's. Her mother was a divorcée and her father was married to someone else when she was born, although they did marry each other when Vivien was thirteen. They met in a pub during the Second World War and started an affair; Vivien was later told that they were delighted when she came along. They assured her she was very much wanted, very much a love-child, and had hoped her arrival would signal a new life for them all. But her father's wife, Constance, would not give him a divorce. Constance knew about Vivien, but could not bring herself to tell her own children, and even when her husband moved in with Vivien's mother when Vivien was four, Constance still refused to relinquish him completely.

Vivien's mother changed her surname, and Vivien's, to her father's by deed poll. Vivien grew up at the centre of what she thought was a happy and loving family, with a mother and father married to each other at its heart. When she found out the truth, she was intrigued rather than upset, and the first thing she told anyone afterwards — including her husband-to-be — was that she had been born illegitimate.

What I find the most extraordinary part of the whole story is Constance's attitude towards Vivien. She did not appear to hate the girl, nor even resent her. Every Christmas, there would be a thoughtful little present in Vivien's stocking without a label. Vivien did not question it when she was a child, assuming this to be an obscure family tradition. She later discovered that the gifts came from Constance, who obviously found her husband's infidelity impossible to come to terms with, but possible to forgive.

Forgiveness is not a word often associated with the stigma of illegitimacy before the permissive age. Even as late as 1969, it was debated 'whether disgrace and punishment should be wholly replaced by kindness and assistance' for unmarried parents and their somehow shop-soiled offspring. In my fairly random sample of the experience of illegitimacy before the 1970s, I have not come across a single instance of an aggrieved mother forgiving her child for being born. To put it another way: if a birth-parent was resentful at the time of the child's birth, as Ella's mother was, that attitude never changed. It might dull a little, but that bitter little flame of animosity never quite died. Most mothers and fathers (assuming the latter even knew about the birth) were *not* resentful, of course; regretful perhaps, and struggling with shame and guilt, but not vindictive towards their child.

There is forgiveness, however, the other way round. Many illegitimate children, whether adopted or not, find a need to absolve the people who brought them into the world so chaotically. 'We don't ask for life,' says the single mother in Shelagh Delaney's *A Taste of Honey*, 'we have it thrust upon us.' But perhaps because bastards are themselves the subject of prejudice and discrimination, they are slow to judge others, and that includes their own parents. This is not always the case; some of the most touching stories I have discovered involve birth-mothers like Imogen, who has written to her adopted son every year on his birthday and at Christmas, and who has not yet had a reply. Or fathers like Gary, who traced his adopted son, even met him once, and who now longs to have a relationship with him, but the son cannot oblige. He is not interested.

This is evidence of a human need to be loved, as much as it is about magnanimity. Children brought up in institutions traditionally dream of their unknown mothers as wronged or unfortunate heroines, like Oliver Twist's. Adopted children might do the same, when they are grafted on to someone else's family tree like mistletoe. Here is the 'ignorance is bliss' idea again.

There is something uplifting in the experience of Dee, born in 1959, and others like her. Dee's mother was living overseas when she became pregnant; she was immediately packed off to England by her parents, to have the baby among strangers, before returning home in complete denial. Dee's birth-father was never told about her; only her maternal grandparents and her mother's siblings knew. Dee was adopted, not very happily, and managed to trace her birth-mother, who was overjoyed but could not bring herself to acknowledge Dee to anyone outside her immediate family. It feels a heavy burden for Dee to bear, to have to keep herself secret from her half-siblings. But she does it for love of her birth-mother, who never even got the chance to hold her first-born child because Dee's adoptive parents were waiting in the next room when she was delivered. The baby was immediately removed by the matron, and presented to them. Her birth-mother was blithely advised to forget about Dee, find a man, get married, have children and lead a 'normal' life. Dee feels so very sorry for her.

A sense of acceptance is shared by other illegitimate children who are proud of their birth-parent(s) for the sacrifices they made, and sympathize with them for the decisions they were bound to take in the supposed interests of their tainted babies. A comment recently posted in an internet chat-room about mother-and-baby homes sums this up beautifully: 'RIP, mum, your secret is out, and it doesn't matter. We all still love you.'

3

The Woman Who Did:
Unmarried Mothers

*A young woman used to be ashamed if she
was not a virgin when she married; in the
Sixties, she would be more likely to feel
shame if she went inexperienced to the
marriage bed.*

I remember the shock when we heard that Tessa
was pregnant. She was sixteen, a year or two
older than I was, and had an air of confidence we
all found utterly captivating. There is someone
like that in every school. In our unsophisticated
comprehensive, her effect on the rest of us was
electric. I was an unpromising child: big and
clumsy, with size eight feet and a shag cut (Bay
City Rollers vintage). Tessa was thin and languid,
with highlights in her long, smooth hair and no
freckles. I was secretly sure that if I tried hard
enough, one day I could be just like her. A little
like St Augustine and his chastity, however, I did
not want to risk trying yet in case it didn't work.

We lived in a comfortable, sheltered community in which everyone I knew, of every
generation, was consumed with curiosity about
the news. It is extraordinary that I can even
remember where I was when I heard it: helping
my mother in the charity shop she ran, no doubt

68

sneezing asthmatically in the dust-clouds rising from the clothes we were sorting out for sale. Someone came in with that special expression which lacks a name, but signifies the imminent breaking of a hugely gratifying secret.

As soon as I was alone with my friends, the speculation began. When did Tessa have the opportunity to conceive? Her parents were known to be quite posh and unbelievably fussy. How far gone was she? What would she do when the baby came? Leave school, or carry it round to lessons with her? Most of all, who on earth was the father? None of us was aware of a boyfriend, and even if we were, we would not necessarily have assumed they were sleeping together. After much discussion, we arrived at the common conclusion that he cannot have been a local lad. He might be a foreigner: Italian, Chinese, or even African? A completely unlikely solution seemed the best answer, at the time, to a completely unlikely situation.

It makes me squirm to realize how ignorant we were in the mid 1970s, and surprisingly naive. I have no recollection of what happened to Tessa. She left school, I know that, and her parents stood by her. I don't think she married the father, so her child was illegitimate. In our rural community, which was a kind-hearted if gossipy one, it was probably welcomed and accepted on its own terms. I hope so.

The scandal died down, more schoolgirl mothers came and went, and as I progressed to university I began to appreciate that pre-marital pregnancy was treated by some students — male and female — as an occupational hazard. It would never happen to me, of course. Like mortal illness and the sort of car crash where everyone dies but a baby, disasters like pregnancy always befell other people, different people. This is the danger of discussing anything like illegitimacy which bears, or bore, such a potent stigma: there is a strong temptation to believe that it afflicts a 'type' of person. It has traditionally been assumed that unmarried mothers must all be promiscuous, feckless, daft, or far too easily taken in. The 'strumpets' of the Elizabethan era found their counterparts in the rampant teenagers of the Swinging Sixties, by way of stridently modern characters like Edith Lanchester and Maud. There have always been irresponsible women who do not think of the consequences of short-term gratification. The 1913 Act equated mental with moral deficiency, and literature is full of ingénues tricked by sexually rapacious men into tragic motherhood. But as we know, there is no such thing as a typical single mother.

There is such a thing, however, as a common attitude towards them. Mr Disgusted Tunbridge Wells, writing to *The Times* about women's emancipation triggering a revolution in morality, was not alone. Indeed, he may well have been a member of the popular Social Purity and Hygiene Movement (of which illegitimate Ramsay MacDonald was a keen supporter), founded to combat the rancid habits of the sexually depraved. Its enemies were threefold: professional prostitutes, who spread venereal disease as well as contaminating the population with bastards; irresponsible 'amateurs' who went about randomly having sex outside marriage, thereby corrupting society; and those who produced and enjoyed pornography, especially people addicted to the solitary vice of masturbation.

The movement's zeal was fuelled by rumours which spread during the early months of the First World War, alleging that the country was in danger of being completely overrun by bastards fathered by urgent young soldiers and their paramours. So intense did the panic become that in the summer of 1915 a Committee on Illegitimate Births was set up. This committee, headed by the Archbishop of York, promptly dispatched 'a skilled lady investigator' to visit sixty-two towns and report, with the help of 'women's patrols', on the sexual behaviour of local women and billeted or garrisoned soldiers. How the skilled lady investigator managed to gather any meaningful evidence on her whistle-stop tour is uncertain, but she concluded that the rumours were unfounded. Instead of corruption and wild revelry she found only continence, she insisted, and nothing alarming at all.

Statistics released during the next few years suggest otherwise. A Royal Commission on Venereal Diseases in 1916 reported that 10 per cent of the male population had syphilis, which was incurable, while far more had gonorrhoea. The number of bastards being born was frightening. In Woolwich, where the Royal Arsenal was based, the illegitimacy rate shot up to an unprecedented level in 1917, as it did around the barracks of Lancaster the following year. The Bishop of Chelmsford raged about moral standards (of Essex girls, presumably), warning dolefully that if 'sickly sentiment' were allowed to influence society — feeling sorry for lone mothers, for example, whose lovers were away fighting for their country, or killed in action — then all would be lost.

More voices weighed in to what was becoming a national and strangely Episcopal debate. The sort of sickly sentiment to which the Bishop of Chelmsford referred was responsible for campaigns to provide funds for war widows and orphans which were indiscriminate (said the critics) in their bounty. There was a move, supported by a more tolerant prelate, the Archbishop of Canterbury, to bring unmarried partners and their children under this welfare umbrella. After all, before the war, a significant number of brides were pregnant on their wedding day; had their soldier lovers been around to marry them during the war, the rate of illegitimacy would be much lower. The frightening statistics about bastards were more about getting caught short, implied His Grace, than about the fruits of fornication. Yet another bishop, the Bishop of London, agreed with the Bishop of Chelmsford. There were too many 'young, giddy girls', he said, 'excited by the presence of young men in khaki'. They were leading the military astray. Not at all, countered the liberals: it was their duty, their war service, if you like, to minister to the needs of Britain's soldiery. A young woman remembered being counselled at the time to be particularly kind to members of the Forces on their return from the hell of the trenches: 'when your men-folk come home, deny them nothing'. This was a complicated response: the commission of a sin justified by compassion. The work of the devil by an angel. Surely no bishop, however progressive, could ever sanction that.

*   *   *

Behind all this squabbling, there was some hard and constructive work going on to address the evident problem of illegitimacy, never mind whether it was an epidemic, and irrespective of whose fault it was. In fact the war gave these radical new enterprises a certain amount of cover, which was convenient for those anxious not to enter into debate, but to *do* something. The National Adoption Society was founded in 1916 as the first networked adoption agency, quickly followed, and eventually eclipsed in scale, by the National Children's Adoption Association (NCAA). The NCAA started out as a local outfit in Exeter, founded by an indomitable refugee-worker, Clara Andrew. Both agencies were not-for-profit, advertising success-fully for support and patronage. The concept of finding war orphans a new home was attractive to the public. War orphans were bound to elicit sympathy; bastards less so.

The National Adoption Society and the NCAA were highly respectable operators in an environment crawling with suspicion and opportunism. Baby-farming was still a fact of life: the regulation of foster-parents had only been a requirement since the Children Act of 1908, less than a decade previously, and three baby-farmers were hanged between 1900 and 1907. Clara Andrew campaigned tirelessly for adoption to be regulated too, something she eventually achieved, in part, with the Adoption of Children Act in 1926.

In 1918, hard on the heels of statistics revealing the illegitimacy rate in England and Wales to be 6.26 per cent (having been only 3.94 per cent in 1907), another fearless individual stepped up to the plate to declare her support not only for illegitimate children, but — more controversially still — for their mothers. This was Lettice Fisher, who founded the National Council for the Unmarried Mother and her Child (NCUMC), which later became the National Council for One Parent Families, and inspired the charity Gingerbread, which still exists.

I first came across Lettice (née Ilbert) while researching *Blue-stockings*, a book about the first women to go to university in England. She was a student at Somerville College, Oxford, from 1894 to 1897, and wrote the most wonderful letters home describing a heady new experience of independence and intellectual freedom. She accepted a research studentship at the London School of Economics after achieving a first class degree in History, only she did not actually receive any formal qualification from Oxford, because its women students were not allowed to graduate formally until 1920. Then she took a tutorial post back at her alma mater, where her husband eventually became the Warden of New College.

Lettice was a natural activist, campaigning for women's suffrage, improved public health and housing reform. She helped develop the progressive Infant Welfare Association, long before the founding of the welfare state, which existed to educate mothers to bring up vigorous and well-adjusted children. The association employed health visitors, ran clinics, organized mother-and-toddler clubs, and gave Lettice the experience and conviction she needed to establish the NCUMC. She had always had the intellectual confidence to analyse society's shortcomings, the political impulse to change things for the better and the energy to attempt those changes herself; now all she needed was support.

Several things came together to help her cause in 1918. Not just the spike in birth-rate statistics for illegitimate children, but evidence that their mortality rate was twice as high as that of children born in wedlock. The incidence of maternal mortality was also higher for unmarried mothers. There were more young 'girl-mothers', having fallen pregnant during the war. Because foster-parents now had to be registered, there were fewer of them, so despairing mothers were forced into prostitution to support their children. The enfranchisement of responsible women fed authority as well as conviction into campaigns like Lettice's, affording the currency needed to influence politicians and public bodies effectively. Enthusiasm for social reconstruction after this 'war to end all wars' meant that the Government's ears were open to reform, and there was a degree of public sympathy for those left vulnerable by the death of husbands and/or fathers who had given their lives for their country. Perhaps unmarried mothers and their children could cash in on this sympathy.

Various conferences were held during the war discussing how best to provide for soldiers' families and several Relief Funds set up. One soldier ambitiously applied to the authorities in Portsmouth in 1915 for help to maintain his '16 wives and one mother'. Such extravagance was a little rich, even for Lettice, but it was clear that radical steps must be taken to re-establish the country's population on a robust and wholesome footing, and that it would take both money and courage to accomplish the task.

The NCUMC was founded on St Valentine's Day — deliberately injecting a sense of romance into what had until now been a steadfastly unromantic problem — and had its first committee meeting on 15 April 1918. There was disquiet from certain quarters about the Council's name. Was the word 'unmarried' not a little distasteful? Might it not put off potential benefactors? Perhaps another adjective would be more prudent? Lettice was never one for euphemisms, though, and insisted on keeping the proposed name exactly as it was. The aims of the organization were published without any shilly-shallying: the NCUMC's mission was to ensure 'the better care of the unmarried woman and her child, also the maintenance of a high

76

standard of morality, and consequently the diminution of unmarried motherhood'. To accomplish that — an aim with which it would be difficult to argue without appearing churlish — it was stated to be of fundamental importance that mother and child should be encouraged to stay together whenever possible. Parting them, except in extreme circumstances of hardship or neglect, caused damage to both parties which was difficult to mend.

If the mother could be helped to bring up her own baby, at least for the first two years of its life, the child would have a better chance of thriving, healthy in body and mind; the mother would have an incentive to behave responsibly and set a good example; and she might even earn a little respect from a hitherto intolerant society. This last point was crucial. Lettice realized that the NCUMC would get nowhere without a wholesale change in society's attitude to illegitimacy. She did not even want the word 'illegitimacy' to be used in terms of children. They were not illegitimate. Their parents might be, but the children were innocent and should be treated as such. It was her ambition that *every* child should eventually be provided for,

ill or well, normal or abnormal, good or naughty, not only from the moment when it is born, but from the moment its mother knows that it is going to be born, [with] a network of services which shall in cooperation with its parents give it the best possible chance of making the most of itself, of

77

developing its personality, physical, mental, emotional, to the fullest extent.

This was radical stuff.

The NCUMC did not ignore birth-fathers. It acknowledged that they had a part to play in their children's lives, and should be held responsible for maintenance. The law needed tightening up on that — as indeed it was, to a limited extent, in the Bastardy Act of 1926, which the Council did so much to influence. But the Council's primary duty was towards mothers desperately in need of help; in 1919 it opened a department which dealt one-to-one with individual cases, and was soon interviewing about fifty women a month, trying to find them shelter, work, affordable and good-quality childcare, legal and medical advice, and financial grants. Funding all this was never easy, but Lettice and her peers were canny and committed people, and no one tried harder than they did to erase the stigma of illegitimacy in twentieth-century Britain.

They faced plenty of opposition. Certain members of the judiciary were reactionary. On sentencing a mother of seven illegitimate children to prison in 1938, a judge complained pettishly that it was 'one of these cases where a woman goes about and produces a mentally defective child every 12 months. It is appalling.' Representatives of the Anglican Church seem to have been the loudest critics. Dr Lowther Clarke, addressing a meeting of the Mothers' Union in 1920, commented that the Church had been asked to 'look upon children born outside married life', by which he presumably meant to include them unconditionally into the congregation. The Church must refuse, he said. No good could ever come of illegitimacy, and it would be unforgivable to 'approximate a human generation to the morals of the farmyard'. He also took the opportunity to have a pop at the 'scanty dress' so many women were wearing these days. Shorter dresses might offer 'facilities for walking' and keep the skirt clean, but they projected an image against which the Church must set its face with stern resolution.

There was controversy in 1934 when a bishop banned women who had had an illegitimate child from membership of the Girls' Friendly Society, an organization founded to support single young Christian women to live responsible and useful lives. 'Bad coin drives good coin out,' he intoned; how many mothers would be willing for their girls to associate with 'those who have had so grave a moral lapse'? To be fair, this bigoted attitude caused revulsion among parishioners and fellow clerics alike, but the Bishop of London was not without his supporters. Allowing fallen women to be members of the Friendly Society would mean the organization's salt would lose its savour, said one; it would bring society down to the lowest common denominator, according to another; the Church should exist to combat moral laxity, not condone it.

There *was* moral laxity involved in illegitimacy. But it was not just the sort of casual laxity that led to sexual incontinence; it embraced far uglier affairs like rape, incest, prostitution, trafficking and infanticide. When stricter controls were introduced over affiliation payments, some cynical women tried their utmost to exploit them for gain. Mothers could be plain cruel, neglecting their children, or victimizing them. Assumptions were made about single mothers — still are — which in some cases appeared to be self-evident. Domestic servants were all empty-headed fools, for example. Particularly parlour-maids.

While it cannot be denied that a significant proportion of single mothers over the years have been girls in service, it is unjust to assume that it is solely because they are foolish. Gertrude was sent into service at fourteen, and three years later, in 1923, gave birth to Monica. Monica's father, Roland, was the son of the house, an army officer, who persuaded Gertrude to join him in a drink after a party to celebrate his homecoming on leave. She may have been innocent; she was certainly unused to drink. But she was hardly culpable for what happened next. She passed out, and Roland raped her. His father paid Gertrude a meagre ten shillings a week to help maintain the child until she was fourteen, on the condition that Gertrude never told anyone who Monica's father was — including Roland himself. Monica was to be kept a complete secret. When the girl was ten, her grandfather died, so the money dried up. Gertrude could not apply to any other members of the family, because no one knew about Monica, and Gertrude was loath to break her promise. There is a difference between foolishness and naivety.

Why were girls like Gertrude so naive, anyway? Tilly was a kitchen-maid at a holiday camp, and remembers ruefully that she used to be extremely popular with 'all the fellows' because she used to go to bed with them. She did not like doing it, and got no pleasure from sex; she just assumed that it was expected of her, and that all the other girls did the same. Phyllis ran away from home when her father hit her; she lived by the coast and was planning to sleep the night in a boat on the shore. But a kind-looking gentleman saw her wandering along the street and offered to take her to his hotel. She was grateful, went with him, climbed into one of the twin beds when he suggested a rest, and then he climbed in on top of her. She did not realize what he was doing. She did not even know what 'pregnant' meant. Girls like Tilly and Phyllis were denied knowledge of the facts of life because it was thought it would corrupt them. That is why reformers like Lettice hated euphemism so much. In 1979, Heather was asked whether she approved of sex-education in schools. 'I think it's terrible. I know when I was a kid and I said once to my mother [was she] going to have a baby, I got a bloody good hiding. I did, honestly. She knocked me all around the room.'

Before they learned about sex and its consequences in biology lessons, or at an excruciatingly embarrassing session with the dowdiest teacher in the school, girls were simply warned not to touch boys, to look after themselves, not to be

81

dirty and never to get themselves into (unspecified) trouble: all admirable sentiments, but lacking in detail. It was rude to mention the word 'pregnant', and you never *ever* mentioned any word beginning with the letters s-e-x. Hence a mother, born in 1930, was able sagely to explain to her daughter that babies came out of your 'back passage'. She had been under chloroform when her own child was born, and had never been taught any differently.

No wonder so many young women were as shocked by their pregnancies as everyone else seemed to be. If you were lucky, your mother might give you some hint of the facts of life on the eve of your wedding, by which time it might well be too late; well into the 1960s less enlightened daughters were being fobbed off with the notion that babies arrived in the doctor's black bag; were somehow encapsulated in pills swallowed by mothers-to-be, like little seeds on which (in one sophisticated variation I heard) their future baby's face was stamped in miniature; they were planted in mummies' tummies by God, or delivered as a wedding gift by an obliging angel. A schoolgirl mother contributing to a radio programme was asked if her parents had ever discussed the facts of life with her. 'Oh no,' she replied, 'we *never* talked about things like that . . . I was well brought-up.' Similarly, a couple interviewed in 1970 admitted to being devastated when their daughter had to get married at seventeen.

Unfortunately she was in the family way, you know . . . It was a shotgun job as usual

82

and it was a bit of a devil, you know, and upset us both dreadfully at the time, because she had a wonderful future in front of her. She was doing A levels and had had a present from the mayor for academic work . . .

Her father had hoped his daughter would go into what he called 'fishology'. There was a future in fish, he reckoned. 'The food of the world, fish.' But fate chose otherwise.

★　★　★

It was difficult to maintain quite such a degree of naivety if you served in His Majesty's Forces during the Second World War. 'Up with the lark, to bed with a Wren': the young, single girls given a chance of independence during this heightened period soon got a reputation for flightiness. If they became pregnant, they were discharged after the first trimester, and were not allowed to attempt to re-enlist until six months after the baby's birth. Local maternity services were said to be finding it hard to cope with the number of servicewomen occupying beds; so much so that in May 1943 the Ministry of Health stepped in to sponsor their care. But in the cold light of peace, it became obvious that there were not as many pregnancies among unmarried service-women as there might have been; according to the novelist Barbara Cartland, who worked in women's welfare at the time, only an infinitesimal percentage of women in the Forces found themselves in trouble. Until 1942, when the supply of rubber from Malaysia was interrupted, condoms were issued to all servicemen; army doctors gave lectures on sex-education; recruits were inspected for sexually transmitted diseases. The girls shared tips on how best to avoid the unwanted attentions of randy soldiers, sailors and airmen. Try not to drink too much before you go to bed, so that you do not have to risk a trip to the lavatory in the night, which might involve walking past the guards in your night-dress. If you are out on your own at night, light a cigarette and loudly stamp your feet, so that you are mistaken for a man. Wear your skirt as tight as possible. Tight skirts are far more difficult for a man to negotiate than boxy ones. Beware of Canadians. And if the worst happens and you need an abortion, there are people you can ask, discreetly, for help — but only at a price.

Women with unwanted pregnancies who were not in the Forces faced different problems. They fell into two distinct groups: the unmarried, and the unfaithful. 'Most of my friends had one particular GI Joe,' remembers a girl who revelled in the company of American soldiers, 'and so did I.' Being suddenly surrounded by men in uniform — especially if they were foreign — was irresistibly exciting to many women who had lived through the drab 1930s in a haze of beige. They did not even have to be in uniform. According to a disgruntled Lincolnshire soldier,

Lincoln women had never seen foreigners here before, it was like Christmas for them.

They'd got Yanks here [heard about the new utility knickers? One Yank and they're off . . .] Germans, Poles, Italians, all Prisoners of War. We never stood a chance. Some of us were getting about 15 bob a week, the Yanks got nearly 15 quid. They could get any woman they wanted, they'd got money, fags, gum, chocolate, and they could get nylons . . . They used to have buses run from Unity Square to the camps. It created a hell of a lot of bad feeling.

Florence fell pregnant to a swarthy Canadian soldier while she was working in the local NAAFI. She was asked to leave as soon as she showed, in case she corrupted the customers. The sort of bad feeling mentioned by that Lincolnshire lad almost overwhelmed Florence's family: when her mother and sisters heard about her being in the family way, their first reaction was to try to abort the baby with piping hot baths and knitting needles. Neither worked, and her daughter Patricia was born with olive skin and long black hair. 'You're not bringing that home,' spluttered Florence's father — but she did, and by the time the Adoption Agency people came round (out of the blue, according to Patricia, because they had heard of a bastard in the house), Patricia's grandpa was so besotted with her that he marched them backwards down the road, nose to nose, and away. This was a family triumph.

For wives conceiving out of wedlock, the situation could be altogether more complicated.

The loneliness of a wife whose husband is in the Forces can be crippling. That did not excuse infidelity then any more than it does now, but does help explain why so many married women had illegitimate children during the war. Strictly speaking, they were *not* illegitimate, since any child born within a marriage is deemed in law to belong to the husband. If the husband failed to acknowledge the child, however, then it was bastardized. Some women found a sort of vicarious joy in making love to other men while their husbands were away, and felt that joy vindicated the act of infidelity: 'If [my lover] had my body, my heart was with my husband, and somehow I didn't feel that I was doing anything wrong.' For others, like Caroline's mother, it was a desperate business.

Caroline's mother was a Dutch woman, multilingual and highly intelligent, who married Caroline's (illegitimate) father in 1939 after a romantic meeting abroad. They came back to Britain just as war broke out. She was training to become a nurse when she discovered she was pregnant with Caroline. When Caroline's father was called up, she and her mother were evacuated to the remote countryside. They were billeted at a small farm where there was neither electricity nor running water. The nearest town was several miles' walk away, and being a foreigner, Caroline's mother was extremely lonely. Caroline is not sure how they met, but at some stage during their stay at the farm, her mother became pregnant by a black American sailor, who also gave her VD. When Caroline's father returned at the end of the war, he agreed to take his wife back, but only if she put the baby up for adoption. So the half-caste girl was taken to an orphanage or children's home; Caroline is unsure which, but knows the child was never adopted.

The first time Caroline became aware of her half-sister was one Christmas when she was about ten. She saw a card addressed to 'Mummy', and when she asked her father about it, he slapped her. He was no doubt dealing with his own demons: his birth-mother never acknowledged him as her son, which affected him deeply. He later apologized, but could not explain. Eventually Caroline's mother broke down, and told her the truth.

After the Second World War, the pressure to conform to an image of perfect family life was intense. Social reconstruction was not just a matter of putting physical services in place; it had moral implications too. A bright new Britain was launched, with a bright new public face. It was peopled with unexceptional, hygienic-looking husbands and wives in smart hand-knitted woollies and tweeds, with a sturdy son and frilly daughter (in that order), perhaps a dear little Scottie dog, and a semi-detached house in the suburbs, as neat as a new pin. This is the contemporary media's stereotype, not mine. When Baby was born, he was elaborately encased in crocheted rompers and matinee jackets, and wheeled in a pram of imperial vastness to clinics, clubs and baby competitions to be shown off and admired. Illegitimacy played no part in this construction, which made it even harder for women like Caroline's mother to bear.

The NCUMC's advice was needed now more than ever, as mother-and-baby homes were filling up fast. Unmarried mothers were usually sent some distance away, partly to avoid the prying and judgemental eyes of the neighbours, and partly so that the baby, if it was sent for adoption, would not be placed in the same locality as the birth-mother. There is a rumour that when a woman fell pregnant on Guernsey in the Channel Islands (where more than 300 illegitimate babies were born during the German occupation) she was automatically sent to neighbouring Jersey to have the baby. When the time came for it to be adopted, the authorities on Jersey treated it as a local baby, so sent it 'away' to be placed — usually, to Guernsey. For the birth-family this could be a cause of danger and delight in equal measure.

Comments in Salvation Army records give us an idea of the different backgrounds their 'girls' came from. Many were fugitives from their families: 'very anxious her father shall not know' — 'father very angry and mother is crushed by the blow' — 'parents heartbroken'; Vera's parents were 'very poor' but they offered what payment they could in return for sanctuary for their daughter, whom they loved dearly. Inverting the usual scenario, they were anxious that she should *not* marry the father. He had taken advantage of her, they claimed, to force her to marry him. A thirty-nine-year-old maternity nurse was admitted because she did not want her relatives to know about her pregnancy. She was a widow, with three children already, placed temporarily in 'an orphanage for middle-class children' while she had the baby. One wonders what became of her, of the child, and whether anyone ever discovered the truth.

★ ★ ★

Imogen and Sarah are friends; they met as young women, and years later discovered that they had both had an illegitimate child at the same mother-and-baby home, but at different times. It was not a Salvation Army home; this one catered to the daughters of professional people, and to independent women. Sarah was a schoolgirl when she conceived. She sat her A-levels in the June, and gave birth in October. Her father was not wealthy, but he was prominent in the local community and a church warden, and Sarah thinks that is why she was referred to this slightly genteel Church of England home. Imogen was a primary school teacher.

Their companions at the home were interesting. Sarah remembers the daughter of a bishop, of a police inspector, an exalted Army officer, a headmaster; a few rich Jewish girls were accommodated there, and some mortified Catholics. The Army officer's daughter was allowed to take her baby home with her, but confessed to being terrified at what her father might do to it. The bishop's daughter was desperate to keep her baby, but he forbade her. She was devastated. The fortunes of Sarah and

Imogen were very different, as we shall see.

Sarah was a teenager when her child was born in 1963, and though not at all promiscuous herself (she loved and had hoped to marry her boyfriend), she suffered from a tendency prevalent at the time, to stereotype all people of her age as obsessed with sex, drugs, alcohol and shocking the older generation. She still feels she is judged by some people, as a single parent. They assume she is easy, racy — and she's nearing her seventies now.

The NCUMC published statistics revealing that in 1961, 2,500 illegitimate babies were born to mothers under sixteen years of age. That was double the previous high, which occurred in the last year of the Second World War. One in eight of all live births in London in 1961 was illegitimate (the national average was one in sixteen) and in the Royal Borough of Kensington and Chelsea — the fashionable place to be for young people in bedsits — the rate peaked at one in five.So widespread was the problem that the massively popular satirical programme on the BBC, *That Was The Week That Was*, featured a 'Lullaby for Bastards' in 1963. It was written by Herbert Kretzmer and sung by Millicent Martin.

Don't you weep, my little baby, cause you
    haven't got a Dad.
Go to sleep, my little baby, things aren't
    really quite so bad.
There's no reason any longer why you ought
    to feel so blue,
The world is full of bastards just like you.

One minute the press blamed the parents of these errant teenagers for allowing them to go out and party all night without adult supervision; the next, the news was all about disaffected children wanting to spite their parents by presenting them with a mongrel grandchild. Arguments erupted then, as now, about what influenced young people to behave so badly. Was it 'X' rated films? Obscene literature ('authors such as D. H. Lawrence', as one journalist rather coyly put it in 1966)? The influence of immigrants from the West Indies who did not seem to care about illegitimacy? Flabbiness on the part of the Churches? The politician Gwyneth Dunwoody probably came closest, when she contributed to a debate in the House of Commons in February 1967. It was her opinion that society had elevated hypocrisy almost to a way of life. How could we encourage young people on the one hand to believe that they could lead 'a wide open sex life', while condemning them bitterly in the very next breath when they produced illegitimate children, making them suffer 'an enormous stigma' and failing to give them the practical support they needed?

Significant numbers of unmarried mothers were students at this time: obviously, university life afforded opportunities for sex unavailable at home. Ten per cent of women on degree courses in 1966 are said to have dropped out due to an unplanned pregnancy. Occasionally students were readmitted afterwards, although this was more common after the 1970s. Carol A became pregnant after a single minimal encounter in 1959, and went to a mother-and-baby home recommended by the principal of her college in Oxford. She was twenty, at the end of her first year as an undergraduate. She found that the support she was offered by her parents, her tutors and her principal was entirely dependent on her decision to keep the pregnancy secret, give birth away from home, and have the child adopted as soon as possible. If she fulfilled these requirements, her parents would continue to subsidize her financially, and her college would welcome her back — even if it was with eyes averted rather than open arms.

Those social commentators who believed that unmarried women usually got pregnant wilfully (echoing the received wisdom of the sixteenth and seventeenth centuries) were not always wrong. Two instances confirm this with some force. They centre around very different women. Margaret was one of the first people I interviewed in connection with the book. She held me spellbound. Her mother Doreen was born in 1906, and by the 1930s was working as a tax inspector in London. It was an unusually responsible job for a woman at the time, and Doreen was obviously well liked and highly respected. It was there, in the tax inspectors' office, that she met the love of her life. He was a colleague, unhappily married, who told Doreen that she had brought him 'back from the dead'.

Doreen made it clear from the beginning that she wanted a child. Her lover had none. His wife used to sleep in her mother's room: it was hardly a satisfactory arrangement. But he was loyal, and told Doreen he could not desert his marriage. He tried to be honourable, too, telling his wife about Doreen. He was committed, in different ways, to them both. At one stage he wrote Doreen a letter, urging her to go and find someone else to give her a child, and they tried to part, but could not manage it.

In 1941, Doreen conceived. Astonishingly, her colleagues were supportive: she was posted to another office in Northern Ireland before she knew she was pregnant, but allowed to return early to London after just a few months and encouraged back to work again after the birth. She had twins — Margaret and a brother — and her lover continued to share his time between his wife and Doreen until the children left home. Doreen wore a wedding-ring and changed the children's surname to their father's by deed poll. They were an alternative family, a loving unit, and the twins were brought up to be non-judgemental and accepting.

It was not an ideal situation, though, and despite her mother's positivity, Margaret remembers a lack of confidence in her youth which she ascribes to not feeling as worthy as other (legitimate) people. It is a feeling shared by Suzanna, whose chaotic childhood seems to have left her somewhat dazed. Suzanna talks of insecurity rather than unworthiness, and there is a sense of pride in her uproarious mother Heidi as well as puzzlement. No resentment, though, which seems, on the face of it, remarkable.

Heidi came from a privileged background. It

was the sort of background that involved a family seat and a coat of arms with a trenchant motto. She had a governess instead of going to school, and grew up to be confident, self-possessed, and extremely charismatic. She married in 1947, and a couple of years later settled in a remote rural area with her husband, who had decided to become a gentleman farmer. Their first child was born in 1950. Sixteen months later, Suzanna came along, looking markedly and suspiciously unlike either her father or her brother. The next child arrived in 1954. According to Suzanna, 'it was after this that my father was caught with the nanny'. He moved away, ostensibly to earn some money, as the farm was a financial disaster.

Baby number four is thought to have belonged to a local farmer, huntsman or headmaster. It is at this point that Heidi's distinguished parents washed their hands of her. Heidi promised after her son was born that she would be a good girl, remembers Suzanna, but it was not long before she confessed that she had 'fallen over a molehill again'. Suzanna and her siblings were sent to the local orphanage when the new baby appeared; there was no one else to look after them. When they returned, Suzanna was dragooned into service as a surrogate mum and expected to bear all the family's responsibilities on her own frail twelve-year-old shoulders.

Heidi and her husband divorced in 1963, shortly before a final child was born, to the local auctioneer (while the others returned for a spell to the orphanage). Life on the farm was brutally hard. Suzanna reckons her mother 'sold herself to keep us all fed; she had sold all the diamonds she inherited, all the family silver and the land off to raise us all'. She borrowed people's husbands — useful husbands like a council repair man who cut all the hedges, the owner of a stable who lent them horses, or a police detective who taught the children to shoot at tin cans. She never found the need to remarry.

Suzanna struggled with her numerous siblings, and sold daffodils and damsons to raise money; meanwhile Heidi continued to make the most of life. She followed the foxhounds in the winter, went otter-hunting in summer, 'and all the time she was having fun being a huge personality'. She thumbed her nose at convention by refusing to acknowledge that her behaviour was in any way blameworthy, to the extent that she became a prominent member of the local church community in later years, after leaving the farm. She convinced her children that to be different was good (luckily) and bequeathed her self-confidence to Suzanna, who believes that nothing is impossible, and shame is a waste of time.

★ ★ ★

On a simplistic level it is not difficult to understand Heidi's motives. She had her illegitimate children because she felt she had a right to, and it was easier to have them than not. A lot of energy was spent on academic papers and conference platforms at the time she was producing her exotic family, and in the decade or so afterwards, about what drove women to 'choose' unmarried motherhood. A ground-breaking study was published in America in 1954 by the sociologist Leontine Young, suggesting that the whole problem was a psychological one. Not in the crude sense understood by the Victorians, that bastards were only born to the libidinous or the mentally dull, but in a more complex, Freudian way. Young maintained that unmarried daughters became pregnant to make a statement, or in reaction, to their own parents. Most single mothers were 'infantile' and in some way 'perverted', and produced a baby partly as a sort of gift to their parents, to gain their approval, and partly (confusingly) as an excuse to break away from them and have someone to love who is exclusively theirs. Either way, we can return to Philip Larkin for the gist:

> They fuck you up, your mum and dad.
> They may not mean to, but they do.
> They fill you with the faults they had
> And add some extra, just for you.

This psychological thesis caught on. In the decade leading up to the passing of the Abortion Act in 1967, illegitimacy was presented as the symptom of an emotionally rather than morally diseased section of society; a problem to be analysed in terms of behaviour and response, and solved not by censure or denial, but by enlightened understanding. So broke the dawn of the permissive age. Not for everyone, though, as a contemporary letter to the *Guardian* proved: 'Sir, How will I know when the permissive society arrives at N13? Yours faithfully, Unmarried Mother.'

In other words, while all this theorizing was going on, in real life things did not seem to be changing much. This is not to say that the theorizing meant nothing. It eventually helped revolutionize sex and the single person. You could hardly get more revolutionary than the Pill, and the provisional legalization of abortion up to twenty-eight weeks. But beneath the ivory towers, on the streets of Palmers Green (N13) and in villages up and down the country, it is clear that illegitimate babies were being born for much the same reasons as they had ever been.

It is not always possible for mothers to articulate the motives behind deliberate pregnancy, if there are any, and not always possible to ask. Feisty Maud and Edith, in the opening chapter, were making a point. So was Heidi, probably. Perhaps the most startling example of the 'political' baby was Sylvia Pankhurst's son by an Italian lover. Sylvia, a founder member of the British Communist Party, announced his birth in the *News of the World* in 1927. He was described, proudly, as a 'eugenic baby'. This caused a sensation. The writer Vera Brittain was outraged on two counts: one, that Sylvia had been so brazen (especially given that her suffragette mother Emmeline had spent so much time and energy trying to convince people that women were responsible members of society) and two, that the baby turned out to be so placid and happy. 'Sylvia was well-rewarded for her 'sin', as people so often are,' complained Vera, a little unkindly.

Doreen (the tax inspector) was not particularly interested in turning her pregnancy into a political statement. She was a mature, intelligent woman who failed to see why her inability to marry should deny her a family with the man she loved. There are other cases like that (but without the romance): a couple who met at a school PTA, for example, both married to someone else. The woman wanted another baby but her husband had said no, and the man was happy to oblige. So they slept together, deliberately not using contraceptives, and the baby duly arrived. The man's wife left him, but it is unclear whether the woman's husband accepted the cuckoo into his nest, or whether the birth-parents built their own. The situation must have been very complicated, particularly for the children involved.

Dot fell in love with a Polish soldier at the end of the Second World War; her father refused to let them marry, so Dot tried to conceive to force his hand. She was successful, but it all went horribly wrong: her father did not relent, and banished her from home, and the soldier disappeared. Eventually Dot's parents adopted the child themselves, but never told him about Dot, and Dot was erased from her family's lives.

Sandra got pregnant so that she should have 'someone to love who would not run away'. Molly did it (at the age of fifteen) to escape her impossibly repressive parents. Rose had been in care, and was terrified of being returned to an abusive stepfather. Trudy was a divorcée, aged forty-three, on the cusp of the menopause and still very much in love with her husband. The urge she felt to have another baby was overwhelming; her husband had refused her, so she turned to one of her children's godfathers, very fond of Trudy, for help. Trudy suffered hyperemesis gravidarum, or acute morning-sickness, during her pregnancy by the godfather, with high blood pressure and hepatitis, and when her own parents blackmailed her into putting the baby up for adoption, for shame, she hardly had the strength to resist. 'It broke her already damaged heart,' remembers her daughter. 'She kept his baby photo under her pillow until the day she died at the age of eighty-nine.'

Years later, Trudy's daughter managed to trace her half-brother — too late for Trudy, sadly — and they are now 'as close as can be', so this sad story does have a happy ending. A surprising one, too: when the daughter researched her genealogy, she discovered that Trudy's mother, who had so fiercely forced Trudy to relinquish the baby for the sake of the family's reputation, went pregnant to the altar herself. So did *her* mother, and *her* mother before that. Not quite a tradition of illegitimacy, then, but as close as it is possible to get. Perhaps respectability is merely a question of timing.

4

Pater Nullius: Unmarried Fathers

*One thing is clear. We need to divest our-
selves of the misconceptions and the
condemning attitudes which have made the
unmarried father a resource, not a person.*

Here is a cautionary tale about the just deserts of
disrespect. It involves a woman called Rose,
several single fathers, and who knows how many
illegitimate children. These days it would
probably involve a court case against the
manufacturers of a certain brand of contraceptives too, but in the 1920s, when this little saga
took place, such litigious thoughts were far from
anyone's mind.

Rose worked on the domestic staff of a
well-known public school. The young gentlemen
there treated her like dirt. There was nothing she
could say to avenge their casual cruelty to her;
answering back might cost her job. So instead,
she hatched a plan. It was her duty to clean the
young men's bedrooms, and she soon came to
know exactly where they kept their most
precious possessions. A surprising number of
them had a cache of French letters squirrelled
away. In those days condoms came coiled in tins,
not individually packed as they are now. With a
glint in her eye Rose took a hat-pin one day,

opened all the tins she could find and radially poked a hole through the contents, thus creating a tiny, discreet puncture or two in each sheath. Then she carefully replaced the lids, put the tins back in their hidey-holes and awaited developments.

Rose's revenge for the pupils' lack of respect probably changed many young lives. There must be children and grandchildren around today because of her. One idle day I should try to find out if there was an unexpected bulge in the local birth-rate round about the time of Rose's employment, and whether the fathers concerned eventually married the mothers. During the period covered by this book, the general expectation would be that they did not. That time-honoured double standard still existed, whereby a girl was required to be pure and a boy to be experienced in the ways of the world. Think of the word spinster, and what do you see? Now think of the word bachelor. The images are somewhat different, and often completely misleading.

In this history of family secrets, no character is so consistently obscured as the birth-father. Over and over again illegitimate children claim they have never had a father. The absence might be inevitable: maybe the mother never confided her pregnancy.

It was decided by my parents to send me away from home. I was told not to tell anybody; I wasn't to tell my friends, not the people I worked with, nobody. I didn't tell the man himself. My mother said, 'Don't tell him because you don't want to ruin anybody else's life.' It was my problem.

A social instinct to protect the putative father was strong. If he was already married that is understandable, secrets and lies often being considered safer than inconvenient truths. We have already met Gertrude, who was raped by her employer's son Roland, home on leave from the army. Roland's father hushed the matter up by paying Gertrude to bring up her daughter Monica alone. What Gertrude did not realize at the time was that Roland had recently married, and that his wife was expecting her own child. The money she received was not so much for Monica's upkeep, as for Roland's protection. But even single men, without responsibilities else-where, were spirited away out of trouble if it was thought they could get away with it. A girl working in a doctor's surgery in the 1930s became pregnant by the doctor's son. While she was found lodgings by her employers, and taken back into service after the baby was born (which was very generous of the doctor and his wife), like so many others the son was sent abroad with a slap on the back 'to start a new life'. And I should be amazed if many of Rose's public schoolboys faced the music. The Surprise Polka. In their case, of course, circumstances were a little different, in that they had tried to act responsibly, but had then been thwarted.

During both World Wars, it was much easier than in peacetime to avoid the responsibility of fatherhood. We should credit those fathers who did not want to avoid it, even in such parlous times. A high-profile case in 1944 involved Nora Carpenter, an ATS girl in Derbyshire, and a married staff sergeant in the US Army. He was glamorous, blond and blue-eyed; they became lovers, and soon Nora fell pregnant. It is an old story with a predictable ending, except that in this case, there was a twist in the tail. On 28 February 1944 Nora gave birth — to quadruplets. One of the babies died a fortnight later, but the other three thrived and instantly became famous, with local or national businesses clamouring to meet their every need, and newspaper articles bringing in mailbags full of donations and letters of support. There was even a short film documentary made about Michael, Maureen, Madeleine and MacDonald, the Carpenter Quads. Their father visited his celebrity babies whenever he could. In 1945 he was demobbed and went back to America, but by the following year he had divorced his first wife and married Nora, who travelled out to live with him there.

There were many other GI brides, married before or after pregnancy; books have been devoted to them. But there were also crowds of women whose lovers left them holding the baby; legions of children, now in their late sixties or seventies, who feel bereft. Figures were published in the US in 1953 suggesting that there were about 70,000 American bastards in Britain as a legacy of the war; fewer than the 100,000 estimated to be in Japan, but more than the

50,000 in Germany. These are enormous numbers. War-babies' fathers were not just white, apple-pie Americans like Nora's lover. To revisit some of the people we have met already: Christopher, who did not realize his illegitimacy until his mother's death, found out that his father was an RAF hairdresser. Caroline's mother was made pregnant by a black American sailor who gave her an STD (and who might himself have been lynched by his white colleagues had they known); Dot's lover was a Polish soldier she was desperate to marry, and Lesley's father was a South African who fought in the First World War; she never knew him, but found comfort at the end of her life in visiting his birthplace; breathing the air he breathed.

There were certain hotspots in Britain during the Second World War where the population of illegitimate babies shot up alarmingly. Tiger Bay in Cardiff was one of them. Nowhere was there a higher proportion of children 'who don't know the names of their fathers', according to a report from the Mass Observation unit. The numbers might have been skewed by the fact that Tiger Bay also had one of the most vigorous red-light areas in the UK. But anywhere hosting a garrison, barracks, training camp or billeting centre was likely to experience a significant increase in illegitimacy. Following the Grenadier Guards' posting to Blackhill, County Durham in 1940, ninety girls were reported to be in the family way, and the newsagents' windows used to display mugshots of certain soldiers with 'Address Wanted' written ambitiously underneath so that putative fathers might be pursued for maintenance.

Not all the women involved were the provincial innocents we might assume them to be; nor were all the men simply opportunists. At a US Army base in Birmingham girls were reported to be arriving in busloads and 'literally knocking at the door for it'. Author Barbara Cartland remembered many of the GIs she came across as gullible and naive. When conscription for women was introduced in December 1941, pregnancy provided some with a means of escape; a weapon of self-defence. It is clear that some women actively sought to take advantage of their lovers for sex, and never mind the consequences. With spectacular insouciance, the married daughter of a well-respected tradesman in a northern country town conceived twins by a Canadian airman. Her husband found out and started divorce proceedings while still away on active service. 'Well, anyhow,' said the girl with a shrug, 'I've had a thrill out of it.' The US soldiers Miss Cartland knew, stationed near Bedford, behaved in an exemplary manner. 'I expected them to be very different,' she confessed;

> after all, they were in a strange country, away from home, risking their lives, lonely, homesick, and young enough to be out for a 'bit of fun'. But on the contrary: they were a credit to their country . . . And there is one other thing which I think should be recorded. When the black troops were brought to this country . . . stories of their behaviour with white women grew and multiplied. There

were no coloured troops in Bedfordshire, but I talked with the Service Police and Welfare Officers of other counties, and all said the same. It was the white women who ran after the black troops, not *vice versa*.

The number of 'unwanted' babies born in Britain during the Second World War put unique financial and practical pressures on the Government, forced to subsidize pregnant service-women and build special hostels to accommodate them all. There was another problem to cope with: the number of claims coming in from foreign women abroad accusing British servicemen of fathering their illegitimate children. This had started during the First World War, particularly in France, where brothels were numerous and a culture of tolerance developed over the issue of Tommy being allowed to slake what were called his 'life urges' in order to fight with keener concentration. Those trusty bishops piped up again in the papers back home, declaring the problem of soldiers' immorality 'to be a greater blow . . . to our national prestige than any falling back of our line in the trenches'.

The situation was complicated during the Second World War by rumours that the Nazis encouraged German soldiers to father as many Aryan children as they could, without regard to the petty constraints of marriage. It was their duty. But it appeared that the Allies were joining in (as those American statistics suggest) and by the early 1950s, when the resultant children were nearing school age, it became obvious that legislation would have to be put in place to determine paternal responsibility. Before the 1954 Visiting Forces Act was passed, it was extremely difficult for foreign-domiciled mothers to extract affiliation payments from British fathers. This spurred the National Council for the Unmarried Mother and her Child to launch a British campaign, somewhat surreally in support of German single mothers. I suspect it was not one of their most popular crusades.

* * *

It is not uncommon for illegitimate children to have been told, when asking their mother about their birth-father, to mind their own business. It is nothing to do with them; it doesn't matter who the father is; it's a secret. The feeling of rootlessness and resentment this has caused is lasting. One can allay it by making things up, pretending he was a brave fighter-pilot shot down in the war, or a dead hero of some other kind. Perhaps he was a tortured but essentially honourable man like Trevor Howard's character in the film *Brief Encounter*, temporarily overwhelmed by a noble and profound passion, and regretful for the rest of his life that he married the wrong woman. One lady told me that after growing up in a family that included her unmarried mother and three children, all by different men, she came to the conclusion that the only father she ever needed — and could rely upon — was God. It is tempting to those who are given no information at all by their mothers to fill the vacuum with more disturbing possibilities. Was my mother raped? Was it incest? Did *she* not know who my father was? Am I damaged goods? Of criminal stock? Carrying some awful malignant gene? There is shame not only in being born of sin, as our grandparents would have put it, but also in having no pedigree, no family history. One feels like a parvenu, an outsider, and somehow not quite real.

These worries cannot have occurred to single fathers who chose to absent themselves from their children's lives. Or if they did occur, they were quickly dismissed, by the RAF officer, for example, who made the mother of his illegitimate child sign an affidavit stating that he was not the father (suspicious in itself, surely?), in return for a sum of money; the barrister imprisoned for helping his twenty-year-old niece falsify the register of their baby's birth, or the gentleman found to be a multiple bigamist, with eighteen illegitimate children and a new seventeen-year-old 'wife' whom he had taken to a registry office, presented with a ring, and confidently informed that they were now completely married.

Dickie is not sure how many bastards he has; in one case it was arranged that the mother's boyfriend would marry her and accept paternity provided Dickie never went near her or the child again, 'which I thought was pretty reasonable, really'. Later on he met a couple of girls on the beach, then 'screwed 'em in the train all the way back. It was the Brighton Belle, actually. The good old days.' At least one of them became pregnant, and again, a gullible boyfriend stepped into the breach. Then there was the black chick in New York, and the girl whose baby — his baby — he helped to abort. These are his 'little peccadilloes', he says with a chuckle. You know how it is.

Michael was feckless, though not as bad as Dickie. He and Jane A ran away together and rented a bedsit while she worked as a kitchen assistant and he lazed around. Unknown to Jane he had recently ended a previous relationship, which produced an illegitimate daughter; Jane was convinced that with her, he would be a faithful, supportive lover. When they got bored with the bedsit, they broke open the gas-meter, stole the coins inside and left via the fire-escape, returning to Michael's home where — he assured Jane — his mother would take them in. It was a relief for Jane to discard the brass wedding-ring she had been wearing for appearance's sake: it was getting harder and harder to scrub the green stain from her finger. Michael told her they would soon be married for real.

'I believed him. I believed him when he would not take me out with him; it was cheaper to go out with his old friends. I believed him when he gave me a STD, but said I would not need to see a doctor, it would soon clear up. He begged me not to tell his mother though; and even though we did not have sex after I began to be symptomatic, it was too late. I was pregnant. I carried on believing him, even when his mother threw me out on to the street. I still believed him, the last time I spoke to him on the phone, when he told me to find a flat, and he would

come to see me, and we would be married
. . . When he did not come to see me, and he
stopped answering my messages to call me, I
slowly stopped believing him. To say I was
devastated is misleading. I was destroyed.'

Surely neither Dickie nor Michael ever grew
into responsible fathers? One lad, caught *in
flagrante delicto* on the parlour couch, blamed
his girlfriend's mother for the resulting pregnancy. She should never have left them alone in
the house together. It was obvious what would
happen. 'I can't do nothing about it.' When his
parents (as well as hers) ordered him to marry
her, he petulantly set the parlour curtains on fire
and then ran away to sea.

Mechanisms were in place to discourage such
irresponsibility. Various Acts of Parliament, from
1845 onwards, were devised to enable single
mothers to name putative fathers and extract
affiliation payments from them. But accusations
of paternity had to be proven, and evidence
corroborated by a third party, which was
distasteful, if not impossible. The whole process
could take months to run its course, and often
involved a mother and her illegitimate child
regularly having to visit an office in the town hall
or police-station or somewhere — very publicly
— to collect the payments due. From the late
1920s, blood tests could be used to determine
who the father was *not*, but support for these
was variable, and suspicions about the reliability
of results was widespread. DNA testing for
paternity did not become available until the late
1980s. So it often came down to word of mouth,

and credibility was closely linked to social standing, which put most women at a disadvantage straight away.

When Lettice Fisher founded the NCUMC in 1918, she stated one of its primary aims to be a change of culture with regard to birth-fathers. They should be acknowledged, without too much censure, and encouraged to support their illegitimate children not only financially, but in whatever way they could. She was one of the first people to articulate how important it was that all children should feel wanted, even bastards, and that parents should work together to the best of their abilities and circumstances to give their children the stability we all need in order to function as useful and trustworthy members of society. After all, the NCUMC was a tool of social reconstruction, as well as a welfare organization. The Salvation Army agreed with this aim, or at least with the acknowledgement and support part, and set up a bureau to trace missing fathers and bring them to justice.

This was all very well, but lost in all the efforts to support single mothers and their babies, the emotional needs of single fathers were completely ignored. It was not until the 1958 Adoption Act was passed that the wishes of birth-fathers were consulted (in a limited way) during the adoption process, and not until the following year that they were allowed to apply for custody of and access to their illegitimate children. By then one man in every twenty-five was estimated to have fathered a bastard. The 1959 legislation followed a test case in 1953, the first time an illegitimate child had ever been entrusted to its father's sole care; the presiding magistrate admitted this was a radical judgement, and his response was pragmatic. 'If we never do anything that has not been done before, we shall never do anything.'

Before that, a father had no legal rights over his illegitimate child at all. That is what illegitimate means. He was not even a parent in the legal sense: *pater nullius*. On the Continent, a birth-father had only to register his name on his child's birth certificate to become a recognized parent. 'Recognition' was a specific state, inhabiting the moral and legal no-man's-land somewhere between legitimacy and bastardy. Such a state did not exist in English law: you were either your child's father, or merely a potential income stream.

This state of affairs could have heartbreaking consequences for those men who felt as closely connected to their children as their mothers did. A case in 1917 particularly caught the public imagination. A little family of children, aged nine, seven and three, had been found wandering the streets. They were all illegitimate; their mother had died, and their father, an elderly clerk in a firm of solicitors, had fallen behind with his affiliation payments. He was desperate to care for them — he would find the money somehow — but the court preferred to put them on the open market. A new mother was chosen from about thirty applicants for the two girls, and from over 100 applicants for the boy. The children were separated and privately adopted. The bereaved birth-father lost all contact, and presumably disappeared from their lives.

In another case, six children were taken from their father and placed in six separate foster-homes when their unmarried mother was arrested for shoplifting. He was devastated, but completely impotent to do anything about it. In 1922 an unmarried father was arrested for abducting the daughter of whom he was 'intensely fond' because her mother demanded sole custody, and he could not bear to lose her. And so the stories repeat themselves, frequently revealing tenderness rather than the expected chauvinism, and a willingness to embrace the responsibilities of parenthood, rather than the fecklessness assumed by a legisla-tive system more used to penalizing single fathers than supporting them.

★ ★ ★

The 'shotgun wedding' was a common prophy-lactic against illegitimacy in working- and middle-class households before the permissive age, usually administered to camouflage the shame of having a bastard in the family. The unmarried mother's pregnancy was held against her lover like a pistol to the head. Marry, my lad, or you'll regret it. Reactions to this ultimatum varied. You could torch the netties and disappear, as we have seen; you could grit your teeth and descend into the abyss, like a young man from Lancaster married to his pregnant wife in 1953. He remembers the occasion with icy clarity: on their way to the reception at the Co-op after-wards, his wife turned to her new husband with a

113

steely eye and put a curse on him. 'I will make you pay for this,' she promised.

Pauline A's adoptive mother was forced to marry at sixteen after she slept with her young man while drunk. Even before pregnancy could be confirmed, the pair was rushed to the altar, just in case. As it happened, her mother later found out she was unable to have children at all — that is why they adopted Pauline — but the marriage endured, luckily, and was a happy one.

Mary would love to have married Derek, baby or no baby. She was a nurse in her mid-twenties, and met Derek, a Royal Air Force officer, at a friend's house-party. *She* invited *him* to a rendezvous at an Oxford hotel afterwards, and when she apparently discovered she was pregnant, she proposed to him in a letter. 'Dear Derek,' she wrote. 'Isn't this the most dreadful thing that could possibly happen . . . I want to bring this child safely into the world, and I shall always endeavour . . . to do my duty regarding it. So for the child's sake, Derek, will you marry me and thus enable the child not to be illegitimate?' Derek obliged, honourably inverting the proposal for form's sake, and allowing Mary to press ahead with wedding plans. But when his mother got to hear of it, all those plans were brought to a shuddering halt. She forbade Derek to commit himself to this dangerous woman — and Derek succumbed.

He wrote to Mary along classic lines:

None of this would matter a damn if I thought we cared for each other enough, but

114

I have to say that I don't think we do, and that marriage started on these conditions would be bound to end in absolute disaster for both of us, and especially for you . . . Don't think too badly of me, Mary, as I don't really think it is right to wreck both our lives like this.

Mary claimed it was the shock of this letter, received four months into her pregnancy, which caused her to have a miscarriage. She subsequently took Derek to court for Breach of Promise — and lost.

There was no proof that Mary had ever been pregnant at all, and the lawyers had no hesitation in finding against her. Paternity suits were notoriously difficult before the certainties of DNA testing, and their ramifications could sometimes be completely bewildering, even for the most experienced of judges. I found one such, summarized in a letter from a barrister to his wife, the novelist Margaret Kennedy, in 1939; quite properly he does not name names, but he does ask for Margaret's opinion.

The defendant was a sailor, aged twenty-one, who used to stay at a pub in Essex when he was home on leave. The publican's daughter was nineteen and worked in the bar. According to her they had sex, consensually, on a single occasion, when the sailor is reported to have told her that he had 'done it wrong'. He said she must let him know 'if anything happens'.

He believed her to be a virgin before this, and claimed that he was too, and that he had not had sex since. When it became obvious that the girl had conceived, he offered to marry her, but her parents refused permission. The baby was born prematurely, whereupon the sailor was issued with a demand from the publican for damages 'for the seduction of X and the loss of her services at the bar'.

The sailor agreed to pay a one-off lump sum of £150, to include child maintenance, which was accepted. On the day the money was supposed to be paid over, the baby died, but no one informed the court, and the payment went ahead. News of the death leaked out, however. The poor child had syphilis, from which its mother was also suffering — but not the sailor. She insisted she caught it from him; he maintained she must have had another lover, and that this other lover was in all likelihood the father of the child. He wanted his money back. There is no record of what happened next. Like one of those court-room dramas, you and I are left to decide a verdict for ourselves.

Sir Charles Oman was an academic at Oxford, a Professor of Modern History, who also held a pastoral post at the university. There, he was responsible for the morals (as he put it in 1924) of 4,000 young men between the ages of eighteen and twenty-five. He was often called upon to deal with reports of wayward women flagrantly seducing the undergraduates in order to get pregnant and blackmail them into marriage. This is exactly what the courts implied Mary had done, and possibly what the sailor's lover was trying to pull off, too. Sir Charles's response was surprisingly robust. He did not know why everyone was so afraid of illegitimacy. Why was it only ever referred to nowadays with a sob in the voice and a mournful expression? That was unnecessary. He had never found that the stigma prevented anyone from rising to merit. Why, he had even known Army commanders whose parents were unmarried, damn it. Society needed to pull itself together.

Meanwhile, beyond the ivory towers, marriage was still regarded as the best treatment — if not the cure — for bastardy. It is not easy to rationalize why Denise and her husband Cliff were wed. Denise was a student nurse, and Cliff one of her patients, twelve years older than she was. They were in love with one another when Denise fell pregnant. But they came from different social classes, and did not have the financial support of their parents. Cliff helped Denise contact the Salvation Army, who recommended the mother-and-baby home where their son was born; afterwards, both parents made the decision to place him in a foster-home while they decided what to do. Both sought counselling sessions, which they attended separately and together. They were thoughtful and mature, but not quite confident enough to face the money problems and social difficulties lying ahead. So they came to the conclusion that adoption would be best.

The boy was eight months old when Denise and Cliff signed him over, but only six weeks old when the welfare officer took him away to his foster-parents. Denise can still remember this clearly, as he beamed at his heartbroken mother and was driven off into the distance.

The irony is that Denise and Cliff got married anyway, and had further children. They made contact with their son again, before Cliff died. In fact, he was a pall-bearer at Cliff's funeral. He had his father's temperament, had followed the same career; they had so much in common. He did not resent their decision, but it must have been hard for everyone involved to accept that what's done is done, and that there's no point in thinking 'what if'.

Gary's experience is somewhat similar. He and his girlfriend got together while they were both undergraduates, aged twenty. They fell in love, she became pregnant, and despite their youth and circumstances, planned to marry and bring up their child together. She was reluctant to tell her parents the news, so Gary turned first to his father, expecting surprise, but some solidarity, and an offer of support.

Instead, Gary's father was stern and clinical. He advised Gary to stop dreaming, do what was necessary to put this unfortunate episode behind him, and try to get on with his life without the girl, and certainly without a baby. Gary was so shocked at this response, and so unsure of his own ability to take responsibility for the child and its mother, that he agreed. He relinquished control, and numbly told his girlfriend that he was not interested in their staying together. In retrospect he realizes he still loved her at that stage, and that if they had had the confidence to marry, their parents would probably have supported them. But he was only twenty, and his

118

own father's approval was important to him.

Gary's girlfriend made arrangements for the birth, and their son was adopted as soon as he could legally be taken from her. Both she and Gary went on to marry other people, but Gary could never absolve himself of the guilt of abandoning her, and never forgot his first-born. He and the boy's mother made contact with each other again when their son reached his twenty-first birthday; by then it had become an emotional imperative for Gary to have news of him. Because his name was not on the boy's adoption papers, Gary had no authority to start the (passive) process of tracing him — to make his name and address available should the boy wish to make contact — so it was necessary for his mother to initiate the search. Together she and Gary found out where he lived, what he did, and what his phone number was. Only then was Gary able to acknowledge how profound an impact the birth and adoption had had on him; how his whole life since had been coloured by a subliminal — or not so subliminal — sense of bereavement. He was ecstatic at the thought of getting to know his son for the first time.

Gary is still waiting for that to happen. His son declined to follow up his parents' overtures, and to answer the cards and letters Gary still sends him on his birthday and at Christmas. That is his prerogative. Now Gary writes books about the issues faced by single fathers, and campaigns for greater awareness of the legal and emotional difficulties they face. No doubt that helps, but surely nothing can quite compensate for the sense of rejection with which both he and his son are trying, in their own ways, to come to terms.

★ ★ ★

Veronica told me about her husband. She met him when she was seventeen. He used to clean the windows at the shop where she worked. He asked her out, and before her eighteenth birthday she had conceived. His parents had her to stay overnight when the news was broken, and gave her gin, Epsom salts and the usual hot bath in an attempt to induce a miscarriage. But the pregnancy progressed. Veronica's mortified father refused to speak to her for six weeks. Her mother was — inevitably — a pillar of the local church, and told Veronica that unless she married, quickly, she would have to leave home.

So the appropriate arrangements were made, and within two months Veronica was wed. She moved in with her in-laws; despite her acquiescence in getting married, she was virtually cut off by her parents anyway. She was not allowed to go and visit them in her pregnant state, or with her baby son, in case she was seen by the neighbours. Life was wretched.

Within a year Veronica and her husband were relocated by the council to a town miles away from home. They had two more children, but were never happy. They argued; there was violence involved; each felt as trapped, resentful and disillusioned as the other. Seven years after they met, Veronica left him. Soon afterwards, he committed suicide. 'I . . . have struggled for years to forgive myself.'

120

It was all about blame. Their eldest child blamed himself for being born, saying that if he had never arrived, his parents' lives would have been much happier. Veronica's mother-in-law blamed Veronica for seducing her son, and at one stage tried to adopt Veronica's boy, to replace her own. 'If I could turn the clock back,' says Veronica, 'I would do so.' Marriage is not always the best solution to illegitimacy, for parent or child. Sometimes it is the very worst thing that can happen.

When talking about weddings, particularly a forced wedding of some sort, it is important to point out that the shotgun did not always point in the same direction. Despite the popular bachelor-boy image of the single father, and the caricature (remarkably like Dickie) of the caddish bounder who loves 'em and leaves 'em, there have always been men who wanted nothing more than to marry the mother of their illegitimate child, just as Gary did before he confessed to his father.

Problems arose if the feeling was not mutual. Some men tried to force their reluctant lovers to marry them, threatening shame and penury if they refused, or emotional blackmail. Kate was a newly qualified teacher when she became pregnant. She decided the father of her baby was not the man she wanted to marry, whereupon he became psychosomatically blind, and when this didn't work (and he suddenly recovered his sight) he threatened to tell her future employers that she was a single mother. That had no effect, either.

Others frenziedly tried to woo the mothers of

their children and *make* them fall in love, like the man who made Johanna pregnant. She was a cook, aged twenty-six, and when she announced her condition (according to her Salvation Army record) he became obsessed with her, besotted, refusing to leave her alone. He carefully arranged to elope with her before the baby was born. The stumbling-block in his case — and it was a considerable one — was that he was already married.

If all else failed, shock tactics were employed by the single father seriously in want of a particular wife. In 1961, a former British Rail employee was fined for taking a steam-engine 'in a fit of pique' and driving it for twenty-five miles. The mother of his illegitimate child had refused to marry him. His defence lawyer conceded that 'one can think of better ways of letting off steam' but pointed out that to the engine-driver, being denied a proper family was disastrous. He wanted — needed — to do the right thing, and stay by his lover and child.

There were other ways of doing this than through marriage, which were common enough even before the permissive age took hold of society and shook it upside down. Doreen, the tax inspector who had twins, was a sort of parallel wife; her lover looked after her while remaining married to his lawfully wedded wife, who had no children. A significant number of the illegitimate people who contacted me were the children of bigamists, or of parents who pretended they were married to each other, but in reality were not.

If you were brazen enough to withstand the opinion of your neighbours and members of your own family (including the children involved), you could do whatever you liked. The wartime wife who had illegitimate twins for the thrill of it is an example of this devil-may-care attitude, as is Suzanna's flamboyant mother Heidi, who was at the centre of an unconventional extended family of lovers, illegitimate offspring, and their several fathers — the farmer, the auctioneer, the headmaster and the huntsman. All the adults seem to have got on quite adequately, while valiant young Suzanna took responsibility for the children.

David is the boy whose 'aunty', or foster-mother, tried to sell him by displaying him in the garden like a little mannequin. Research into his own rather distorted family history revealed that his birth-father lived next door to his mother. He was married, but his wife could not have children so he turned to his neighbour instead. David's mother was sent from London to the country to have the baby when the time came; David was then handed over to his father and his father's wife. But they soon got divorced, and David's father realized he could not take the responsibility of a child after all; that is when the boy was committed (without his birth-mother's knowledge) to the dubious professional care of aunty.

Luke did not care what people thought of him, either, but in his case this reflects on his sensitivity rather than his fecklessness. His story does not have a promising beginning. He dropped out of sixth-form college at the age of sixteen and went to live in a commune, where he met Joyce A. Joyce was illegitimate herself, and a disturbed character; she was older than Luke, and had just left her husband when she and Luke embarked on their unconventional relationship.

Joyce became pregnant when Luke was seventeen. The general idea was for the child to be adopted, and Joyce agreed (as did Luke) on the condition that she was never shown the baby. Three days after it was born, however, an unwitting nurse brought it along to Joyce, whereupon Joyce refused to let it go. The novelty of parenthood appears to have waned quite rapidly with her, so Luke took over the baby's care. Joyce began to drift away from Luke, who — against all advice — applied for legal custody of the child, and was granted it. This was in the early 1970s. His parents agreed to help, and Luke returned to college as a single parent.

At about the same time as Luke became the guardian of his own child, another single father was making headlines because of his unorthodox efforts to keep an illegitimate baby. John's story appeared in The Times in 1969. His family life was complicated: he got married at seventeen ('it shouldn't be allowed. It's much too young'), had three children, and then separated, but did not divorce. He met another girl, to whom he became 'engaged', even though they could not marry. Baby Ricky was born soon afterwards. When Ricky was three months old, his mother told John she had decided she did not want the baby any more, and was going to have him adopted. John was appalled. He gave up his job to care for Ricky, and his girlfriend left.

John tried his best. He fed the baby on the latest bottled foods, and bought him new-fangled disposable nappies; he took him to Brighton on the train at the weekend to see his own parents, and thought he would be able to manage, until the money ran out. It only took a fortnight. Not knowing who else to turn to, John phoned the Samaritans, who immediately put him in touch with an emergency foster-mother. Three foster-mothers later, John realized that this was not going to work. By then, his battle to keep Ricky was attracting publicity. He appeared on television — the *Eamonn Andrews Show* — with startling results.

After that I had masses of letters offering us homes — they were mostly [from] unmarried mothers.

But I picked out one or two that seemed hopeful, and that's how I met the lady we are living with now. She's divorced with two kids of her own — I don't want her name mentioned because people round here don't know we're not married ... but we are going to be as soon as this new divorce law goes through. And if it doesn't, well we'll live together.

John might have phoned the NCUMC rather than the Samaritans. In 1970 it changed its name from the National Council for the Unmarried

125

Mother and her Child to the National Council for One-Parent Families, and was always ready to help single fathers. By then the tide was turning, and illegitimacy was beginning to be treated as a social condition involving not just one person, but at least three. In the middle of the nineteenth century, those who sired bastards fell into fairly distinct categories: the predator, the reprobate and the fool. They were rarely mentioned in public except as literary characters or as criminals, where they were likely to be punished either by the courts or by fate (think of Alec D'Urberville in *Tess of the D'Urbervilles* or William Latch in George Moore's *Esther Waters*). The perceived shame surrounding illegitimacy was more potent in society than the welfare of the child involved, just as adoption by a married couple was deemed more desirable, in all circumstances, than the sole care of a birth-father. If an unmarried father could feasibly deny his paternity, he probably would, even if this meant surrendering to blackmail.

A hundred years later, and the single father is unrecognizable. According to a book published by the NCUMC in 1951, he has become 'the decent young fellow seduced by some hussy. He is a boy, frightened by the raw, new power of sex. He is a respectable married man in a good position. He is the soldier killed before he could marry.' In other words, he is human.

He is not, however, very vocal; nor has he ever been, except in his own defence in court or in private. For every contact from a single father, I have had scores from single mothers. Where are

126

they all? Why will they not discuss things? I get the impression that few seem to think their story worth telling. Or maybe they feel the sense of shame involved in illegitimacy even more keenly than the unmarried mother? Being men of a certain age — not used to emoting in public — perhaps they just *can't* talk about it.

Those who are brave enough to describe the impact of having an illegitimate child often reveal themselves to be straightforward and frightened people at the centre of a catastrophic situation, fast losing control. A young man so mortified at his girlfriend's pregnancy, perhaps, that he rushes headlong into a loveless marriage with her as a sort of penance, too eager to blame himself. It was so easy to father a child. Most courting couples before the 1970s relied on *coitus interruptus*, on 'taking the kettle off the stove before it boiled', or jumping off the train before it got to Blackpool. That proved about the most unreliable method of contraception imaginable.

It was not an uncommon view, before the Pill became available to unmarried couples, that using contraception during sex was somehow more culpable than not using it. It implied a degree of premeditation that was faintly filthy, and denied the act any association with hearts and flowers. Getting carried away was rapturous, and girls liked a bit of rapture. Being prepared for intercourse implied that you were deliberately immoral. Any useful knowledge of the facts of life for young men was almost as patchy as it was for women; even if they were aware of what happened and how, they appear to have been chronically naive about the practical implications of becoming a father.

In 2003 some research was published into the attitudes of single fathers to their children and their children's mothers. Those who had not been consulted about the adoption of their babies, and had no documented relationship to them, could be crippled by bitterness at being written out of history. Those memoirs and TV programmes about reunions between adopted children and their birth-mothers, which talked about lives being 'complete' once the connection had been made, all ignored the role of the birth-father. How could a child's life be complete if it failed to acknowledge its 'real' father? And how could that father rest content until he knew the fate of his child?

Of the thirty men interviewed in the course of the research, most of whom became fathers in the late 1960s, only fifteen saw or briefly held their children before they were adopted. Six of the men greeted the news of the pregnancy with unalloyed joy; the others worried how they were going to cope financially and emotionally. One ran away; the rest felt proud as well as shell-shocked, and walked with a skip in the step at the thought of being a dad.

The parents of the girl in question appear to have been the most influential people in all these stories. If the girl was under-age — below twenty-one, for the purposes of this book — then her parents could decide what to do with the baby without reference to anyone else, least of all its birth-father. This understandably caused a good deal of distress, with men suffering profound anger decades later, or profound regret. Ian was nineteen when his baby was conceived in 1963, and his girlfriend fifteen. Her parents had the child adopted, but Ian insisted on getting married to the girl as soon as he could, just in case the child should one day need to get in touch. He wanted to be ready. Ten of the fathers concerned met their adopted children in later life; one voice speaks for the twenty who did not: you never stop thinking about them, he says. 'There has never been a time when I was completely free.'

The jury is still out on whether or not it is generally wise to seek contact with an adopted son or daughter. I suppose the truth is that it is not generally *anything*: each case is unique, each of the personalities concerned is different, and everyone's expectations of such a meeting must vary wildly. Gary is positive that it would be the right thing for him; his son appears just as certain that it would not. There are some horrible stories of all the festering resentments of a lifetime exploding in the faces of birth-fathers when they present themselves to their children (and if the birth-father is available, it seems to be he who is expected to shoulder the blame these days rather than the birth-mother). One of my correspondents described her late husband Ken's life as being totally overshadowed by his rage at having been abandoned. His mother left him on a workhouse doorstep when he was a baby; she had presumably been deserted by his father, whom Ken never knew. Ken's personality was defined by his reaction to the circumstances of his birth. To an extent, his widow's was, too.

'Why am I writing to you about him? Because he is not here now, and it matters little to anyone else, illegitimacy. I cannot say he was a bad man, plainly he wasn't, he was clever as well, good-looking, and well presented. But I am sorry to say I never really understood him during the thirty-seven years of our marriage . . . What was the problem? Well, I have never ever seen it mentioned anywhere about illegitimacy, but he said categorically that he did not know what love was, and sex and closeness were a 'no no' as well . . . I was very angry and hurt, and to put it bluntly I did not love him. Did I?'

To counterbalance that unenviable bleakness, it is cheering to realize that more people speak about forgiveness and redemption than blame and resentment. Malcolm was born in 1942 and adopted as a baby by a friend of his mother: the two women worked in the same munitions factory. He managed to trace his birth-mother and, despite her strenuous silence on the subject, his birth-father too. He turned out to be a rear-gunner in the RAF, shot down before Malcolm was born. He was married (to someone else) with two children. Malcolm's elderly birth-mother refuses to communicate with him still, but he enjoys a relaxed relationship with his father's relatives; there is no stigma, no outrage, only a new and happy family he never knew he had. With their help, Malcolm feels he has been able to 'get all the ducks in a row' regarding his birth. Those are his father's legacies: love and acceptance. He prizes them both.

5

Black Lamb of the Black Sheep: Moral and Legal Judgement

The real stigma of bastardy is social, and it cannot be removed by any legislative declaration.

In a pragmatic spirit of social reconstruction, the legal approach to illegitimate children and their parents changed after the First World War. While building a homeland fit for heroes, the uncomfortable truth had to be acknowledged that many of these heroes had fathered bastards when home on leave. Pressure groups like the NCUMC and the newly formed Women's Institute, both led by women of vision and energy, campaigned for the passing of the Bastardy Bill in 1920. That campaign triggered off a series of legal and practical reforms which culminated (as far as this book is concerned) in the Abortion Act of 1967 and the availability of the Pill to unmarried women attending family planning clinics in the early 1970s.

Society's attitude to illegitimacy always tended to lag well behind any change in the law. Lynn was unaware of being on the brink of the permissive age in 1961 when she became pregnant. It happened after her first sexual experience at seventeen, when she was still at school. Her father instructed her to say that she had been raped, thus accessing the possibility of an abortion, but Lynn refused to betray her boyfriend. Father warned her she could not live at home if she had the baby; nor was she allowed to accept an invitation from her boyfriend's parents to live with them: they weren't 'good enough'. When Lynn retorted that at least they were better than *him*, for the first time in her life her father smacked her.

There followed several grotesque episodes of being douched with disinfectant by Lynn's stepmother; she was made to crouch in scalding-hot bathwater, to run upstairs two at a time and leap the last three steps on the way down. She was repeatedly slapped on the backside while standing at the kitchen sink to do the washing-up, and given a noxious cocktail of hot stout and Epsom salts to drink, while parading round the room to prevent her being sick.

When none of this had the desired effect of flushing out her baby, Lynn's parents decided on adoption. Lynn was adamant that she was going to keep her child. The months she spent at a distant maternity home were designed to put her off motherhood and persuade her how sensible it would be to give up this unplanned baby and return to normal life. They had the opposite effect. After caring for her daughter for the first six weeks of life, Lynn was incapable of leaving her. Perhaps she sensed a tiny change of heart in her parents' attitude: Father finally agreed that she could live with her grandmother in a neighbouring town. Lynn loved her Nan, and acquiesced. Nan accepted the situation — and the baby — with delight.

Still Lynn was forbidden to visit the family home, which seemed ridiculous, as everyone she knew from the village would stop, chat and admire the baby whenever they met. However, those who did not know her made a point of ostentatiously checking her left hand for a wedding-ring, and whenever Lynn visited the baby clinic, the nurses seemed to relish the opportunity to bawl out 'Miss' so-and-so instead of the courteous (but spurious) 'Mrs' when they announced her appointment. The accepted code at the time for an unmarried mother, incidentally, was to call her 'Mrs Green', and several of the women who wrote to me asked to be given that name in this book, for old times' sake.

All this was embarrassing, but Lynn was too happy to care. 'I have never regretted the decision that I made back in 1961,' she insists; 'the fight to keep my daughter was worth every moment, but my heart goes out to those mothers who had no choice but to give up their babies.'

Even then, as the sixties began to swing into action, for many women in Lynn's position there really *was* no choice. Society's attitude to illegitimacy could still be unbelievably intransigent. It is unbelievable because this was, comparatively, such a short time ago, and legislators and reformers had been busy trying to improve the situation for decades. It is difficult to understand how public opinion could rescue *Lady Chatterley's Lover* from the imprecations of the Obscenity Act in 1960, and yet primly purse its lips at a girl like Lynn. D. H. Lawrence wrote his notorious book in the 1920s; it was first published in Italy in 1928, but not to be had in an unexpurgated version in the UK for another thirty-two years, when Penguin famously made it available to wives, servants, all-comers. Before that it was thought pornographic, too morally subversive for public consumption, and potentially lethal to the sensibilities of women readers. Not only did its hero and heroine, Mellors and Constance, discuss sex and graphically indulge in adultery, but Constance conceived a child out of wedlock. What is more, she defiantly demanded a divorce from her impotent husband Clifford because she would rather the baby were known to be illegitimate than assumed to be his. D. H. Lawrence never told us what happened to Constance, nor how she and the baby were treated.

A report commissioned by the NCUMC in 1957 argued in favour of tolerance. It stated that the unmarried mother should no longer automatically be regarded as 'ruined'. Now, illegitimacy could be recognized as a symptom of emotional maladjustment rather than moral degeneration; the result, perhaps, of an unhappy childhood, loneliness, a lack of wholesome interests in adolescent and adult life and of the right kind of attention. Therefore, insisted the NCUMC, it followed that to remove the illegitimate baby from its mother was merely to remove a symptom, 'leaving the chronic disease uncured'. The founder of the NCUMC, Lettice Fisher, died the year before this report was published. The

Council launched an appeal for funds in her memory to train young mothers for work, and provide suitable housing and childcare for them meanwhile. Times were changing, claimed the Council, and society must rise to the challenge of nurturing the nation's new generation, whatever its parentage. Being shocked at the sort of behaviour that got people into trouble helped no one.

Dr Eustace Chesser was a controversial sexologist, whose books included a guide to birth-control for which he was arrested on obscenity charges in 1940; a study of the causes and effects of illegitimacy (*Unwanted Child*, 1947), and a dispassionate account of homosexuality in men and women (*Odd One Out*, 1959). He agreed with the NCUMC's philosophy. 'Traditional morality is based on clear-cut definitions,' he wrote in *Is Chastity Outmoded?* in 1960. 'It must obviously be reconsidered when the old definitions and categories begin to disintegrate.' To Dr Chesser and his wide readership, the argument was simple. Women were becoming more independent finan-cially, professionally, in their own homes, even in their own heads. They did their own thinking nowadays, and made choices in the workplace and the bedroom. This was what he called 'emancipa-tion'. Emancipation was a good thing. Traditional morality was holding emancipation back. There-fore traditional morality must change. This was nothing to do with some strident political theory, according to Dr Chesser, but a simple matter of humanity. 'When we hear that Mrs X's daughter is 'in trouble', do we not more often say, 'I knew that girl would come to no good' than, perhaps, 'Nice girl, difficult background, I'd like to help her'?'

* * *

Dr Chesser's belief that sex should be validated by love rather than by law might have been a step too far for some of his readers, but as the 1960s progressed his and others' call for a more forgiving attitude to pre-marital sex made sense to a newly invented section of the community, the modern teenager.

What did teenagers do, according to the rest of society? They treated school, work and parents with contempt. They listened to shrieking pop-music, went to unsupervised parties, smoked strange concoctions, consumed vast amounts of alcohol and — to use their own uncouth terminology — shagged each other at every opportunity, indiscriminately and with unashamed enjoyment. They also got wantonly pregnant. While experts like the officers of the NCUMC and Dr Chesser advocated practical measures to make life easier for unmarried parents (of any age) and their children, the British press reported alarming statistics and blustered commentaries about a rise in teenage illegitimate births. It was easy to conflate the two issues, and think in terms of cause and effect. Give young single parents an inch, and they'll take a mile. Lift your guard against conventional morality, and you'll find yourself not in the new Jerusalem, but in Sodom and Gomorrah. And you'll be paying for it through your taxes. Levels of prejudice against the young single parents sponging off the state through self-indulgence and sinfulness were as high — in certain sectors — as they had ever been. It was as though illegitimacy were as new as sex itself (invented, according to Philip Larkin, in 1963), a symptom of the permissive age, proof that our so-called civilization was going to the dogs.

The truth is that illegitimacy was being discussed in public for the first time; the difficulties it presented for the child involved, and its implication for the economic and emotional health of the nation, were openly being assessed. The old belief was that talking about sex, even confiding to young people the facts of life, was dangerous. You were more likely to do bad things if you knew what those bad things were. If ignorance is bliss, so is naivety. The attitude of a pregnant fifteen-year-old's parents illustrates this perfectly: 'the family seem to think that by expressing immense surprise at the baby's arrival it makes it into a virgin birth'.

The statistics did appear to be worrying. In 1964, sixty-six out of every 1,000 babies born were illegitimate. The rate in London was almost twice that of the national average. Fifty thousand bastards were born in England and Wales in 1961 and over 56,000 the following year: every fifteenth child born then was illegitimate. Every seventh child was conceived (if not born) outside marriage; every third or fourth mother conceived her first-born before her wedding day, and over half a million babies were born to girls of thirteen or younger. This was shocking, but what most people failed to realize was that it was nothing new.

In 1918 the rate of illegitimate births was over 6 per cent, although admittedly this was partly due to a glut of war-babies. The lowest rate was in 1936 (nearly 5 per cent) and the highest, predictably, in 1945 (9.33 per cent). The figures for 1964 do not seem so terribly high in comparison. In fact they are exactly the same as those for 1842, when such statistics were first collated in England and Wales.

Moral indignation is a tempting luxury, however. During the 1950s and 1960s there were plenty of households and communities in Britain — urban and rural — still clinging to the trousered-piano-leg school of probity. Brides at shotgun weddings would be showered with ashes rather than confetti. 'You was the scum of the earth,' remembers Liza, if you married at a registry office rather than a church. Even if you weren't 'showing', the choice of venue was enough to label you a woman 'gone' before her time. Liza was showing, and felt utterly miserable. She wore a vast dress four sizes too big for her to accommodate the bump. Only her parents, her husband's brother and a friend came to the reception, which was a cup of tea and a piece of cake at her Aunty Nell's.

Immorality was still considered to be contagious in the most basic of ways. Patricia's parents probably thought they were being remarkably progressive when they sent their pre-pubescent daughter to visit the local mother-and-baby home (or 'Home for Fallen Women', as they put it) when she was eleven or twelve years old. Their idea was to show her how awful life was for unmarried mothers, and so frighten her off illicit sex — even though she had no idea what sex was, illicit or otherwise. The poor child was expected to recite improving poems to the inmates, which must have been a mortifying exercise for all involved.

As well as segregating the sinful from the righteous, which has been part of the ethos behind every kind of mother-and-baby home from the earliest days of the workhouse, removing unmarried mothers from society before, during and immediately after their confinements was necessary for discretion's sake. Out of sight, out of mind. In Catholic Ireland, Magdalene homes hid whores and bastards away until the 1990s, and were themselves hidden away by decades of denial and chilling euphemism. My adopted cousin Sue became close to a birth-relative later in life. He wrote a poem for her, a poignant articulation of society's attitude to unwanted children. In it, he talks of 'the pawning of truth; the ego enshrined/The bland acceptance of the double-think'. There is an 'eternity of debt' to be paid, he admits, both by the child for being a bastard, and by society for labelling it so.

In some cases, those born illegitimate before the First World War refused to collect their pensions in the 1960s and 1970s for fear of their secret being revealed. The permissive society meant nothing to them. Several of my illegitimate correspondents said their mothers never applied for child benefit, for the same reason. They were too ashamed. The novelist

Dorothy L. Sayers, creator of Lord Peter Wimsey and the sublimely modern Harriet Vane, never publicly recognized her illegitimate child, even though he lived with her. Politicians fathered and mothered bastards, as they had always done, and feared the scandal of their discovery as fervently as ever. Family secrets are still being uncovered now, all the time, proving that secrecy itself is far more enduring than shame.

* * *

A prospective undergraduate wrote a letter to *The Times* in 1944 complaining of the multiple handicaps conferred on her by her illegitimacy. The greatest hardship of all was the lack of a complete birth certificate.

> My early education was accomplished privately and finished abroad, in which I may or may not have been more fortunate than some. But when at 19 I found myself alone (my dear inconsequent and rarely seen mother dying, having kept me in the dark for 19 years), and facing then both shock and poverty, I found college entrance barred, for, though I managed an exhibition [a type of scholarship] I could not produce that shaming document. Nor could I obtain any help from societies giving help in training. It has kept me forever from matrimony. Or should one give false information for one's marriage certificate and risk spending one's honeymoon in gaol? A useful war job in the Foreign

Office, another in the Passport Office, Censorship — all inaccessible for the same reason.

She was wrong in almost every instance. She could indeed have gone to college, married, worked in a respectable job, despite being illegitimate. That is not the point. She didn't *know* she was wrong. No one had told her the facts, and she had never had the courage to ask. Like Liza (though from a different world), she assumed herself to be the scum of the earth. The letter was signed 'Spero Meliora' — I hope for better things. It is a hollow hope; she obviously felt marked for life, as though society had blackballed her in some arcane secret ballot, and voted her out.

The problem was not that one had no birth certificate at all if one was illegitimate (as Spero Meliora implied); it was rather that the space for 'Father' had an indelible line through it. One of Lettice Fisher's proudest achievements at the head of the NCUMC must have been the success of her campaign to regularize birth certificates by the introduction of a 'short form' in 1947. After registering the baby's birth, parents could choose to take a copy of the full registration, or a brief but entirely valid certificate showing the child's name, date and place of birth, but with no mention of either parent.

The purpose of this abbreviated document is obvious: looking at it, no one would be able to tell whether or not you were illegitimate, including you. A surprising number of people only discover their illegitimacy when reading their own full birth certificate for the first time. The drawback of the document is equally clear. Because there was a choice, people assumed that a short certificate meant you had something to hide, just as they assumed a registry office wedding meant a baby was on the way.

The period between the wars, and up to the 1960s, was such a polite age. One did not care to offend people. Social nicety was a badge of middle-class sensibility, of good breeding (appropriately enough), and the barriers erected between members of a community, even members of the same family, were almost as inviolable as they had been in Victorian times. Reserve, reticence, call it what you will; that is what stopped people asking for each other's secrets, or for more information than they needed to maintain some sort of emotional equilibrium. But doubts fester, just like secrets, sometimes for years.

This collective need for life to be nice and shiny impeded the progress of reformers like the NCUMC. A little like the parents who hoped that not mentioning their daughter's unwanted pregnancy would somehow metamorphose the sordid details of her seduction into an immaculate conception, people preferred not to talk about the unfortunate stains in the fabric of everyone's life, the frayed edges and the patches, especially in the decade following each World War. Lettice Fisher and her colleagues had to work doubly hard, first to bring the problems of illegitimacy to public attention, and then to catalyse change.

Mrs Fisher had help. Some of her staunchest support came from what might be considered an unexpected quarter: the Women's Institute. The WI was founded in the UK in 1915, with a joint purpose. It had originated in Canada in 1897, set up as a support network for farmers' wives in isolated rural communities. Transplanted into British soil, just as the First World War took hold, its members were immediately mustered to boost the country's food resources, which they did extremely effectively while enjoying the novelty of getting together with new friends and working cooperatively.

The movement had a political ethos, too. This was nothing to do with party politics, but with political awareness. Many of its founders — male and female — were suffragists, campaigning hard for votes for women. Some were full-blown suffragettes, like Edith Rigby from Lancashire, who torched various local landmarks and hurled home-made bombs and black puddings at passing politicians; she was imprisoned seven times, went on hunger-strike, was force-fed — and believed the Women's Institute to be 'a temple of national enlightenment'. However extreme their views, or militant their actions, the WI's pioneers had a common cause: to educate the women of Britain to use their vote, when it came, with responsibility and understanding.

This meant giving them confidence, which was achieved through encouraging members to speak about personal and practical concerns in the comfort of their own WI meetings, among friends. It soon became obvious that certain common subjects about public affairs were troubling institutes all over the country. So each year, from 1918 onwards, members were asked to vote on which of their collective concerns they would like to bring to the Government's attention by way of a national resolution at their Annual General Meeting.

That first year, the main resolution was about state-aided housing. Many WI members and their families lived in appalling conditions, lacking running water or drainage, and with unhealthy levels of light and ventilation. They urged the Government to do all it could to build new and affordable homes for its post-war heroes. There was no public affairs resolution in 1919, but in 1920, there were two. One involved access for women to decision-making bodies about local health and housing; it asked for support for those considering joining parish and council committees (uncharted territory for most housewives at the time). The other was in support of the Bastardy Bill.

It is astonishing that a national movement of women, still wary about being taken seriously, should have the courage to raise its head above the parapet so early in its existence by allying itself to such a controversial subject. Then, the stereotypical WI member was a homely body in her floral pinny, or a hand-knitted twinset and tweeds, more concerned with pickles and preserves than cutting-edge activism. That image was as misleading then as it is now; there were over 60,000 members in 1920, and they chose only to campaign about subjects which urgently affected themselves and their communities. The moral and practical implications of illegitimacy

144

obviously fell into this category. They were courageous enough to admit that, and fight for change.

The champion of the Bastardy Bill was a Birmingham MP whose sister Hilda was a prominent WI member, and who later became uncomfortably prominent himself. His name was Neville Chamberlain. There had been no significant legislation covering illegitimacy since the Poor Laws and their Amendment Acts (the most recent being in the 1870s). By 1920, when Chamberlain introduced his Bill, endorsed by the Women's Institute's experience and conviction, he was able to quote statistics to prove that 201 illegitimate babies out of every 1,000 died before their first birthday. The figure for babies with married parents was ninety per 1,000. There had to be a remedy in law for this. There was a procedure for single mothers to claim affiliation payments from the putative father, but it was so complicated, or obstructive, that in 1913 (for example), of the 38,000 illegitimate babies born in the country, only 7,000 were officially supported by their fathers. Mothers were required to name the father within a year of the baby's birth (not always easy, for a variety of reasons); his paternity had somehow to be proven beyond doubt; he must be brought to court, and even if he was ordered to pay, if he subsequently left the country or could not be traced, he got off scot-free. The mother was liable for the cost of summonsing him if he fell into arrears; she must physically collect the payment herself from an intermediary, and was not entitled to any support from the putative father during her pregnancy.

Chamberlain could not understand England's reluctance to face up to this problem, although the WI managed to overcome it by not being polite, and daring to air their own and others' dirty linen in public. How was it, he argued, that we had school clinics, special schools, infant welfare centres and so on, but no system to care for bastards? In Scotland they could retrospectively be legitimized by the parents' subsequent marriage, as they could in other countries. Not here. In France they had a right to inherit half the property which would have been due to them if they had been legitimate. Not here. In Hungary, they could claim maintenance from the state until they were twelve, and in Norway, the children of married and unmarried parents were equal in the eyes of the law. Even Germany had the decency to call unmarried mothers 'Frau' instead of 'Fräulein'. There was some small comfort in the fact that we did not behave as the Inuits traditionally did. If the mother of an illegitimate child died in Greenland, her inconvenient mistake was promptly strangled.

The NCUMC printed a poster in support of Chamberlain's proposals, on which it listed the principal aims of the proposed legislation, and answered imagined objections. The Bastardy Bill would divide parental responsibility between the mother and the father 'as equally as possible'; it would provide for the guardianship of a bastard should either or both parents be unable to care for it (at present, if the mother of a bastard died

146

in childbirth, and she had not named a father, her baby would have no legal family — in fact no legal identity — at all); it would throw the responsibility of establishing paternity and enforcing affiliation payments on to the state by appointing dedicated 'collecting' officers, thus improving efficiency; it would introduce more discretion into affiliation proceedings, abolish a limit on affiliation payments, and — crucially — allow for a child to be legitimized by the subsequent marriage of its parents.

There were only two main objections to all this, according to the NCUMC: that bastardy would become more difficult to conceal, and so offend public morality to an intolerable degree, and that the incidence of it would increase, endorsed by an over-generous state. The NCUMC countered these by arguing that concealment is dangerous to both mother and child, and illegitimacy will never be eradicated. Social sanctions have not helped in the past, so plainly, 'new methods are needed to deal with an old evil'.

In fact Chamberlain faced many more objections than these two. The greatest was the name of the Bill itself. 'Bastardy' was a harsh word, a rude word, and its coarseness made the whole subject unpalatable. 'We are hampered in this matter by the existing law and its phraseology,' explained Chamberlain, 'but surely we are not going to allow substantial improvements in our social order to be delayed or defeated because of the necessity of using a word which we dislike?' 'The Children of Unmarried Parents Bill' was suggested as a mealy-mouthed compromise that appealed to none, instead of offending all.

The new name did not stick, and the Bill as Chamberlain envisaged it was never passed. The Bastardy Act of 1923 increased affiliation payments for unmarried mothers, but not much else. The Legitimacy Act of 1926 was more far-reaching. Now, for the first time in England and Wales, a child's illegitimacy could be erased by its parents' marriage, provided both would have been free to marry at the time of the child's birth. If either was married to someone else when the child was born, even if they were subsequently divorced or widowed, the child remained a bastard all its life. Another innovation was the provision under the Act for an illegitimate child to inherit from its mother should she die intestate, providing she had no legitimate issue. A mother could also inherit from her illegitimate child in the same circumstances.

The clause about retrospective legitimization was not repealed until 1959. That is when parents were allowed to rescue their children from bastardy by marrying after the birth, whatever their marital circumstances when the child was born. It was an important distinction, but did not necessarily make life any easier for the people concerned. I have come across children — now grown up — who thought that they were legitimate because their parents married before 1959 after one of them got a divorce from a previous spouse. And people who assume that they are illegitimate even if their parents were free to marry one another when they were born, but did not get around to it until later.

Several of my correspondents remember occasions in their childhoods when mummy and daddy disappeared for a day and then came home wearing shiny new rings, but with no explanation (then or ever) of where they had been or what they had done. Vivien was taken out to a Chinese restaurant in 1965, when she was about thirteen, an occasion of sufficient rarity and splendour for her to remember it for years. She later found out that it was the day of her parents' wedding. This was the problem with both the 1926 and the 1959 Legitimacy Acts: to make everything all right by marrying after the birth of a child meant admitting that everything was *not* all right before. And the problem still persists for people of a certain age: acquiring legitimacy later on does not always cancel out the inherent shame of being born a bastard in the first place.

* * *

In many families it is difficult to separate the issues of divorce and illegitimacy. Both carried a stigma, yet often one was necessary in order to deal with the other. This presented some ticklish dilemmas. Will my child be teased more for being illegitimate, or for having a divorced parent? If I have had a child by someone other than my husband, will it still be assumed to be his, by law, if we divorce? Even if I subsequently marry the real father? If I marry the divorced mother of my illegitimate child, will the fact that we cannot do so in church mean that we are not

149

really married at all? And if I am a Roman Catholic and I marry a Protestant or someone from another faith, will that mean that because the marriage is unrecognized by my religion, our children will be bastards? If my marriage is annulled, surely that makes my children illegitimate, as I have never truly been married at all? Say I marry and father four daughters, then take a mistress, have a son by her, divorce my wife and marry the mistress. This will make my son legitimate, but how will it affect my daughters? Will they have equal rights, if I die intestate, with my only son? These are all real problems, faced by real families.

Here is a complicated scenario. John was married in 1897. He and his wife Eliza had a son the following year, but by 1901 they had separated; John had left Eliza and the child and moved on. In 1903 he appeared on the birth certificate of a daughter by another woman, Hannah, whose surname was apparently the same as John's. They had another child the following year. Hannah died in 1911, whereupon John was wed for a third time, to Georgina. The marriage certificate for this ceremony has been found, proving — as his first wife Eliza was still very much alive — that John was a bigamist, possibly twice over.

When John was killed in action in 1917, third wife Georgina was listed as his next of kin. She was informed of his death, but in a slightly elliptical manner. The Army chaplain wrote her a letter commiserating with the loss of her 'boy'. Georgina was by now looking after two stepchildren — the late Hannah's (second wife) — as well as her own daughter; she was poor, uneducated, and times were hard. She had also lost her sight since John's departure to the Front. When she applied for her widow's pension, Georgina was curtly informed that John's (first) wife had already claimed it, and that she and her family were owed nothing.

Georgina was devastated. She appears never to have known why the pension was refused; what has since emerged is that John's first (and only legitimate) son, by Eliza, enlisted at sixteen and may well have met his father during the war. Perhaps John, for an easy life, agreed to his son letting Eliza know where he was, and either he or Eliza told the authorities.

Through no fault of her own, Georgina was left penniless to cope with her children and Hannah's, and the mortifying possibility that she had never been properly married. I was told this story by John and Hannah's granddaughter; when she informed her aunts — Hannah's and Georgina's daughters — that she was investigating the family history, they both wept and begged her not to do it. They must have known the truth, and it terrified them.

Bigamy was a fairly straightforward problem: it was a criminal offence, and that was that. Perhaps the most complicated question faced by lawyers trying to accommodate illegitimacy in the twentieth century was the one posed by artificial insemination. In December 1958, a child conceived in America by artificial insemination using donor sperm (AID) was judged to be illegitimate. AID was deemed 'tantamount to adultery' — and yet the practice was growing, and bringing joy to an increasing number of happily-married couples both in America and elsewhere. Surely it was inhumane to discriminate against such a child because its biological father was not its mother's husband? Resolution came in the UK with the Family Law Reform Act of 1987, when it was decreed that as long as the husband had consented to AID, the child was assumed in law to be his.

The concept of legal equality for single mothers and illegitimate children is a fairly modern one. Neville Chamberlain was aware that not enough was being done to support them; to him that was a matter of natural justice. But when legislation was passed in other areas, even apparently unrelated ones like workmen's compensation or pensions, it became evident that illegitimate children would have to be classed with their legitimate counterparts (with certain checks and balances) or else face an insupportable degree of discrimination. If an unmarried father was killed by an accident at work, for example, his longterm partner and their illegitimate children must have the same entitlement to compensation as a lawful wife and family would. If he was killed while serving in Her Majesty's Forces, there must be equal financial support for the presumed widow, as well as for the real one.

Thus, little by little, in the arcane rubric of Acts of Parliament and the abstruse arguments of courtroom lawyers, official attitudes to illegitimacy began to soften. That is what made the permissive society permissive. In 1926, the same year as the Legitimacy Act, the Adoption of Children Act was passed, which legally formalized the adoption process in England and Wales. Adoption agencies were regulated for the first time by an Act in 1939; ten years later Local Authorities were ordered to supervise all adoptions and to appoint someone to represent the child's interests, and in 1950 secrecy was enshrined for birth-parents and adopted children. All of these laws affected illegitimate children, gradually giving them a voice and inalienable rights. The 1948 Children's Act impacted on the care of illegitimate children separated from their parents, and the Family Law Act of 1969 changed the rules on inheritance. The latter was one of the first pieces of legislation not to use the word 'bastard', but not until 1987 was the concept of a child's illegitimacy in law finally abolished.

Most of my correspondents are pleased by this relaxation. Their own children might be living with partners rather than married, and their grandchildren blissfully unaware of the tawdry label which would have been pasted to their foreheads, metaphorically speaking, just a couple of generations ago. Some feel cheated, though. Why couldn't society's attitude to illegitimacy have changed sooner? Why have the rules changed so quickly, so completely? If nobody thinks it important now, why did I suffer so much then? These are difficult questions to answer; indeed, I have found them impossible.

Maybe there is comfort to be had in knowing that if you feel like this, you are not alone. I don't mean just that there are others feeling exactly as you do; but that throughout the course of your life there have been people trying to fight your corner, trying to make life better, and lift the leaden weight (as someone tearfully described it to me) from your soul.

★ ★ ★

The first task of everyone concerned with helping unmarried mothers and their children was to tackle the question of guilt. The 'lewd woman' of the Tudor Poor Laws was evil, wilfully polluting herself, her lover, her child, and her community. She was punished for it. During the nineteenth century the idea began to develop that she might possibly be as much sinned against as sinning. Maybe fate conspired against her, or she was like Alfred Lord Tennyson's 'soft and milky rabble', too weak and impressionable to resist temptation. There were always going to be vicious mothers who transgressed because they were mentally and morally defective, but now there was room for manoeuvre.

As in so many areas of life, the First World War was a catalyst for change. The novelist John Galsworthy wrote to *The Times* on 22 February 1918 to urge that illegitimate war-babies be protected by the state. In responding to his letter, a welfare worker shared an experience connected with a recent visit to a workhouse.

I have, within the last two days, been present at a meeting of a committee of women Poor Law Guardians in one of our great provincial cities. They were engaged, no doubt unconsciously, in a game which, for want of a better name, I must call girl-baiting. I saw a young expectant mother, cruelly handled, and tortured with bitter words and threats; an ordeal which she will have had to endure at the hands of four different sets of officials by the time her baby is three weeks old. These guardians told her, in my presence, that they hoped she would suffer severely for her wrong-doing, that they considered that her own mother, who had treated her kindly, had been too lenient, and that her sin was so great that she ought to be ashamed to be a cost to self-respecting rate-payers. They added that the man who was responsible for her condition was very good to have acknowledged his paternity, but expressed the belief, nay, rather the hope, that he would take an early opportunity of getting out of his obligation. Meanwhile, a pale, trembling girl, within a month of her confinement, stood, like a hunted animal.

It's like something out of Dickens.

This account prompted, in turn, a response from Lettice Fisher, announcing the creation of the NCUMC. On the Council's tenth anniversary, Mrs Fisher published a progress report, celebrating 'a considerable change in the general attitude towards the problem of the illegitimate

155

child'. Now it was widely understood that illegitimacy was due to many separate causes: some women were betrayed, some dissolute by nature, some trapped. 'All were different and needed individual attention.' This was a breakthrough. Even the occasional bishop agreed that more humanity was needed in dealing with the problem. We must be careful where we apportion blame, said the Bishop of Birmingham in 1919. If an unmarried girl finds herself with child, it might be because her parents 'neither taught nor warned'. The state must take responsibility for the evil environment in which she may have been brought up. The Church — his Church — has never really 'got hold of the young nature'. It should be more understanding. And public opinion has much to answer for. He believes that a mother might 'rise' through her illegitimate child, not just fall; a little love and respect goes a long way. Her sin might be the making of her. Surely we owe her the chance, in a Christian spirit of forgiveness?

Prominent figures like John Galsworthy, Lettice Fisher and the Bishop of Birmingham worked on the public consciousness of illegitimacy. Meanwhile, the Women's Institute was again the most practical of the NCUMC's allies. As well as campaigning for the passing of the Bastardy Bill, it produced a Resolution for the wider treatment of sexually transmitted diseases (passed on by soldiers returning from front-line brothels). There was a particularly high incidence of STDs in illegitimate babies; if their mothers could be treated while pregnant, instead of reviled and left alone, their children might be saved. The WI fought for an increase in the number of women police officers, too, understanding that pregnant mothers who had been raped, or who needed non-judgemental help, would be more likely to speak to another woman than to a big, burly copper. It publicized the need for district nurses and local clinics for every mother and child; as one village in three had its own Institute by 1939, and the membership of the movement peaked at 467,000, theirs was an authentic, powerful and influential voice.

Between the wars, a network of maternity homes and hostels was created by the NCUMC, the Salvation Army, other religious and charitable organizations, local authorities and private enterprises. The black sheep of the family and her black lamb were slowly assimilated into mainstream health and social care, and for the most part, treated with a measure of forbearance and sympathy, if not forgiveness. What the NCUMC called 'the better type' of unmarried mother might even be welcomed into a respectable family household as a lodger, with her baby. The diary of a Scottish Mass Observation contributor, written in 1944, illustrates how well this could work.

[A] lassie came to cook, but she has a wee baby, eighteen days old. She has very little gear, I borrowed Margaret's old pram and fixed up a drawer for a bed . . . She knows very little about babies and is rather frightened but [we] reassured her. She kept on saying it was lovely to be able to keep him.

Lydia was a married but childless restaurateur in Edinburgh during the Second World War. When she found that Carol B, one of her waitresses, was pregnant, she summoned her to her office, to try to discover the facts. She managed to cheer the distressed girl up a little, then delivered 'an awful warning against any attempt at abortion — just in time as she informed me that a lady she knew had offered to deal with the matter for £1'. Lydia took it upon herself to visit Carol's parents. Her mother had bought some abortion pills; her father was 'a drunken bully', and the house was crawling with children. Lydia took Carol back to the restaurant and put her up there, before finding a nursing home where she could have the baby (whose father Carol steadfastly refused to reveal) and where she would find help to arrange an adoption afterwards. 'The matron,' said Lydia, 'is a perfectly grand person — a little tough bouncing woman with an inexhaustible sense of humour and the kindest heart in the world.' This matron was just the sort of character the NCUMC would like to have installed in all its mother-and-baby homes, and Lydia's attitude the perfect modern response to the age-old problem of a terrified girl in trouble.

Not everyone aware of the plight of the unmarried mother and her child was as sensible as this. There were a few high-profile mavericks. George Bernard Shaw got rather over-excited on the subject of how best to bring up a bastard. It was his opinion (unsupported by evidence) that 'Kaiserin Augusta's House in Berlin reared children with scientific efficiency, trained nurses, worked under the best advice, and the infants died like flies. Among the families living in mud cabins in Connemara there was no infant mortality rate.'

He was obviously one of those who thought love and common sense were all any baby needed. Never mind the busybodies who tried to regulate everything; they had probably never had children themselves. 'It was always the plain, withered virgins who had never been tempted and never had the opportunity of going wrong who had the most to say.' Without those busybodies, however, organizing beds in mother-and-baby homes, arranging clinic appointments, applying for grants and referring problems, life would have been intolerably hard for many of the people who have written to me about bearing, or being, a bastard. Sympathy is all very well, but sentimentality is distinctly unhelpful. In *Orphans of the Living*, published in 1968, the author Diana Dewar rhapsodizes about 'the greatest human grief apart from death: lost love and forlorn children, children in mourning for phantom parents.' I can imagine Lettice Fisher reading that, if she were still alive, with exasperation. Don't witter on so: *do* something.

In 1987, the Family Law Reform Act was passed. This was the first piece of legislation in this country not to mention 'illegitimate' children. It spoke instead of children whose parents were not married to each other at the time of birth. 'Illegitimacy' has not been used as a legal term referring to children since. In 2012 it was reported that for the first time, more children in England and Wales were born outside marriage than within it.

That sort of statistic represents exactly what reactionary commentators feared most, back in the Swinging Sixties. They warned of an anomic society, a general implosion into moral turpitude, a domestic apocalypse. 'It hardly seems possible to eliminate the stigma attached to illegitimacy without at the same time weakening the family as a social institution,' cautioned someone in 1966. '[T]here is one sure way of abolishing illegitimacy,' someone else declared, 'namely, by eliminating marriage and the family.'

More than half a century later marriage still survives; so does the family. It might be a different sort of family than we aspired to in the 1960s, and teenage pregnancies are still a worry, but most communities in this country have developed a *modus vivendi* which does not necessarily depend for its success on whether or not the parents of children are married to one another. Whether that is a good thing is still up for debate — but not, I suspect, for much longer. It is eminently possible that in another fifty years, the concept of illegitimacy will be remembered with nothing more than a puzzled shrug of the shoulders.

6

All the Way to Blackpool: Sex, Pregnancy and Birth-control

Bad girls don't have babies.

The National Council for the Unmarried Mother and her Child did not concern themselves exclusively with practicalities. As well as trying to change society's attitude towards illegitimacy and those involved with it, they campaigned for better sex-education in schools, 'right from the earliest age'. It was not nice to talk about sex before the 1960s, and there was no concerted approach to teaching children the facts of life at school before the National Curriculum was introduced in 1988. It is still not compulsory in England and Wales, except in so much as children must be taught about the reproductive system in science. I remember a session in our school's lecture theatre in the mid 1970s taken by an unmarried teacher blazing with embarrassment; it involved her unwrapping a condom with shaking hands and trying to fit the thing on to an outsized wooden phallus, while we twelve- and thirteen-year-olds whooped with excitement and disbelief.

I expect that was considered quite progressive at the time; before then, most schools addressed the subject of where babies came from in biology

161

lessons about lady and gentleman rabbits. John was at school in the 1930s; he recalls a sententious clergyman visiting one day to lecture the class on the importance of 'avoiding self-abuse' and 'honouring women'. There was no elaboration. Girls were warned not to let themselves and their parents down, and to save themselves for their husbands. This advice, without context, was meaningless.

Even at university, before the Second World War students at women's colleges were advised, if they needed to sit down on a chair recently vacated by a man, to place newspaper on the seat first. The suggestion was that the ambient warmth of the boy's behind might kindle unsuitable stirrings. Telephone directories served much the same purpose. In mixed company, young ladies should always keep at least one foot on the ground. If any male had occasion to visit their rooms, even if it was a family member, the bed must first be removed. They should never initiate a conversation with a man they did not know, or to whom they had only just been introduced, in case things got spontaneously out of hand and they ended up ruined. It must have seemed as though sex were some rampant and unpredictable monster lurking at every corner, liable to leap out at any moment and devour them whole.

A firmly-held belief among many men and women was that kissing a girl made her pregnant. Even if they were aware that sexual intercourse was involved, they often thought it was the act itself that did the damage. What that act was, they were unsure. They knew none of the sophisticated details involving sperm and eggs and things. One of my correspondents was a midwife in the 1960s; in those days even *she* did not know how babies got themselves into the womb — only how they were supposed to come out.

Most of us, before the 1970s, learned what sex-education we could from family and friends. Mine was initiated after asking my mother the meaning of that stark, black-and-white enamelled notice screwed on to the inside of every public lavatory door. It was faintly menacing, about contacting a 'VD' clinic and how you should do it straight away and need tell no one else about it. First I asked what VD was; then whether or not you could catch it from the lavatory seat, the chain or the door handle. That led to a fairly full revelation of the facts of life, with the sage (but at the time utterly bewildering) advice that 'once you start, ducky, it's terribly difficult to stop'.

Joan's mother clammed up when asked about sex in the 1940s; instead she gave Joan two books, supposed to explain everything her daughter needed to know. One was the infamous *The Awful Disclosures of Maria Monk, as Exhibited in a Narrative of Her Sufferings During a Residence of Five Years as a Novice and Two Years as a Black Nun*, first published nearly 100 years previously in 1836. This was a sensational (and apocryphal) account of a young girl's incarceration in a convent which turned out to be a sort of clergy brothel on an industrial

163

scale. Maria and her sister novices were repeatedly raped there by priests, and the resulting offspring dipped in quicklime and tossed into a mass grave. Maria managed to escape before giving birth to her bastard daughter, and her sorry tale was published — ostensibly — as a grim warning against undisciplined sexual urges and Catholics.

The other book was Radclyffe Hall's *The Well of Loneliness*, which at first glance might appear to be a love story between a gentleman called Stephen and a lady called Mary, except that Stephen is really a woman, as is Radclyffe Hall. Presumably Joan's mother was unaware that this was a pioneering lesbian novel, one which the editor of the *Sunday Express* considered morally lethal. 'I would rather give a healthy boy or a healthy girl a phial of prussic acid than this,' he wrote, shortly after the book's publication in 1928. It was banned soon afterwards. Much more useful to Joan was a book circulating under the desks at school at the time: *Lady Chatterley's Lover*, not yet freely available, but obtainable abroad.

Publishers faced possible obscenity charges for non-fiction books, as well as literature. Any enlightened doctor hoping to educate young people about their sexuality — like Eustace Chesser — was forced to couch their advice in oblique scientific or sociological terms, which was not always helpful to those who might benefit from it most. Dr Marie Stopes managed to avoid such censure. Perhaps that is because she was a Christian woman advocating marriage, responsible parenthood, and complete fidelity.

Dr Stopes was originally an academic, a paleobotanist who lectured at Manchester and London Universities. *Married Love* was published in 1918, after she divorced her first husband on the grounds, ironically, of non-consummation. It champions birth-control in fairly anodyne terms as an essential part of any happy and responsible marriage. She wrote further books and pamphlets covering sexual education for the young, sexually transmitted diseases, and how to manage the menopause. These subjects were all more or less taboo before Dr Stopes articulated her views and offered her advice; the response she received from her readers ensured that for married men and women, at least, the discussion of sexual matters need not necessarily be considered smutty, vulgar, or morally subversive.

In 1921 Dr Stopes and her second husband set up the UK's first birth-control clinic, 'The Mothers' Clinic' in North London, offering advice to married women of the working classes on how to limit their families. Dr Stopes believed in eugenics, optimizing the intellectual, physical and moral calibre of the next generation through selective breeding. The clinic's motto in these early days was chillingly evocative, in hindsight, of things to come in Nazi Germany a decade or two later: 'Joyous and Deliberate Motherhood. A Sure Light in our Racial Darkness'; it was designed, she said, to uphold 'reverence for the Race, that it shall be represented on this earth by the most perfect and God-like individuals that it is in our power to call forth in His image'.

Marie Stopes's Mothers' Clinics gradually spread around the country; staffed by midwives, with visiting doctors, they even took to the road in caravans. They offered cervical caps, condoms, and 'female sheaths'; if these were distasteful for any reason, they recommended alternative contraception involving sponges soaked in vinegar, or suppositories of quinine or oil. Soon Dr Stopes was employing full-time secretaries to deal with sacks of letters arriving every day, thanking her for her willingness to face up to an age-old problem, for her practical sympathy for the hard-worked housewife and mother, and asking for her advice for sexual problems. All help given was non-judgemental, as long as the patients were married, and did not seek an abortion.

Dr Stopes's violent opposition to abortion was a hallmark of her approach to contraception. Better for a child not to be conceived, than to light the spark only to snuff it out later. Her first child was stillborn, which must have influenced her passion for the right to life. With a dual purpose to prevent conception and discourage over-population, Stopes felt her clinics fulfilled a public service, a crusade. They helped ensure that the population did not become overrun by ill-nourished, ill-educated children; they also husbanded the population's resources and encouraged stronger stock by supporting parents not to dissipate their energy and finances by producing endless, increasingly feeble offspring.

This sounds a little Machiavellian, but Dr Stopes genuinely wanted to empower married women to choose whether or not to add to their families. Thousands of people wrote to her, husbands as well as wives, even unmarried men and women (who got short shrift). Her response to them proves that she believed passionately in the right of the current generation to regulate the next. This letter, written to her in November 1922, helps explain the strength of her conviction that contraception should freely be available to all wives who wished to have it.

> I was very strictly brought up and when I married knew nothing of sex relations, realisation coming as a dreadful shock. My husband was well-off then and both of us very, very fond of children. Although a public school girl, with a 'finishing' abroad, I had a rooted conviction for years that contraception of any kind was immoral and indecent. Hence my large family.

This woman had nine children, as well as several stillbirths. And now, her husband's fortunes having taken a turn for the worse, all the children were in the workhouse. How much better it would have been, she implies, if most of them had never been born.

* * *

The result of a report on young people's attitudes to birth-control was published in 1965. Given that the Pill had now been available for four years, it revealed a remarkable degree of naivety. True, the NHS did not prescribe the Pill to unmarried women before 1974, but the publicity surrounding its sensational debut in the UK was hardly discreet. In this report, a nineteen-year-old girl was quoted as being completely ignorant of sex. Her parents had never discussed it with her. 'My mother always says it's filthy.' Another claimed that the only advice she had ever heard on birth-control was from her father, who told her to 'keep your legs crossed and say no'. A boy of sixteen confided this bloodcurdling fact about contraception: 'Apparently, one can temporarily sterilize oneself by heating one's sex organs in boiling water.' There were comments on the desirability of condoms: 'Oh no, I won't use them. It destroys the whole thing.' 'If it were natural to use them, we'd have been born with them on.'

Attitudes like this were not confined to the young. A Dr Routh wrote to *The Times* in 1921 to express his learned opinion that the 'artificial avoidance of conception' could never be carried out without 'the probability of serious disturbance of health in both parents' even within marriage. Later on, in the so-called 'Little Kinsey' survey of sexual behaviour carried out by the Mass Observation unit in 1948, twenty-nine people in every 100 demonstrated complete ignorance of what birth-control meant. Most thought it was something to do with the birth process itself. Pain relief, maybe. Of those who did understand about contraception, only 63 per cent approved of the concept. 'The people who practise that are all more or less prostitutes,' said one. Some agreed with Dr Routh that its unnaturalness was bound to cause harm. 'Well I don't know. [Childless women] get tumours and die, and that. I had a lovely friend die because she hadn't had any [children].' For others, it was simply a matter of good taste. Making love to someone wearing a rubber glove on his you-know-what was perverse. 'I think women very cheap if they allow that.'

Generally, especially among the older generation, the consensus of opinion seemed to be that withdrawal was the best method of contraception. In fact it hardly counted as contraception at all. There were a number of euphemisms for *coitus interruptus* involving kettles not coming to the boil, trains not coming into the station, or — a particular favourite — not getting 'all the way to Blackpool'.

A few mavericks tried more imaginative methods. One girl used to keep a sturdy hatpin about her person in the 1940s to deal with any unwanted advances. A married woman, sexually frustrated at home, chose a Roman Catholic for her lover because she knew Catholics did not believe in having illegitimate babies; therefore she would be safe. Jill says she knew about condoms when she was twenty in 1967, but would not have had the courage to ask a boyfriend to use one. So she relied instead on refusing to imagine herself pregnant. There is a limerick people used to recite, along the same lines:

There was a young lady so wild,
She kept herself pure undefiled

> By thinking of Jesus,
> Venereal Diseases,
> And the dangers of having a child.

Jill concentrated very, very hard on not being pregnant, but it didn't work.

Perhaps the most extreme method I have encountered comes from a Lancashire woman born in 1908.

> My mother told me about a young woman and she went with this young fellow in the park and he tried it on with her. It upset her that much, she arranged to meet him again. This time she took a razor with her and she cut it . . . you know what I'm talking about, don't you? His 'tea-pot'. She cut it and she nearly cut it off. She said that would teach him, as he asked for it. It nearly killed him.

Although apparently so much easier than all the alternatives, the Pill was not greeted with universal applause. Even non-Catholics thought it tampered with nature, and must be unhealthy. Not that it was available to most of the women who appear in this book. Its champions argued that it 'mopped up what had previously been the spilt milk of accidental motherhood' — as Germaine Greer put it — and gave women a choice only available in the past to men. That is not quite true; Dutch (or cervical) caps were introduced in the 1880s, and intrauterine devices as early as the 1860s. For centuries, women have used a variety of suppositories as a spermicide

— citrus fruit jellies, perhaps, or quinine — and an assortment of objects such as lemons, leaves or (as recommended by Dr Stopes) sponges, as barriers. But the Pill was so simple, so discreet, so magically powerful. It came to symbolize a whole era: the permissive age, the age of Aquarius, the summer of love, and all those risky concepts like feminism, sexual emancipation and the modern teenager.

Requesting it, though, was embarrassing for those not on some political or ideological mission. Even if one was married, using the Pill could seem mechanistic, as though one were somehow soliciting for sex. 'Bad girls don't have babies,' said Greer Garson in the film *Blossoms in the Dust* in 1941: they know how *not* to have them. It sounds simplistic now, or crass, but even as recently as the 1960s women were unused to the idea of enjoying sex for its own sake, as a right rather than a duty. Asking for the Pill made them feel self-indulgent, incontinent, greedy, especially as it was a clear signal that they were denying their natural function by choosing not to have children. That might have been a redeeming factor for those unmarried women who sought contraception, but for the married, it smacked of selfishness and guilt.

In 1962, Helen Brook was working as a director of the Marie Stopes Memorial Clinic in London. She was a married woman with three daughters, who did not personally advocate 'free love', nor abortion, but who appreciated how damaging an unplanned pregnancy could be for all concerned. While Lettice Fisher's National

Council for the Unmarried Mother and her Child concentrated on the child, Helen Brook saw a need to focus on mothers *before* they could conceive. In direct opposition to the ethos of the Family Planning Association (founded in 1930) and her colleagues at Marie Stopes clinics, she determined to welcome young and unmarried clients to her consultations, and when the Stopes organization objected, she left to set up an alternative service, the Brook Advisory Centres, addressing the problems associated with unprotected sex, particularly for the young.

In the mid 1960s it was reported that an average of 75,000 illegitimate babies were delivered every year; 45,000 more appeared within nine months of a shotgun wedding; 30,000 were 'unwanted' within marriage, and 100,000 were aborted. This was appalling to social reformers. A Family Planning Act was passed in 1967, allowing local authorities to provide advice to everyone, regardless of their marital status, and for social as well as medical reasons. But only a quarter of authorities were offering this advice a year later. Mrs Brook recognized why this was. People under forty were generally in favour of the sort of practical and non-judgemental help she offered; it was the older generation who were too deeply embedded in their own prejudices to support her. 'I think it is due to a dog-in-the-manger attitude,' she wrote in 1968. 'They are envious of the new freedom which we are giving the young, largely because they didn't have it themselves.'

By 1974, a free family-planning service was

available on the NHS, and Brook Advisory Centres still exist today. So do Marie Stopes clinics (as 'Marie Stopes International'), although they now offer advice on abortion as well as contraception. Nothing stopped children from being born out of wedlock, however. Nothing ever will, as long as wedlock still exists.

★　★　★

Alison bravely wrote to me about the birth of her baby in 1967. She does not mention what sort of sex-education she received at home or at school; in her case, it would have been irrelevant. She was nineteen when her son was conceived, in her first year at teacher-training college, far from home. One day, Patrick strode into the common room, and Alison was smitten. He was wearing a long greatcoat, high riding-boots and a fedora hat. He was a drama student, tall, with a droopy moustache, and looked impossibly romantic.

Patrick and Alison started meeting each other, just once a week, and in secret (which was Patrick's idea). They never kissed in public, nor even held hands, but Alison adored him. Towards the end of term he suggested they see other people, to mask their relationship, and Alison agreed. The secrecy, she says, was delicious. She accepted a date from another first-year student — and was raped. When the man told her he was sterile, having had mumps as a teenager, Alison stopped struggling. Besides, he was a six-foot rugby player while she was an eight-stone girl. She told no one.

173

That Christmas, she returned home for the holidays. Her mother suspected she was pregnant, so as soon as she got back to college in the new year, Alison went to her GP. It was confirmed. Alison realized that she would have to leave college immediately, even though she hoped to be accepted back after the baby was born. She did not tell Patrick the news; in fact when a friend offered to supply the Pill to her (available from family planning clinics) Alison agreed, and pretended to take it, as by now she and Patrick were sleeping together. Perhaps she was in denial; she was certainly in love with him, and convinced he would leave her if he knew what had happened. He was stunned when she did eventually find the courage to tell him, on the last day of the Easter term. That was the day she left college.

Alison's parents came to collect her in their little Austin A30. They asked to meet the baby's father, and Alison introduced the man who had raped her, aware of the fact that she was now expected to marry him. They had not exchanged more than a couple of words all term, and Alison had no intention of keeping the baby, never mind marrying. It was Patrick who followed her the 300 miles from college to see her at home, and who visited her, later on, in hospital.

Home offered Alison absolutely nowhere to hide. Her mother was active in the Church, and a member of the Women's Institute and Mothers' Union; she had been unusually relaxed with Alison and her friends, letting them have a garden shed for an impromptu youth club. Her argument was that she would rather know where Alison was than have her roaming around the streets and possibly getting into all kinds of trouble, even though the more purse-lipped of her neighbours warned her against such liberality with gloomy predictions that things would come to a sticky end if she wasn't more strict with her daughter.

Alison could not bear the thought of subjecting her mother to the gust of *schadenfreude* which would surely greet the news of her downfall, and so decided to abort the baby. There was no possibility of this being done officially; instead Alison's mother got a recipe for a soap mix, and some rubber tubing. Alison says she can smell that soap mixture to this day: it had to be heated on the stove, then poured through the tube into the uterus. She and her mother could not get the tube bit right, and the abortion failed. She was desperately disappointed; she had tried to abort the baby in college using the time-honoured gin-and-hot-bath method, but that had not worked either.

The only solution now was to run away and have the baby secretly. London seemed a suitably anonymous place. Her parents gave her £20, and the bus fare to get there, and Alison found herself digs in north London. She was lonely, miserable, and rapidly running out of money, until she found a temporary job as an au-pair. Patrick visited her regularly, took her out, introduced her to friends, and tried to cheer her up.

She remembers attending a single antenatal

class before her confinement; when her waters broke, some weeks early, she had no idea what was happening. She had arranged a place at a mother-and-baby home, but everything was happening too soon. She took a taxi to the nearest hospital, and was admitted.

What happened next is best left, for now.

Alison's attempts at home abortion were not uncommon. In many ways, that has been the hardest thing to deal with in researching this book: hearing about the desperate botches done to or by expectant mothers. The soapy solution she mentions was well-known. One woman was told to shred some Lifebuoy soap into a jug, melt it with boiling water, then use it as a douche. 'That'll do the trick.' She was too anxious to realize that she was supposed to let the stuff cool before she used it, however, and the resultant burns eventually killed her.

Another favourite was to use the stairs. Lynn, in the last chapter, did that, when she was told to run up two-by-two and jump the last three steps when coming down. Variants included leaping from top to bottom and landing on a mattress, or (in what Jill admitted was a very half-hearted attempt) trying to climb the stairs on one's knees.

Gina went to the 'steamie', or public baths, and emptied a whole tin of mustard powder into the water before climbing in for a soak. A girl in Sheffield heard that skipping worked well, so she skipped and skipped until she could skip no more. Florence's sisters and her mother tried to abort her baby with knitting needles; when her daughter was born with a birthmark on her chest, Florence was convinced it was because of damage sustained in the womb (otherwise, the baby was fine). There used to be a woman called 'knitting-needle Nelly' in Hayes, Middlesex, in the 1920s, to whom you could apply if found to be inconveniently in the family way.

I am not sure whether knitting-needle Nelly was a midwife, but she might well have been. Midwives were often the first port of call for anyone faced with an unplanned pregnancy. Traditionally, they were the women in the community who knew about the properties of herbs and natural abortifacients like slippery elm (the bark of *Ulmus rubra*), aloe vera, or ergot (a type of fungus). Before the First World War — for generations — those who delivered babies also laid out the deceased, and could often be prevailed upon to procure dead babies. They used pencils, candles, needles, crochet- and button-hooks; they offered enemas and douches of carbolic acid, turpentine, or castor oil. Some of their infusions were horrifying: in water they steeped nails and pennies, gunpowder, gold leaf from painters' shops, lead scrapings, or rat poison. No doubt these concoctions dealt with the baby, but all too often the mothers succumbed too.

Back-street practices continued into the 1960s, although seldom involving registered midwives by then. Some doctors performed abortions on demand, for a price, from Harley Street to the Liverpool Docks; when their patients died, as they frequently did after contracting septicaemia or peritonitis, charges were brought, there was a

177

sensational little flurry of publicity, then all went quiet again. Meanwhile, quacks calling themselves 'Dr' this or that peddled pills and potions said to correct female infirmities, or remove obstructions. Dr Reynolds sold special 'Lightning Pills' as a 'sure and prompt cure for all irregularities and all complaints incidental to the female system', while Dr Gardiner, at his hairdressing salon in Villiers Street, London, obligingly offered 'regulating' pills for delayed menstruation at ten shillings a box. If those pills failed to work, he prescribed double-strength ones at £1 a box (although the pills were exactly the same as the original ones). This was in 1920, when the value of the pound was equivalent to about £175 today.

Gardiner's pills were probably fairly harmless, but he also operated as an ad-hoc surgeon, inducing abortions by using catheters and other appliances, for which he was tried at the Central Criminal Court. He faced two charges: one for the manslaughter of Edith Daynes, a cook, and the other for causing Frances Smedley, a nurse, to miscarry. No doubt when he went down there were plenty of other practitioners ready to pop up and take his place.

When the Abortion Act came into force in early 1968, it was a little like the introduction of the Pill: relevant only to relatively few women. It permitted termination of pregnancy before twenty-eight weeks (reduced to twenty-four weeks in 1990), and then only on conditions involving mental or physical health. Legally, a pregnancy resulting from rape was not covered by the Act, although in practice it was often included. Social considerations — whether or not the parent(s) actually *wanted* the child — counted for nothing. So again, it hardly impacted on the number of illegitimate babies being born, especially given the increase in recreational sex during the 1960s. The only abortion available to most single parents was an illegal one. How sad, that messing about with knitting needles or turkey-basters charged with carbolic acid were acceptable alternatives to giving birth to a bastard.

Before leaving this dispiriting subject, here is the story of Elisabeth, who wrote to me right at the beginning of my research. It illustrates how very bleak life could be for a young woman faced with an unplanned pregnancy, and how limited her choices were.

I am using her own words.

'Where do I start? I suppose at the beginning. 1963. I was a very naive seventeen-year-old and became pregnant during a relationship with a boy at the college I was attending. I knew nothing about contraception. My mother had given me only vague guidelines about what not to do with boys and there was no education or information within the media (or I didn't see it if there was). I suppose I thought it wouldn't happen to me. I remember a few years prior to this, hearing about a girl at a school in the area who had become pregnant and we were all very shocked. I can even remember her name now. Anyway, after some fumblings in the back of this boy's father's car, I realized the worst had happened and I made a secret appointment to see the family GP. He confirmed my fear and to be honest I am not sure what I planned to do next.

'This was taken out of my hands as a couple of days later my parents were waiting for me outside the college as I came out, as the doctor had telephoned them. As you can imagine it was just awful. I can picture them outside but don't remember much more detail. I was very frightened. I am honestly not sure if I had told the boy at this stage. My parents rang his parents and they came round to our house to have discussions about where to go next. All I can remember is my mother saying that if we married, we would probably be on social security for the rest of our lives. It turned out that my parents had thought of an alternative. (I must stress in all this that I am in no way blaming my parents for their views or plans — it was just how things were at the time.) Secrecy at all costs.

'My mother worked at the time and one day a contact of hers came and made some attempts to remove the baby. I am really struggling with this now as I haven't thought about it for many, many years and I cannot go into detail. Thinking about it now fills me with horror because of what I now know of the dangers. Suffice to say, the baby remained. I remember my father chain-smoking in the other room and obviously being so frightened. Such was the stigma at the time that my mother and father had resorted to this. I am going to pause now for a while . . .

'My brother was working in Scandinavia at the time and arrangements were made for me to travel and see doctors over there to see if an abortion was possible under the law there. To this day I don't know how I managed the journey overland and on ships on my own. I cannot overstress how much of a child I was mentally. I obviously didn't fulfil the criteria and can only imagine that maybe my parents had hoped that Scandinavia might be a little more lenient in things like this, but I don't know for sure. I returned to England briefly and then it was arranged for me to return there [to Scandinavia] to spend time as an au-pair girl until the baby arrived. I must stress also that my parents were by no means rich and it must have cost them a great deal to do this. No one outside the immediate family was told apart from the mysterious lady who came [to attempt the abortion]. I have no idea if anyone had guessed.

'I contacted an adoption agency where I was living in Scandinavia (I'm being deliberately vague here) and arrangements were made for the baby to be taken away at birth. I remember going to antenatal checks and not understanding a word as no one spoke English but I was with a good family who knew the situation. I had stayed initially with a friend of my brother and had advertised my services as an English au-pair. All this sounds as though I was confident, but actually I was consumed with fear the whole time. The family I stayed with literally gave me a home so that I could converse with their two children to improve their English and there was very little housework involved. They were obviously very forward-thinking and made no judgement. I moved to the capital to stay with one of the adoption society ladies when I was nearly due. I never saw the baby and I think I just wanted to put the whole thing away afterwards as I can honestly say I was afraid to think about it. I knew it was a girl because the card I was given had it on.

'I soon returned to this country and carried on relatively normally but always with this fear that someone would find out. I do wonder if one of the friends I still have now had an inkling. I went on to marry, but didn't tell my husband . . .

'I must sound so unfeeling to you and I am really not. I think I had just put the whole thing in a box and wanted it to stay there. I still to this day would like it all to go away. That again must sound so selfish, but I have never ever had peace of mind.'

★ ★ ★

Neither Alison nor Elisabeth had to endure the mortifying business of breaking the news of their pregnancy to their families. In Alison's case, her mother guessed; Elisabeth's doctor told her secret. The awful telling-of-the-parents was usually when full realization dawned; when the truth of what had happened, and was going to happen, first sank in. The NCUMC recognized what a difficult time this could be. In a thinly disguised publicity feature appearing as a piece of journalism in 1957, a spokesperson for the Council tried to put a positive spin on this most dreaded of encounters.

It is a cruel thing to be presented suddenly with an illegitimate grandchild, whereas the woman who has her daughter's confidence and shared the burden can say 'My girl told me and I helped her out.' When broken courageously, the news is nearly always better received than the girl had expected, and [a] social worker will, if necessary, be present at the interview or draft the letter.

Draft the letter? I wonder how many daughters really wrote to their parents in these circumstances? Or sons? The only time Jill ever saw her mother cry was when she heard about her pregnancy. Sarah's mother was more understanding than Sarah had dared hope, but her father was desperately disappointed, more wounded than angry; Sarah felt she had let him down terribly. Jane B's mother, Emma, was similarly stoical and supportive. But when Emma broke the news to Jane's father, he was shattered. 'The stupid little idiot. My God — the stupid idiot ... If she had to sleep with someone, she might at least have seen that she didn't bring some luckless little bastard into the world.' When he had cooled down a little, and faced Jane herself, all he could manage was 'Hard luck, chum.'

One very angry woman told me that although she has had two children, she has never been a mum. She first fell pregnant on Christmas Day, a few days before her sixteenth birthday; her boyfriend was a keen motorcyclist, who was killed the following New Year's Eve in a road accident. She did not realize she was pregnant for some time. When it became obvious, she broke the news to her parents. It is difficult to credit how badly they treated her. Their first concern was to find out who the father was, so that he could be prosecuted for having sex with a minor. Her mother, a Catholic, marched her straight off to an adoption agency to arrange for the baby to be taken away as soon as it was born. The only reason her father did not beat her, she says, is because he had a slipped disc at the time. There was no sympathy, no compassion, and an overwhelming sense that after this, she would have to spend the rest of her life making up to her parents for her ungrateful wickedness.

Two years later, and still unmarried, she became pregnant again; the reaction this time was even worse. When one of her sons managed to trace her in later life, he was shocked to learn how unsupportive his grandparents had been. This woman is still consumed with rage and sadness. Many of my correspondents cried when they told me their stories (as did I), usually when talking about having to relinquish the baby if they were parents, or having been relinquished if they were illegitimate; about what tenderness or possibly resentment they feel for their mother or child now — a generation or two away — or about how coldly they were treated by others. This woman only cried when she remembered an aunt had once told her that she loved her.

Until this book came along I thought, probably naively, that not many relationships were innately closer than a child's with its parents. I grew up in what appeared to be a cheerful, well-meaning rural community in the 1960s and 1970s, and most of my friends, like me, appeared to thrive in an atmosphere of mutual respect (within limits) and unconditional love. Perhaps we were not as ready as modern families are to articulate our emotions and *tell* our family members we loved them, but it was deeply understood. A neighbour in our village had an embroidered motto on her wall: 'I loved you once, I love you still; I always have, I always will.' I coveted that, with its silken border of pansies and its fancy frame. It says exactly what I sensed at home as a child, and what I hope my children sense from me today.

It was therefore no real surprise that Tessa, who went to my school, was supported by her parents when she became pregnant, and I am pretty sure mine would have stood by me in a similar situation. So what were all these hard-hearted mothers doing sending their confused and pregnant daughters away? Maybe no love is completely unconditional, and everything snaps when it's stressed too far. 'A woman's chastity consists in not being asked,' said Ovid. Perhaps our sense of security consists in not being threatened. It is too easy to make ill-informed judgements when we hear stories of blind parental panic, induced abortions and fantastically elaborate under-cover operations designed to keep secrets and protect reputations. These were the days when mothers did not even tell their daughters about menstruation; they were left to face the shocking evidence of 'the

185

'curse' completely unprepared. The past is, indeed, a different country.

That said, we should not forget the many, many loving parents who accepted their unexpected grandchildren with love, who forgave, and who tried to be positive. It is tempting to impose our own terms of reference on others, particularly our forebears; to imagine how we would react in the same circumstances today, and judge them accordingly. But it is unhelpful to compare the despair of a well-respected couple in a provincial town in the 1930s, say, with a laid-back, metropolitan parent's attitude a couple of generations later. There can be no comparison. Yet one cannot help being a little bemused by the man — for example — who felt such vicarious shame at his unmarried daughter's condition that he gave up his job and moved the family to the other end of the country, or the father who hid his daughter in a caravan in the garden for most of her pregnancy. One girl was kept in seclusion as soon as she broke the news. Her parents arranged for her medical appointments to be at home, so there would be no chance of being spotted in the surgery (several other parents insisted their compromised daughters only visit the GP at the end of surgery hours, and use the back door). Another, when her waters broke early on the top deck of a London bus, was so used to trying to be anonymous that she immediately put her coat over her head, like a convicted prisoner. It was as though these women accepted their condition, and the attitude it evinced — at best dismissive, at worst plain cruel — because they felt they deserved it. This was the burden they must bear in return for doing wrong, the wages of sin.

This would chime well with the defensive attitude of neighbours and friends who, perhaps in superstitious fear of being visited by similar misfortune, were shrill in their condemnation of other people's ruined daughters. Respectable folk would cross the street to avoid speaking to such ungodly young women; they would warn their own children to keep away, lest they become polluted. It was easier to assume the pregnancy was a result of promiscuity than risk being sympathetic. Only 'fast' girls fell pregnant; girls who were not properly brought up. And once a certain type of young lady conceived a child, it was a common belief that she was then liable to ricochet around having sex almost uncontrollably, so that she could pick a putative father from as wide a field of candidates as possible.

The irony is that being 'nice' is often what caused the trouble in the first place. Being nice meant not mentioning things like sex, and not mentioning things like sex meant the sort of institutional naivety which led to agencies like the NCUMC being run off its feet. 'There but for the grace of God go I' is as ineffective a method of contraception as hoping you'll be able to keep enough wits about you to get off the train before it reaches its fateful destination.

What the eyes don't see, the heart doesn't grieve over. Frequently, mothers-to-be were dispatched by their parents to stay with distant

187

family members or unknown vicars' wives, who could be trusted to keep their mouths shut (often for a fee). Others were found jobs as companions or au-pairs, like Elisabeth in Scandinavia. A proud couple in Trinidad sent their poor daughter all the way to England to give birth in 1959. She knew no one. She duly had the baby, left it in the UK and went home behaving — outwardly — as though nothing had happened. More than half a century later the repercussions of that course of action are still echoing around the family on both sides of the Atlantic.

Perhaps the most common reaction to an unplanned pregnancy in the family was to send the mother-to-be to a purposely-run maternity home. Most mother-and-baby homes were accessed through agencies like the NCUMC, the Church, the Salvation Army, local authorities or adoption agencies. You were admitted about six weeks before the baby was due to be born, and left six weeks afterwards, either with or without the child. There, you were expected to help with light domestic duties until the confinement, and were offered medical and practical support by the staff. Not always emotional support: that came, if it came at all, from your fellow inmates.

Smaller, private residential homes were available, too. Most were in London and other big, anonymous cities. There was a glut of them on the ultra-respectable Isle of Wight, masquerading as seaside guest-houses. If you could afford it, you could send your embarrassing daughter into one of these as soon as her swelling belly began to show. In 1966, a home like this could cost as much as 50 guineas a week — twice the average weekly wage — so it is no wonder so many of these expectant mothers felt themselves to be under an intolerable obligation to their parents afterwards. One girl remembers being 'incarcerated in a nursing-home for affluent old ladies' for most of her pregnancy. Barbara went to work in a 'legitimate' maternity home, as a menial domestic, long before anyone could have guessed she was pregnant at seventeen. As time went on, and the fact became obvious, she was so derisively treated by the patients there that she ran away. She was not allowed home: she stayed with friends instead until a place could be found for her in a less exclusive mother-and-baby home elsewhere. She soon settled in with the other residents. They were all from different backgrounds — a girl from Ireland, a Welsh girl in her late twenties, a lady in her thirties who was an accomplished pianist, a hairdresser, and someone she describes as being 'one sandwich short of a picnic' who could knit absolutely anything without a pattern, and it always fitted perfectly. They did not judge each other, because as single mothers they were all in the same boat, all up the creek without a paddle.

In special cases, homes run by Barnardo's or the Salvation Army would take young women early, too. Sue B was only fourteen when she and her teddy-boy lover (aged eighteen) discovered they were expecting a baby in the early 1960s. She was three months pregnant when she was sent to a Salvation Army home, where she stayed until twelve weeks after the baby's birth. The child was adopted, but traced Sue, and now, being so close in age, 'we're really good friends'. Stephanie managed to avoid her parents' wrath at the news of her pregnancy at sixteen by simply not telling them. She and her boyfriend secretly arranged a place in a Barnardo's home in London; one night she packed a suitcase, and leaving a note the next morning, she left.

Imogen did not tell her father (her mother was dead). She was not exactly a skittish teenager when she conceived in the early 1960s; she was a primary-school teacher, in the midst of an affair with an unhappily married colleague fourteen years her senior. She was not comfortable with this duplicity, and imagined that if she could move away, disappear, her lover would subside into marriage again, and she could start afresh. She researched jobs in Canada, even the Falkland Islands, but her lover talked her out of it. She did manage to move to a different county, but he followed her, with his family, and the affair continued.

Then Imogen became pregnant, because of a 'failure of contraception'. She had just secured a post as a deputy head teacher. Never mind, said her doctor, you'll just have to get married a little sooner than planned. She blurted out that the father was already married, and a few days later a postcard arrived at her flat, from social services, asking if she needed support. A *postcard*, not a letter: anyone could have read it.

The baby's father put Imogen in touch with a local branch of the NCUMC. In October she moved into a bedsit in the home of one of the NCUMC staff. The baby was due in December. She resigned her shiny new job, telling the school that her father was ill and she needed to leave to look after him. Then she did her Christmas shopping, far in advance; she even wrote her cards, which a friend said she would post at the appropriate time. Every time she left her bedsit Imogen was terrified she might meet someone she knew, and betray her secret.

When she was admitted to her mother-and-baby home, she was finally able to relax a little. She felt safe there and could sense herself becoming meek and submissive, taking the line of least resistance. This was a relief, although it was heart-breaking not to be able to give the name of her next-of-kin to the nurses. Her father still knew nothing about the baby, and the baby's father, though he often came to see Imogen, was simply not free. A lack of antenatal care intensified Imogen's fear of the future, but for now, among friends in a sort of suspended reality, she felt temporarily content to wait for the next episode in this strange and unpredictable new life.

7

Ungentle Birth: The Confinement

Where the Dickens did that come from?

Imogen spent the timeless days before her child's birth at the mother-and-baby home sewing its layette. The repetitive, anaesthetic stitching focused her mind and body with gratifying numbness. Those, like her, who had already made plans for adoption were issued a list of things to provide for the baby; a sort of trousseau with which to launch it across the Rubicon into another world. Susan remembers being given a cardboard box, which she covered and lined with bright nursery wallpaper. Inside she put three 'Cherub' envelope-neck vests with sleeves (her baby was born in April, an unpredictable month), three flannelette nightgowns, three matinée jackets, eighteen terry-towelling nappies, eighteen muslin squares, some bibs, a shawl and a pram blanket. Many mothers smuggled in little extras. Susan added a beautiful broderie-anglaise top, and a small blue teddy-bear.

Tokens like this remind me of the tiny treasures left with foundling babies on Thomas Coram's doorstep in the eighteenth century. As well as being proofs of kin, they were like charms, to keep the baby safe and link it secretly to the mother whose love, though intangible and unacknowledged, would never leave her child.

By the time Susan and Imogen had need of one — in the early 1960s — most registered mother-and-baby homes in the UK had lost that air of guilt and culpability which used to eddy sourly through the corridors and dormitories of Victorian maternity homes for fallen women. Thanks to the efforts of the NCUMC, such places were not so much about penitence these days, as about giving an illegitimate child the best possible start in life (according to the mores of the time) and making sure its mother gave birth safely. In the 1920s the mortality rate for illegitimate babies was about twice that of babies born in wedlock, and more single mothers than wives died in childbirth. The Curtis Report on the care of children 'deprived of a home life' was published in 1946, and revealed that only 37 per cent of unmarried mothers in local authority care were offered the services of a doctor during childbirth, or analgesia, compared with half of married women. More illegitimate babies were bottle-fed than legitimate ones. Staff at the mother-and-baby homes of the post-Second World War period were supposed to discourage discrimination like this — yet when Susan shouted for help while left alone during her labour in 1961, she was told by a nurse to keep quiet, because 'this is your punishment'.

Both Susan and Imogen found themselves at establishments run by religious organizations, which formed the majority of homes for unmarried mothers before the 1970s: there were about 100 of them in the UK in 1963. The

Church of England and the Salvation Army sponsored most of these. Local authorities also ran homes, which evolved from workhouses, although workhouses themselves were still admitting indigent or ostracized unmarried mothers until the 1940s. When asked to describe her confinement there, one elderly and (then) unmarried lady recalled, 'I was put where they were put in them days. My mother put me in the workhouse . . . because she thought it was wrong what I had done.' Her baby was born two months premature, and weighed a puny 3lb 2oz.

Unregulated mother-and-baby homes were risky. In 1960, the matron of the sinister-sounding 'Pixey Hollow' in Ramsgate was charged with selling her residents' babies to Americans, and spending the proceeds herself. It was not unusual for large, lugubrious houses in the suburbs, or even in country villages, to be filled with a transient population of pregnant lodgers sent from the other end of the country to give birth in anonymity. Specialist homes for married ladies, for schoolgirls, or for professional women (like Imogen) were available to those with the nous or the contacts to access them. All these places aspired to comfort and efficiency, in variable degrees, in preparing to deliver the residents of their unfortunate little burdens.

Irish Catholic girls who conceived out of wed-lock were considered to be singularly disgraceful. Many of them were sent to Magdalene homes, with associated industrial schools and laundries. These had a threefold purpose: to remove rotten apples from society, to teach them the error of their ways, and to employ them profitably. They were run by religious orders: nuns from the Sisters of Our Lady of Charity, the Sisters of Mercy, the Religious Sisters of Charity, or the Sisters of the Good Shepherd. They were not exclusively Irish, and some were run by Protestant orders. In fact the first ever Magdalene home was opened in London in 1758. But the Irish Catholic variety is particularly notorious, synonymous with cruelty, exploitation and religious bigotry of the worst kind.

The Magdalene home at Tuam in Co. Galway dealt with fifty-one confinements in 1954. The local county council paid £1 per week for each single mother in residence, and most young women stayed for a year. In return for their board and lodging, they were expected to do domestic work. At the end of the year, they were allowed to leave, either with or without the baby. If it was the latter, the child would be sent for adoption, or held in the home or an industrial school, a sort of borstal, until old enough to fend for itself. If by any wicked mischance an inmate should conceive again, or if she already had an illegitimate child or children, she was sent straight to one of the commercial laundries, run by the sisters and in many cases contracted to the state on behalf of the police force or the armed forces and other organizations. A typical one of these in the 1950s was staffed by seventy-three girls, of whom 70 per cent were unmarried. The rest were arbitrarily described as 'backward', so unfit for life outside. If they mended their ways and had a suitable place to go, after a period of labouring in the laundry, some 'Maggies' were allowed to leave, while others became 'consecrated penitents' and stayed for life.

A report into state collusion in the Magdalene laundry system was published in 2013, together with an acknowledgement of the Irish Government's regret to former 'Maggies' for all that they had been put through. The report found that half the women incarcerated in laundries between 1922, when the Irish State came into being, and 1996, when the last one closed, were under the age of twenty-three. (The history of the Magdalenes stretches back to the eighteenth century, of course; by 1922 they had over a century of experience behind them in dealing with the detritus of a religious society.) Ten thousand women were sent to the laundries during that seventy-four-year period, and at least 988 of the women buried in laundry grounds are said to have lived there all their lives. Many of the 2,500 women committed to the Magdalene system by the state were sent against their will for being unmarried and pregnant. They were put away, and if they tried to escape, the Gardaí were instructed to pursue them and return them to the custody of the nuns. Maggies were never subject to the fair wage clauses that applied to the rest of the Irish workforce, nor to any social insurance benefits. In effect, they were slaves.

One hundred and eighteen women volunteered to contribute their experiences to the 2013 report. They spoke of abuse (more emotional and psychological than physical or

196

sexual): 'the nuns never hit me in [the home], I'll give that to them. But they gave it to you in your mind.' They issued you with a number or a new name when you arrived, and cut your hair; they taunted you with insults and jangled rosaries in your ears; they censored your letters, stopped visitors, and refused to explain why you were there or when you might leave. And the laundries were hellish.

The floors . . . were constantly floating with water — often soapy dirty water streaming out. There was constant inhaling of steam from the large colander (large ironing board). Young women stood either side of the colander for up to two or three hours in the morning and again in the afternoon. Large buckets of boiling water were scattered around the floor used for starching and steaming. The light was poor and their only view from the windows was more iron bars. There was often a foul smell in the air from the extensive, industrial laundry of soiled sheets from hospitals, hotels, convents, farms and more.

Some of the women who testified to what life was like on the inside did so anonymously. I don't mean merely that their names were unpublished: they told their stories clandestinely, stealing in and out of a back door in the building where the interviews were taking place, for fear their families might find out that underneath a hard-earned veneer of respectability they were

Magdalene girls. They felt too ashamed to admit their past, even to those closest to them. Samantha was, and is, happy for her name to be known. She was not a Magdalene survivor herself; she testified on behalf of her mother, Margaret — a non-survivor.

Margaret's story is appalling. She was born in a mental hospital in Dublin, where her mother was a resident patient. Her mother used to be allowed visits home, and on these occasions conceived six children, who were left in the care of their father. He tried his best, but in the early 1950s he was reported by a neighbour and brought to court for neglect, with the result that the youngest four children — including Margaret — were put into care. That is what we would call it now; in reality, 'care' had nothing to do with it.

Margaret was sent to an industrial school. Her record shows that she was punished at two years old for persistently wetting the bed, and by the age of five, her working day began with kneeling by the urine-soaked sheets to say her rosary at 4 a.m. before going to the kitchen to prepare meals for seventy children. As she grew older, Margaret's IQ was tested to see what level of education might be appropriate. It was decided that with a score of 50 (which her fiercely intelligent daughters dispute) she was unfit to be educated at all. Instead, she must work.

At sixteen, Margaret was transferred from the industrial school to a Magdalene home, and began her career as a laundress. She spent most of her life washing the sheets and clothes of inmates at another sort of prison, Mountjoy

Gaol in Dublin. When not busy from dawn till dusk with her hands immersed in freezing cold water, or inhaling the chemical steam from the boilers, she would be set to cleaning in the Home or in the local church. Cleaning clean things; cleaning for the sake of cleaning. 'Cleaning their souls, I suppose,' says her daughter Samantha.

The conditions inside the Home were grim. There was a nicely furnished reception room for visitors (who were a rare luxury), but behind the façade, the residents' quarters were squalid, damp and cold. They were not paid for their work. The doors were locked behind them and they were forbidden to leave, except on the odd trip to a shrine or some other holy place. On these uncommon occasions, they would be given a little pocket money to spend on sweets or cigarettes.

In the summer of 1971, when Margaret was about nineteen, the nuns organized a visit to Wicklow. Margaret remembered taking her pocket-money to a sweet-shop there, which was run by a man much older than she. Nine months later, back in Dublin, Margaret gave birth to twin girls, one of whom was Samantha. The nuns accused Margaret of running away from the Home and being raped on the street — or even soliciting for sex — but Margaret herself insisted she had never been let out except on supervised trips. 'Sure, I'm not allowed to leave and where would I go anyway?' She said the girls' father was the sweet-shop man from County Wicklow.

Margaret was committed to a mother-and-baby home for the confinement, and for six or seven weeks she cared for her daughters herself, insisting on breastfeeding them. During the day she was expected to carry on working, scrubbing in the laundry, but afterwards she would come back to her babies. One evening, however, her babies were not there. Without her knowledge or consent, they had been transferred to another part of the mother-and-baby home, and Margaret was returned to the Magdalene.

Samantha's compassion for her mother is very moving. Before Margaret was traced, Samantha imagined she was just 'an ordinary young girl who made a mistake'.

'I assumed she moved on with her secret, met a nice fella, and lived somewhere in Dublin with three or four kids and thought about us sometimes . . . [I] hoped that she was able to cleanse herself from the guilt of giving away twins. Because, I never thought that people did that flippantly, I always thought that even if it was impossible to keep your baby or babies in our case, that you always did that with a heavy heart. But no matter what your circumstances were, that you didn't want the baby, you didn't want the blot on your reputation, but once the baby was born, God you wanted the baby. And I know, I know now from giving birth myself . . . sitting on the edge of the bed staring at him in his Perspex cot in the hospital ward and the nurses were coming down to me saying, do you want, do you want us to take him for a while, you don't have to sit up looking at him, he's asleep, and I said: 'I can't stop looking at him. I can't believe I'm a mother.' And I thought of Margaret, looking at the two babies and then they were gone.'

1. 'Able Bodied Inmates' at a Leeds workhouse in the 1920s. For many young women who fell pregnant out of wedlock, there was nowhere else to go.

2 & 3. Foundlings were left at Coram's Hospital with distinctive tokens to identify their origins. Some tokens (*above*) were ordinary objects personalized with a motto; others were lovingly worked and elaborate. From the nineteenth century, receipts were given instead (*below*).

HOSPITAL *for the Maintenance and Education of Exposed and Deserted Young Children.*

The *Thirteenth* Day of *January* 1937.
RECEIVED a *Male* Child *E.*

Reginald E. Nichols

Secretary.

This must be produced whenever a personal enquiry is made after the Health of the Child (which may be done on Mondays, between the Hours of Ten and Four), and also in case the Child should be claimed: if enquiry is made by letter, the full date of admission, the sex of the Child, and the letter of the Alphabet must be stated, but this parchment must not be sent.

4. Captain Thomas Coram, who established the Foundling Hospital in London in 1739.

5. The grandeur of Coram's Hospital and its illustrious patrons made his charity fashionable, despite its connection with illegitimacy.

6. At the Babies' Castle, a Barnardo's home in Hawkhurst, Kent, it is time for a non-negotiable nap, October 1934.

7. Saying prayers at the Babies' Castle, 1963.

8,000

orphan and destitute boys and girls always being supported and prepared for an industrious and self-reliant future.

EASTER
OFFERINGS

are earnestly asked for to maintain the Charter of the Homes.
"No destitute child ever refused admission."

10/- will feed one child
for a fortnight.

£35 will support a healthy
child for one year.

Cheques and Orders payable "Dr. Barnardo's Homes," and crossed, should be sent to Dr. Barnardo's Homes, 92 Barnardo House, Stepney Causeway, London, E.1

8. A magazine appeal for Dr. Barnardo's homes, 1930s. Illegitimate children were more tastefully described as 'orphans'.

9. It was important to Barnardo's and other agencies that children should be taught to support themselves. Here, boys are being trained as wheelwrights.

10. Chastened single mothers sew church embroideries at the Horbury House of Mercy in Wakefield.

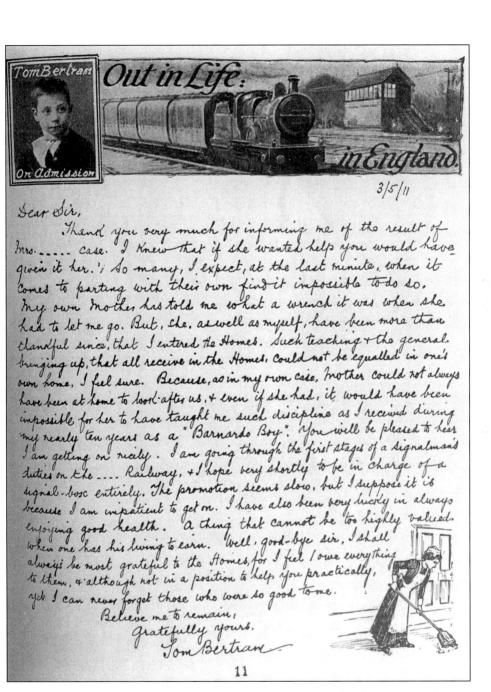

Out in Life: in England

Tom Bertram

On Admission

3/5/11

Dear Sir,

Thank you very much for informing me of the result of Mrs. _____ case. I knew that if she wanted help you would have given it her.'; So many, I expect, at the last minute, when it comes to parting with their own find it impossible to do so. My own Mother has told me what a wrench it was when she had to let me go. But, she, as well as myself, have been more than thankful since, that I entered the Homes. Such teaching + the general bringing up, that all receive in the Homes, could not be equalled in one's own home, I feel sure. Because, as in my own case, Mother could not always have been at home to look after us, + even if she had, it would have been impossible for her to have taught me such discipline as I received during my nearly ten years as a "Barnardo Boy". You will be pleased to hear I am getting on nicely. I am going through the first stages of a signalman's duties on the ____ Railway, + I hope very shortly to be in charge of a signal-box entirely. The promotion seems slow, but I suppose it is because I am impatient to get on. I have also been very lucky in always enjoying good health. A thing that cannot be too highly valued. when one has his living to earn. Well, good-bye sir, I shall always be most grateful to the Homes, for I feel I owe everything to them, + although not in a position to help you practically, yet I can never forget those who were so good to me.

Believe me to remain,
Gratefully yours.
Tom Bertram

11

11. Success stories like Tom Bertram's were publicized to prove that illegitimate and disadvantaged children were not inherently corrupt.

12. Maud was inspired by the suffragettes in exercising her right not to marry the father of her children.

13. A birth-control nurse outside one of Marie Stopes's mobile clinics in the 1920s.

14. A cautionary tale is told in the Christmas edition of *Lucky Star*, 1936.

THE

DELIVERER

BLOOD AND FIRE

THE SALVATION ARMY

ORGAN OF THE WOMEN'S SOCIAL WORK

MONTHLY, ONE PENNY   Registered for the]   LONDON: AUGUST, 1909   [Canadian Magazine Post   YEARLY, 1s. 6d. Post Free

A FRONT VIEW OF IVY HOUSE HOSPITAL
WITH COLONEL SAPSWORTH, THE SUPERINTENDENT, AT THE TOP RIGHT SIDE

15. *The Deliverer* reported the Salvation Army's mission to rescue unmarried mothers and their illegitimate children between 1889 and 1993.

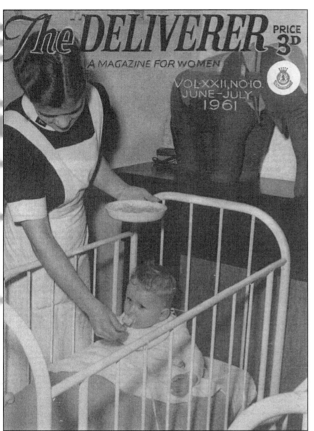

16 & 17. Feeding-time was part of a strict routine at Salvation Army mother-and-baby homes. These images from *The Deliverer* suggest it was an impersonal affair in 1961 (*left*); later it became a precious opportunity for a mother to bond with her child (*below*).

18. A group of children set off on SS *Oronsay* for Fairbridge Farm School, Molong, Australia, 1938. The new outfits in their suitcases were usually confiscated on arrival.

19. For illegitimate emigrants, life in the colonies was supposed to promise independence and freedom from prejudice. These are 'future landowners' working in Canada, photographed by Barnardo's in 1912.

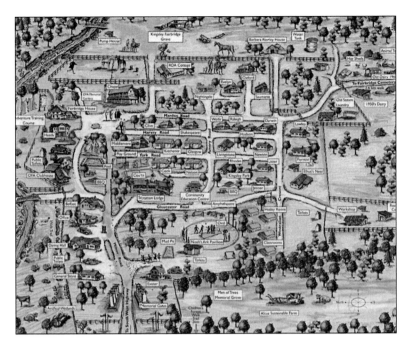

20. Plan of Fairbridge Village in Pinjarra, Australia, where children lived in dormitory houses named after bracing heroes like Darwin, Nelson and Nightingale.

21. Clearing the ground at Pinjarra in order to expand the Fairbridge Village. Much of the burning-off and building was done by children.

22. Good Shepherd Magdalene asylum looms over the Co. Cork countryside. It was abandoned in the late 1970s.

23. A memorial to deceased single mothers – or 'Penitents' – from the Mecklenburg Street asylum in Dublin. Toys are tucked around the cross.

24. The unwelcoming door of Gloucester Street Magdalene asylum in Dublin, where Samantha's mother, Margaret, spent thirty-five years of her life.

25. Mealtime in the nursery at Sean Ross Abbey, Co. Tipperary, in the mid-1950s, where Philomena Lee lived with her illegitimate son before his adoption in America.

26. An empty cradle in a convent wall is ready to receive modern foundlings in Poland. 'Okno życia' translates as 'the window of life'.

Would you be more careful if it was you that got pregnant?

Contraception is one of the facts of life.
Anyone, married or single, can get free advice on contraception from their doctor or family planning clinic.
You can find your local clinic under Family Planning in the telephone directory or Yellow Pages.

The Family Planning Information Service

27. The Health Education Council fronted its family planning campaign in the early 1970s with this shocking image of a young father 'in the family way'.

What happened to the twins we shall find out later. Margaret, meanwhile, became pregnant again after four years, and again her daughter was taken for adoption. Margaret would — or could — never talk about the circumstance of this child's conception. Nor, in later life, could she remember giving birth at all. In 1996 the commercial laundry closed, but the home and its regime remained. Margaret died in 2003 at the absurdly young age of fifty-one from Good-pasture's Syndrome, an auto-immune disease of the kidneys and lungs caused by prolonged exposure to industrial chemicals; in Margaret's case, detergents.

I once came across the death certificate of a Victorian baby who perished at a few days old. It had died, according to the doctor, 'of itself'. Margaret was a little like that. She died of herself: of being Margaret, a person institution-alized and exploited all her life, who accepted it because she knew nothing else. The fault was not hers that her parents could not look after her when she was a child, but she was still punished for it. The fault was not hers that her illegitimate babies were born, but no doubt their birth was seen as an endorsement of her flawed morality, her grubby soul. It is wicked, what was done to Margaret and the thousands of other women like her in the Magdalene homes, most of whom were there because of unplanned pregnancies. We can acknowledge that wickedness now, and must never forget it. In his official apology to these women, made in February 2013, the Irish Taoiseach, Enda Kenny, made this statement.

What we discuss today is your story. What we address today is how you took this country's terrible 'secret' and made it your own. Burying it, carrying it in your hearts here at home, or with you to England and to Canada, America and Australia on behalf of Ireland and the Irish people.

But from this moment on you need carry it no more, because today, we take it back.

Samantha does not cry often. But when she heard this, she cried for Margaret, and for all that had been denied her. And I wept, when I read Samantha's testimony, for all those secrets so much darker than the truths they tried to hide.

★　★　★

In 1964, while those who ran the Magdalene homes were still busy with their secret work across the Irish Sea, the NCUMC in London published a blueprint for the ideal mother-and-baby home. It had fifteen to eighteen guests, with three or fewer to a bedroom. There were sitting rooms, an interview room, a milk room for preparing feeds, a laundry (for the convenience rather than the employment of the residents) and a pram shed. The beds were comfortable, and a generous three feet wide; each resident had a bedside locker, and the use of a public telephone. The home looked cheerful and welcoming. It is a nice image. And sometimes, the ideal was realized. This is Jane A's description of the home to which she was dispatched in 1970, at the age of nineteen.

'The matron is very kindly, and fails to be intimidating though I'm sure she tries. She introduces me to the cook/housekeeper Betty. Matron explains that I will be in the house until the baby comes, and for six weeks after, at which time I will either surrender the child for adoption, or go to whatever accommodation I have been able to arrange with my social worker.

'I will not spend my time in idleness, but will be required to assist Betty with a little light housework and assistance in the kitchen. I am lucky, she goes on to explain, that as I am the only resident at the moment, there will be very little for me to do anyway.

'I am shown to my room, which is comfortably furnished with a divan bed, a dressing table and a small wardrobe. I receive state unemployment benefit, and maternity benefit and I am required to surrender 50 per cent of this in lieu of rent and food.

'During my six weeks' antenatal stay Matron, who is a registered midwife, will educate me in the rudiments of childcare, as even if I do the sensible thing (it is always the sensible thing) I will probably have children in the future, if I am lucky enough to find someone who'll have me (me being damaged goods, of course), so it will not be wasted.'

Jane soon settles into a gentle routine, as more guests arrive. In the morning residents are expected to gather in the front parlour to start the day with a bracing hymn and a prayer. Then they move through to the kitchen, where breakfast is prepared for them. There is always a choice of cereal or toast, and then a variety of goodies which sound as though they should be residing under silver salvers on a sideboard (perhaps they were): boiled eggs, bacon, kidneys, or sausage, depending on the day of the week. On Saturdays, Betty's morning off, Matron herself cooks a full breakfast, and on Sundays they have a light meal before going to church mid-morning. Sunday lunch is ready on their return. Jane does not recall being asked whether she is a Christian, or what denomination she is. It is assumed that for the duration, like everyone else she's a High Anglican.

The afternoons are when Jane feels at her lowest ebb. She sits in the front parlour, alone, and wrestles with her conscience and her fate. 'In this room I plead with my father and God to forgive me. I ask the heavens to witness that I never wanted to cause so much trouble.' As tea-time approaches, she collects herself, washes her face, and emerges into company again, 'and if I am still red and puffy-eyed at the table, Betty and Matron never comment'.

Jane may have been lonely, and privately struggling with her parents' disapproval, but on the whole she had a pretty easy time of it, until the baby arrived. One woman, at a mother-and-baby home in south London in 1960, likened the experience to being at a boarding-school without the lessons. The handyman at her home was particularly popular: he was kind, and used to stop the delivery men from jeering at the residents.

Susan's home was a large one, with about thirty beds. She was taken there under cover of darkness from her angry parents' house, and installed about eight weeks before the baby was due. The home was staffed by a matron; a deputy, who was very stern but had a huge dog which Susan loved; a cook and a gardener. Every Sunday morning the 'PGs' (pregnant girls) would be marched to church; in the evenings they were expected to attend again, for Evensong, but this time unaccompanied. Most, it was rumoured, went to the pub instead. Susan always volunteered to look after the babies on Sunday evenings.

Elsewhere residents were generally called not PGs but EMs — expectant mothers — and were *never* allowed to miss church. They had to parade two-by-two through the streets, like a primary-school crocodile. This might not have been too bad in somewhere like Blackpool or Bournemouth, both well known for a prodigious number of maternity homes; in a neat market town in the Home Counties, for instance, or a close-knit Yorkshire village, it was mortifying.

The typical mother-and-baby home was a big house in extensive grounds. They were imposing, sometimes overwhelming, but often became welcome sanctuaries for the frightened women inside. Like Imogen, Susan felt safe in her mother-and-baby home. The camaraderie was wonderful after months of feeling alone, and the residents were supportive of one another in the way that only those who are in the same situation can be. Their ages might range from twelve to forty-something, and their backgrounds be as diverse as can be imagined, but all of them had two things in common: pregnancy, and the stigma it brought in its wake.

Sarah conceived shortly before taking her A-levels. In her home she was surprised to find herself in the company of a middle-aged woman, an incredibly bright and intense young lady who smoked like a factory for the whole of her stay, someone whose lover was a married Spaniard (terribly exotic), and assorted daughters of the great and the good. More often than not, their shared predicament brought them together, even if individual circumstances were unique. There would always be a few stand-offish ones — probably too terrified to be friendly — and the odd misfit or maverick who refused to join in, but the general atmosphere among the residents in these places seems to have been one of affectionate solidarity.

Naturally, friendships could not last long; this was an intense and limited episode in these women's lives which was usually screwed down tight and forcibly forgotten about afterwards. To maintain a relationship made in the mother-and-baby home would be counter-intuitive. The whole experience was like side-stepping out of ordinary life for three months; afterwards you were supposed to resume the old routine again, rejoin the dance, with or without a new baby.

Yet however earnestly you were encouraged to deny your confinement, you could never entirely block it out. Samantha's mother, Margaret, had horrifying flashbacks. She was having her hair cut one day, years later, when suddenly she started to scream and cry at the searing, unbidden memory of her lost babies. Others are aware of a soft undercurrent of melancholy, with occasional gleams of bright recollection like kingfishers darting above a dark river. 'Fifty years later, I remember every detail of the room . . . ' 'Everything smelt of wood-polish and Dettol.' 'There was a school close by and I could see the Christmas decorations in the classrooms.' 'Matron liked China tea whilst having her daily bath.' And, most poignantly, 'I shall never forget Jean, whose red dress was perpetually sodden with milk and tears.'

★   ★   ★

Poor Jean-in-the-red-dress must have looked back on her experience of giving birth with a desolate heart — as did Pauline B, who was extremely anxious that I should not reveal the name of her home. I am not revealing *any* names — though sometimes wish I could, since it is obvious to me that several of the women to whom I have spoken were at the same place, and possibly at the same time. Would it help if they could share memories? Possibly not.

Pauline became pregnant in 1964, when she was seventeen. Her parents were disgusted, she was 'worse than a prostitute', and they promptly committed her to a Salvation Army home not for the usual twelve-week stay, but for five months. Most Salvation Army homes are remembered with some affection and gratitude; complete devotion in some cases. Pauline considered hers a prison. She was taken there — like Susan — at dead of night and dumped on the doorstep. Presumably she would have been checked for evidence of sexually transmitted disease, as most residents at mother-and-baby homes were; then she was set to work. The house was dark and forbidding, like something out of *Wuthering Heights*. Meanwhile the Swinging Sixties were roaring away outside the walls, without her. People used to point at her and her friends walking in the grounds, from the top deck of passing buses, and the staff lost no opportunity of rubbing in the 'naughty girls'' guilt.

There was a maternity ward on the first floor, where respectable (i.e. married) women were also admitted; girls like Pauline were required to use the servants' staircase rather than the main one, in case they were spotted by the private patients, and to sleep in the attic. Members of staff were never cruel, but they were relentlessly strict, and expected to be obeyed. The atmosphere was awful.

The NCUMC interviewed residents in mother-and-baby homes in 1968 as part of a survey into maternity care for single women. There appear to have been plenty of jolly matrons regarded by the residents as mother-figures, and most homes clearly tried to offer kindness and support. But rules and regulations were legion; there was a curfew in the evening — perhaps as early as 6.30 p.m. — and very few places allowed mothers and their babies to sleep together. If the home accommodated married and unmarried women, like Pauline's, it was common for the wives to be allowed to see their babies at any time, while the 'girls' could only see them at feeding time, regardless of whether the babies were destined for adoption.

A number of the interviewees confessed to

disliking their matron, or even worse, fearing her. Several complained about the culture of blame in their homes: 'They think we don't realise what we've done wrong, but we do. We know and we want to forget and we don't need it rubbed into us all the time.' According to my correspondents there were locks on the fridges. Mail was read. One was told to clean the parquet flooring with a toothbrush. 'The worst job was kitchen duty; that entailed helping the cook prepare the meals ... The worst aspect of kitchen duty was emptying the pigswill bin every morning. The smell was disgusting and used to make me throw up continually. Other jobs included cleaning Matron's bathroom every day and taking away the teapot and tea things ... '

Wendy was exhausted by the time her baby was born, after five weeks' stay in a home in London. There was no sitting around in the parlour, like Jane, for her. Wendy's particular jobs were polishing the floor, including the upper storeys, which involved lugging a heavy metal 'bumper', or buffing machine, up the stairs in an advanced state of pregnancy. Then she was expected to carry all the bedside mats outside and shake them clean. She was in charge of cleaning the staircase with a brush and dustpan for the treads and a damp cloth for the risers, and had to take her turn boiling up nappies in a sort of cauldron; transferring them with a large stick into three sinks, one after the other, to rinse them; putting them through the mangle, and hanging them out to dry. If it started to rain, she had to waddle outdoors and un-peg them all, put them through the mangle a second time, and then load them into industrial driers.

A Scottish lady who contacted me about her experience of illegitimate birth in London in 1969 had not one good thing to say about her home. Indeed, her story has a Magdalene-like bleakness to it. Hardly anyone there spoke to anyone else. All the expectant mothers had jobs — this girl's was endlessly to roll butter-balls — and everybody had to be in bed by 9 p.m. When the girl suspected she was going into labour, she was told by one of the nuns to climb on to a table, so she could be examined. An ambulance was called, and the girl was sent to wait for it in the nursery. She might as well clear up the cigarette butts littering the floor in there, said the nun, until the ambulance arrived. No one accompanied her to the hospital. She had made her bed; now she must lie in it, alone. I doubt either she or Wendy or any of the mothers in this book complained at the time. Treatment like this was all part of the package of repentance and — maybe — redemption.

★   ★   ★

Alison is the girl who fell in love with that dashing drama student Patrick in the hat and the high black boots, but who subsequently became pregnant after a date-rape. We left her working in London, living in a bedsit, still in touch with Patrick, and waiting to be admitted to her chosen mother-and-baby home six weeks before the expected birth of her child. Her mother, though comparatively liberal, tried to help Alison procure an abortion, but the attempt failed. Now — terrifyingly early — her waters have broken, and she has been admitted to hospital.

'A young, male student must have been assigned to be with me, because he answered all my questions and 'held my hand' during the next twenty-four hours. It was around 5 p.m. the following day that I gave birth. It was a forceps delivery, and I was left alone for a long time after delivery. My notes were on the bedside table next to me, and on the top was written 'Doesn't know she's had twins. To be told tomorrow.' On my way back to the ward, I explained that I had read the note, and 'my' student came along to explain that one of the twins had been stillborn, and the other was in intensive care.

'I was in hospital for five days. Patrick came to visit, but refused to visit the baby, who was [still] in intensive care. My father came, too. He was on a works conference, and brought me the biggest basket of fruit I had ever seen. He did come and see his grandson, and seemed very moved by the sight of him. At one point, I was feeling much better, and bored, so I decided to go along to the nursery at the far end of the corridor, to see if I could help the nurses. I was met by one senior nurse, who hurriedly and determinedly took me angrily back to bed, and told me in no uncertain tones that I was not to mix with the other patients. I don't know if she was afraid I would harm one of the babies, or that by being a single mum I was contaminated — she was extremely hostile, however. I was told to vacate my bed and I took the train home, having gone back to my employer's house to collect my belongings, leaving my baby in hospital.

'I had been home for seven days when the hospital phoned to say my son had died.'

The boy had cystic fibrosis, and was unable to digest food properly. On her postnatal visit to the hospital, Alison was given his plot and grave number in the local cemetery, which she visited. He was buried behind someone else's huge marble statue of an angel. 'My arms were empty, and I was grief-stricken and guilt-ridden.' Now she was expected to put all that behind her: the shock of being raped, the realization of her pregnancy, the trauma of running away from home so that she would not betray her parents, repeated attempts at abortion, going into premature labour, learning that she had had twins and that one was stillborn, and then losing the surviving child. All this she had to bear, and to forget.

Alison went back to college; she qualified as a teacher, married, and had two more sons and a daughter. When they were teenagers, she told them briefly what had happened to her, using her own case to illustrate that when a girl says 'no', she means no.

'Fate is weird. Instead of finishing their lives before they were born, it allowed one child to die in the womb three weeks before he was born, and the other to come into this life and die after only twelve days. But twelve days of such agonizing pain and worry for everyone. Why? To teach me a lesson I'll never forget? Oh, I won't forget. He'll be buried in an unmarked grave because his father, naturally, won't give me the money for a headstone. Yet I'd like to put one over them, and I shall, somehow. Just a small one, like they were.'

Forty years after the twins' death, Alison was finally able to afford that headstone.

Alison's experience of childbirth, the first time around, was just about as distressing as one can imagine, and she does not even mention the physical pain and terror involved. For Pauline B, incarcerated in her suburban Wuthering Heights, the pain was beyond description. She reported to the delivery room upstairs when it got too much to bear, but was told there was nothing going on, to get back to her room and stop moaning. On the change of shift some hours later, the new nurse on duty took one look at Pauline and summoned an ambulance. Her baby, like Alison's, was stillborn, and again, she was told to forget all about it. When Marilyn's daughter was born dead, she wrote a single sentence in her diary: 'At least I don't have to make any decisions about my baby.' She was sent home, with no sympathy, support or compassion. After that, she admits, 'I behaved rather badly for a while.'

There really does seem to have been an attitudinal divide between the home and the hospital bed in many cases. When unmarried mothers turned from guests into patients, all the old prejudices came flooding back, just when the women were at their most vulnerable. Perhaps medical staff, being busy and harassed, resented the 'unnecessary' work created by single mothers. Claire

Rayner trained as a nurse before becoming a writer and agony aunt; she remembered keeping a box of curtain-rings on her desk to hand out to self-conscious single mothers visiting the antenatal clinic. But other staff were not so sympathetic, and appear to have taken pleasure in humiliating unmarried patients.

Evelyn loved her mother-and-baby home — in fact she wanted to stay there for ever — but the hospital to which she was sent was horrific. The doctors and nurses ignored her; when they did get round to dealing with her, they gave her an enema and then sent her to crawl down the corridor (literally) to the lavatory. When she arrived at the labour ward, no one spoke to her, and the two young girls in uniform in her room stood gazing out of the window while Evelyn tried to get on with the terrifying business of giving birth. No analgesics were offered. Luckily, the baby 'shot out like a rocket' and physically at least, all was well.

Susan did not have a clue what was going to happen to her when she left the other PGs in her comfortable mother-and-baby home in the back of an ambulance. Everything was strange, and very scary. She had not been prepared at all for any of the procedures likely to happen to her in hospital, so when she was shaven, and given a huge glass of orange juice and castor oil to drink, she was utterly bewildered. Her baby was induced, which naturally involved rupturing the membrane, but at no stage can Susan remember anything being explained to her — not even when she was given an episiotomy during the birth.

Visiting time on the maternity ward was usually reserved exclusively for husbands, and many single mothers recall hiding under the sheets and weeping or pretending to be asleep for the duration. The other mothers' happiness only threw their own isolation into deeper relief, and emphasized the stigma of illegitimacy. It was as though the medical staff assumed that illegitimate babies were not as lovable as legitimate ones. Or perhaps they were subtly trying to prepare mothers whose babies were due to be adopted? Maybe they hoped their detachment would encourage some sort of emotional remoteness between the single mother and the child she would soon be losing? If so, it occasionally worked, but at a cost. Penny prepared no clothes for her baby, gave it no name, and refused to breastfeed it. Another girl was sent a small bouquet by the owner of the café where she worked. It was the first time anyone had ever sent her flowers, and she cherished them. 'I was so thrilled that I kept them till all the petals had dropped off.' But for her daughter, she felt nothing at all. 'I remember signing her away and not even realising she was my own child.'

By contrast, Jill cried with love when she first held her newborn daughter, and Hannah 'truly loved the baby, long before he was born'. The strongest sense I had when my sons were born was one of recognition. Oh, it's *you*, I realized, as soon as I saw them. I knew them so well already. That feeling of complete familiarity must be common to most mothers, surely. That is what makes loving so easy, and parting so hard.

* ★ ★

Most children born in the UK after the First World War first drew breath in the company of a midwife. But not all of them, and one of the reasons for the high mortality rate associated with illegitimacy was the fact that some unmarried mothers were forced by shame or circumstance to conceal the birth. In the worst cases, this led to infanticide. An Act of Parliament was passed in 1624 'to prevent the murthering [sic] of bastard children'. It included the following clause:

> Whereas many lewd women that have been delivered of bastard children, to avoid their shame, and to escape punishment, do secretly bury or conceal the death of their children, and often, if the child is found dead, the said women do allege, that the said child was born dead . . . be it enacted . . . in every such case the mother so offending, shall suffer death as in the case of murther, except such mother can make proof by one witness at the last that the child . . . was born dead.

A willing witness to the birth of a secret bastard is as likely as a witness to its conception. One of the few conditions for the death penalty to be commuted in a case of this kind was, ironically, the pregnancy of the accused. You could not put to death a woman heavy with child.

In parenthesis, I came across one law case involving a wife who was accused of conceiving a baby out of wedlock in 1921. Her husband was a soldier, who was away from home from 4 October. The baby was born on the first of the following September, 331 days later. The lawyer defending her against a charge of adultery insisted that an eleven-month pregnancy was perfectly possible. The case, astonishingly, was dismissed.

That same year, the NCUMC took up the cause of single mothers convicted of murdering their children after a widely publicized case involving an unmarried twenty-one-year-old factory worker called Edith Roberts. Edith was the daughter of respectable parents; her behaviour had always been exemplary and — according to her father — she could not have been a better daughter. It is believed she was raped, and managed to keep her pregnancy secret from everyone in her family, including the sister with whom she shared a room. On the night of her confinement (which her sister denied knowing anything about, despite Edith giving birth in the same bed), she insisted that she did not touch the child, except to kiss it. Its cheek felt cold.

Edith wrapped her baby up and stowed it in a wooden box under the mattress, where its body was found three days later by Edith's unsuspecting stepmother. A post-mortem examination suggested that the child had been alive when it was born, and was then suffocated by a camisole put over its mouth, and Edith was arrested on suspicion of murder. Her counsel successfully challenged the fact that there were women on the jury; he claimed he only wanted a fair trial for Edith, and 'did not think that women were fair to their own sex'. But even with an all-male jury — perhaps because of it — Edith was convicted of murder, and sentenced to hang.

The sentence was subsequently commuted to penal servitude for life, but when she appealed against her conviction, pleading manslaughter due to diminished responsibility rather than murder, Edith lost. Five hundred people took to the streets of Leicester, her home city, to protest. The following year, the Infanticide Act 1922 was passed, with the support of the NCUMC and a host of other women's political and welfare organizations who lobbied MP Nancy Astor, the only female Member of Parliament at the time. The Act abolished the death penalty for mothers convicted of killing their newborn babies while the balance of their minds was assumed to be disturbed. This did not prevent Elizabeth Humphreys from being sentenced to death in 1933 for throwing her illegitimate baby into a canal, however, despite the jury's 'strong recommendation to mercy'. Elizabeth was only sixteen, and the father was a married man. But she was still considered responsible and evil enough to have premeditated her child's demise.

Bertha, a midwife, remembers a girl she attended one evening in the 1930s, who might well have suffered the same fate as Edith Roberts or Elizabeth Humphreys had she done what she meant to do. The girl had been to work that day, as usual. When she came home, her mother (on her way out to the pictures) suspected nothing, but her father was uneasy. He asked the girl if she was feeling all right. 'Is there anything you

218

want to tell me?' She assured him there was not, but he sent her upstairs to lie down, all the same. A little while later, she reappeared with a baby in her arms. 'Look what I've got!' Her father fainted. When he came to, he phoned the doctor, who called for midwife Bertha. Bertha takes up the story.

'Anyway, she'd torn the cord, she'd broke the cord. I don't know how she'd done it. She hadn't cut it, she'd just broke it . . . So the doctor looked, he says, 'Oh, you attend to her, I'll look at the baby.' So eventually we got the afterbirth and we got her cleaned up and tied off the cord and that, but he lived, that baby, he lived in spite of all that . . . And the girl she was all right and to this day she would never tell anybody who the father was. And her mother coaxed her, she did everything, threatened her, but nobody to this day knows . . . You see, she'd never told anybody and she had intended to do away with the baby. She'd bought a new suitcase and in that case was sheets of brown paper and string. And she'd intended to do away with the baby, but once it was born, she just couldn't, you see. And she loved that baby so much so that you could hardly take it off her to bath it or do anything with it.'

Betty had her baby in the house where she worked as a live-in maid in 1937. When her periods stopped, she assumed it was because she had been out cycling too much. She loved cycling. She and her boyfriend used to go for rides into the country on her day off, and sometimes they would get off their bikes for a cuddle in the fields. Those cuddles got quite elaborate, but Betty did not realize that what she and the lad were doing might lead to pregnancy. One day Betty — always a well-built girl — was overcome by awful stomach-ache. She took to her bed and not long afterwards gave birth to a baby. Understandably, the girl panicked. 'Where the Dickens has that come from?' The mistress of the house was called; instead of offering sympathy, she ordered Betty and her bastard out of the house, forbade her to come back, and informed her she would be docking the expense of cleaning the sheets from Betty's wages.

Betty was beside herself. She knew nothing about new-born babies, and feared the umbilical cord was a permanent fixture, an aberration, and that she was destined to spend the rest of her life physically attached by it to her daughter. When she eventually got to hospital, and the nurse chided her for having the baby, Betty was indignant. 'Well,' I said, 'I didn't know I *was* going to have her.' In a spectacular example of shutting the stable door after the horse has bolted, the nurse then explained to Betty the facts of life.

To avoid situations like this, the Salvation Army and other agencies did their best to welcome last-minute admissions who had not been through the usual route of interview and formal acceptance, and maternity wards were unlikely to refuse a mother in labour, whatever her marital status. There are still reports each year of babies found abandoned, alive, on doorsteps, in the back of taxis, in phone-boxes or shopping-bags, under shrubs in public parks or even in litter-bins. They may be named after the person who found them, perhaps; if it is Christmas they will inevitably be Holly or Robin. A call will go out to the mother, urging her to visit a local hospital for her own sake, and we are never told what happens to the infants.

Today, in many parts of the world you can post unwanted babies through a sort of cat-flap in a hospital or an orphanage wall, where they land gently in a heated cot, and an automatic bell rings to alert whoever is on duty inside. These are the modern equivalents of the 'turning wheels' installed outside foundling hospitals in the eighteenth and nineteenth centuries. In Japan, such a hatch is called a 'stork's cradle'. In Poland, it's *okno życia*, or 'the window of life'. That almost sounds romantic.

8

Love-child: The First Six Weeks

I truly loved the baby, long before he was born.

My mother was a searcher after truth. She was brought up in the Church of England, but flirted with Catholicism, Buddhism and Humanism, eventually settling for a slightly uncertain cocktail mixed from the best bits of everything. Between the ages of about five and twelve, I accompanied her, in an Anglican phase, to our tiny village church every Sunday. Ours was the least important church in a widespread group parish, with the result that we always got the graveyard slot: three o'clock Evensong, without the song. Drowsy after Sunday lunch, and unashamedly bored — or bewildered — by the long sermon, I found solace in the *Book of Common Prayer*. Its language was intoxicating and went on to inspire my university and subsequent career. Its suggestiveness was equally seductive. Every week I would check the 'Table of Kindred and Affinity' at the back, telling me who might or might not marry. Obviously I would not be able to marry my father or son when I grew up (although if I had a son, wouldn't I already be married to *his* father?). But nor could I wed my husband's son's son, my father's mother's husband, or my son's daughter's husband. It all took some thinking about.

The other thing that fascinated me, along with the 'Form of Prayers to be used at Sea' and the 'Denouncing of God's Anger and Judgements against Sinners', was the 'Churching of Women'. Properly called the Thanksgiving of Women after Childbirth, this was a short service of blessing for new mothers. It was nothing to do with babies alive or dead: they had ceremonies of their own.

The service opened with some instructions. 'The woman, at the usual time after her delivery, shall come into the Church decently apparelled, and there shall kneel down in some convenient place.' Then the Priest read a Psalm about deliverance from the snares of death, or about how happy is the man whose children are like arrows in his quiver: 'they shall not be ashamed when they speak with their enemies in the gate' (not bastards, then). He said a prayer of thanks for the mother's survival after the pain and peril of childbirth, and vowed on her behalf to walk henceforth in the ways of the Lord. And that was that.

In Christian tradition the churching of women was done on the fortieth day after confinement. Its roots are in the purification ceremony of the Jewish faith; following it, mothers were deemed 'clean' and ready to take an active part in society again. There was nothing about forgiveness either in the text or the invocations. Yet many of the women whose stories form this book are convinced that they were encouraged — or

223

forced — to be churched to atone for the sin of bearing an illegitimate child. Those who found themselves in mother-and-baby homes run by Church establishments remember weekly visits throughout their stay from a clergyman of some kind, who would urge them, after the delivery, to make things right with God and try to start afresh.

In Wales, it was not uncommon for chapel attendance to be barred to the mothers of illegitimate children for three months after the birth; churching was therefore irrelevant to them. Catholic priests could not offer the ceremony to unmarried women — it was reserved for more conventional, God-fearing mothers — so they sprinkled holy water on them instead. Pauline B, in a Salvation Army home, was encouraged to enquire of God each evening, with due deference, whether or not she had been forgiven yet. Marilyn's flesh creeps when she recalls the vicar who used to ask her, in urgent tones, whether she was thinking about God while her baby was conceived. Sarah's was a Church of England home; her friend and fellow resident the bishop's daughter was appalled at Sarah's resistance to churching, but the nursing sister at the home took Sarah aside. 'You don't have to do it, dear, if you don't want to,' so she didn't.

It is easy to appreciate why many frightened young mothers felt they must go along with this ritual, especially when it was given the gloss of repentance. Even if they had no faith in God themselves, and did not concur that what they had done was sinful, they were powerless in those first weeks after the birth. Hypocrisy was all around them. Why bother resisting this manifestation of it when you had failed to resist the rest?

For feisty young women like Sarah, however, it was the last straw. Her situation made her angry, as a teenager sent away from home, asked to consider relinquishing her baby and behaving as though the whole unfortunate episode had never happened. Why should she be expected to make that sacrifice? Why waste time and energy in pursuit of spurious spiritual redemption? What had a ceremony of purification and thanksgiving to do with her? She reckoned that she had been offered a stark choice by fate: sink (on other people's terms) or swim (on her own). She decided to swim.

Churching was not compulsory, even in the 1960s when I was so engrossed in my prayer-book and Sarah was having her baby, but certain cultural and administrative rites of passage were unavoidable during the first six weeks of a child's life, so that its existence could be made official. From 1915 onwards, every new arrival had to be notified to a local medical officer within thirty-six hours, in order for one of the new health visitors to come round and check that all was well. The birth had to be registered within three months, and a baptism arranged as swiftly as possible, especially if it was a sickly baby. In most mother-and-baby homes the staff and visiting social or 'moral welfare' workers would help with this. In hospitals, it would be the almoner's job.

As we know, not every baby was born with the benefit of medical care and advice. Hence Thomas Coram's foundlings, and the babies offered through the 'window of life' and similar devices. These were the lucky ones, comparatively speaking. The unlucky ones were left to a far more uncertain fate: neglected, abandoned, or simply thrown away. Violet d'Estrelle was an Irish dressmaker who became pregnant by a chauffeur while living in London in 1929. He disappeared, and when Violet's son was born, she abandoned him on Camden Road, South Croydon. She had appealed to her brother for help, who was reputed to be well-off — 'at least, he has more than I have' — but he hit her on hearing her news and knocked her down, before ordering her out of the house. So she left the baby where he would be found, and could not resist writing him letters afterwards, which she sent addressed to 'Robert d'Estrelle, the unknown Croydon foundling', care of the Croydon Poor Law Guardians at the workhouse.

Violet was traced and remanded in custody. At her trial it emerged that this was not the first time she had abandoned Robert; he had been found on the Fulham Road before, and returned to his mother. There was little hope, now, of a similar reunion.

The police had been anxious to trace Violet for her own sake, as well as the baby's. The hours and days after the birth of a child can be critical, and stories of carelessly repaired episiotomies, or dangerous infections, are common in the annals of mother-and-baby homes. Most mothers were instructed to sit in salty baths after the delivery and were kept in bed for anything up to ten days. If they wanted to breastfeed they could, with a degree of practical help if they were lucky, but breastfeeding was not recommended for those planning an adoption. They were given pills to dry up the milk supply and expected to bear the tenderness — emotional and physical — without complaint.

New-born babies in the care of mother-and-baby homes were routinely tested for syphilis and underwent a careful medical examination. They had to be 'perfect', according to a former member of Barnardo's staff, before they could be considered for adoption. It was not just physical and mental deformity the doctors were checking for; any genetic abnormality had to be taken into account, too, and the possibility of disease was as damning as its actual presence. In one case, a baby was refused by an adoption society because its grandmother and great-grandmother had both happened to lose the sight in one eye during middle age. Imogen's son had a problem, although no one bothered to tell his mother. She only realized something was wrong when the doctor on his round of the maternity ward turned to a colleague and airily said, 'This one's got it,' before moving on. 'It', Imogen later discovered, was jaundice, which would not prevent her son's adoption, but was enough to keep them both in hospital longer than normal.

Poor Jane B's baby was far less fortunate. She was a student nurse supported by her parents but not by the father of her child. He married someone else during the pregnancy, attracted to her, according to Jane's mother, because she had not slept with him. Jane's baby was induced ten days after his due date: he was growing too big for her. The plan was for the child to be taken away as soon as he was born, to prevent Jane's bonding with him. He would go to a foster-parent, and then be put up for adoption. It was a difficult delivery, involving forceps which damaged the baby's skull. With howling insensitivity, Jane was put in a recovery room beside an empty cot afterwards. She was frantic to see her son, but the nurse urged her not to give in.

Soon the news filtered through that Jane's son might be 'mentally defective'. He was certainly too ill — imperfect — to be considered for adoption at the moment. But he rallied, and was allowed to leave hospital for a foster-home before being placed with another family at six months of age. And Jane carried on with her life, vowing never to forget him, not knowing how damaged he was or what his future held.

* * *

The routine was strict for healthy babies in all maternity homes, whether for 'naughty girls' or nice. New-borns slept in the nursery; they were usually brought to their mothers only to be fed and if they cried were stoutly ignored. My mother used a childcare book published in 1948 by Anne Cuthbert. It recommends five feeds a day, at 6 a.m., 10 a.m., 2 p.m., 6 p.m. and 10 p.m. Baby's digestive system will soon learn to accommodate itself to this regime, unless he is particularly highly strung or irritable. 'It is a debatable question whether it is ever wise to feed an infant during the night,' according to Mrs Cuthbert, 'even during the first few weeks of his life. There is, I think, no doubt that every effort should be made to make him wait . . . ' Sarah remembers with a shudder what happened if any baby dared to cry for its feed before 6 p.m. in her mother-and-baby home: 'God almighty! Matron would go mad!'

In Magdalene homes, where mothers were prohibited from feeding in bed in case of what were darkly referred to as 'accidents' (the clear implication being a deliberate infanticide), babies were lined up in the nursery with bottles propped in their mouths at the appointed time. When their feeding slot was up, the teats were removed, whether or not the baby had been able to drink enough — or anything at all. In Moira's rather liberal mother-and-baby home, one of the girls hit on the great idea of making the hole in the teat bigger, so that her bloated baby would finish feeding more quickly, and she would be free to go down to the pub. After daytime feeds, babies were habitually wheeled outside in their prams (donated, perhaps, by Barnardo's) and left to cry themselves to sleep, under a tree. I have a strangely precise recollection of being supine and looking up at the light through a complicated tracery of leaves. It must be one of those acquired memories, although my pram was certainly vast enough to accommodate a toddler of two or three.

Once new mothers had returned from hospital to the home with their babies, the daily round would be much as before. Laundry and cleaning had to be done, laying the table and doing the washing-up, and people took turns to mind each other's infants. The Salvation Army maintained that working was good for self-esteem, and the National Council for the Unmarried Mother and her Child saw it as preparation for life beyond the mother-and-baby home, when with the right support, a single mother might be expected to earn her own and her baby's keep.

Just as a good home could be a welcome sanctuary for confused and ashamed mothers-to-be, it provided somewhere safe and curiously static for the six weeks (or longer) after giving birth. You were still told what to do by the firm and confident adults in charge; your baby's needs were met, and you found comfort in the friendship of your peers. Evelyn did not want to leave. 'I loved it there; yes, we had jobs to do, but everyone has to clean where they live.' The staff could be almost unbearably kind, like the nun in one of them who secretly sewed intricate little gowns for the fatherless babies, or the matron who brought you a cup of tea, told you to put your feet up and cracked surprisingly robust jokes to raise your spirits. Residents would stay up late together, if they had the energy, just talking, as though they were carefree college students. When they grew hungry, they would break into the fridge and then tiptoe back to someone's room to put the world to rights again, fortified by bread and cheese or a companionable mug of cocoa.

Part of the charm of going away to college, in retrospect at least, is the realization that the experience is like an oasis in time. It is ephemeral, and all the more precious for that. The same holds true for many alumnae of mother-and-baby homes. It was a long time until Evelyn was as happy again. There is often a fondness in reminiscences of what life was like as an inmate, before reality kicked back in without the baby, or a new joint life began.

Sarah was fortunate: although only nineteen, and fresh from school, she was never pressurized too strongly to give her baby up for adoption. She made the decision to keep the child as soon as her family agreed to welcome them back into her own home. Shortly after she returned to the village from her mother-and-baby home, a neighbour came to call expressly to see Sarah, congratulate her, and admire the baby. That meant so much, in a world where no one sent cards to welcome the birth of an illegitimate child, and friends and relations might be expected to cross the road to avoid acknowledging an unmarried mother. That simple gesture helped give Sarah the confidence to step out into society again and begin to make a life for herself and her daughter.

Jo never felt ostracized. She came from a small community, but found it embraced her rather than casting her out. The most unexpected people 'came up trumps' to help her keep her baby, and she and her mother became closer than they had ever been before, more like sisters than parent and daughter.

Nancy B fell pregnant when she was about seventeen, between the wars. She screwed up the courage to tell her mother, who responded with astonishing equanimity. 'It's not the end of the world, my love, there are worse things in life than having a baby, and you don't have to get married if you don't want to.' Nancy was sent to a comfortable mother-and-baby home in the neighbouring county; when the child was two weeks old she was allowed to bring it home. Nancy's mother looked after it while Nancy got herself a job as a cinema usherette. Eventually she married the baby's father and probably lived happily ever after.

Not all happy endings involved a wedding; Victoria is in her seventies now and has never married nor had any kind of lasting relationship since her child was born in 1965. But she lives life on her own terms, enriched by her daughter and a grandchild. Not that it has been easy. Her own parents were less than supportive at the beginning.

'My mother, a very strong character whom I loved, but with whom I had always had a fairly stormy relationship, was particularly distraught, being extremely sensitive to the social stigma, and I came under a great deal of pressure to disown the baby, one way or another. It was . . . hard to resist; I was made to feel that I was destroying my parents' lives. Even my friends, my contemporaries, believed the child would have a better life if adopted. However, there were supportive voices. A childless married couple living in the flat above my parents invited me to supper and encouraged me to keep the baby. That was a real life-line. When I threw down the gauntlet and told my mother that I intended to do just this and she must either accept it or disown me, she began cautiously to explore the attitudes of her friends and found, to her surprise, that they were less critical than she expected. One even said, somewhat unflatteringly, that if she had an unmarried twenty-six-year-old daughter, she would positively advise her to go out and get pregnant deliberately. A breath of fresh air!'

When the time came for Victoria's baby to be born, several days early, labour was painful but blessedly rapid. The fact that Victoria was a midwife probably helped. Her mother, who had driven her to the hospital, suggested an old family name, which Victoria loved. 'I think we were lucky that [she] was the first grand-child, because she was loved from the outset and never discriminated against in any way.' Unlike Sarah and Nancy, Victoria was determined to look after her baby alone, and did so by finding a live-in domestic job, then working as a resident midwife in a mother-and-baby home before renting a tiny cottage and eventually returning to hospital midwifery.

Very occasionally one hears the positive story of an unmarried mother who — unlike Victoria — had no family support at all, and yet still managed to keep her baby with her and earn a living successfully. This is what the NCUMC was all about: empowering single parents to make informed decisions of their own, and if possible, to bring up their children themselves. In order to make this possible the NCUMC appealed constantly for grants, for new foster-parents, suitable housing, open-minded employment opportunities and forbearance. To some extent, nearly a century after the Council was founded, this is still work in progress.

I have come across no evidence to suggest that the NCUMC, nor any other agency, was able to offer meaningful support to the minority of single mothers whose babies were stillborn, or who died as neonates. Alison, who was not told she had given birth to twins, lost one of her babies at birth and the other within two weeks. There was no bereavement counselling available at that time, no letter from the hospital, no visits to her home, nothing. Marilyn's baby died of encephalitis. She received 'absolutely no words of comfort or sympathy' from the hospital staff. This denial of an illegitimate baby's death matched the denial surrounding its birth: least said, soonest mended. Out of sight, out of mind. What the eye doesn't see . . . and so on: all nonsense.

★   ★   ★

In 1908, foster-care in England and Wales was regulated for the first time. Before then, it was a risky business with too many opportunities for exploitation and brutality. Coram's hospital, Barnardo's homes and similar organizations used foster-parents as part of the structure of care for lone children. Abandoned or relinquished babies would be homed with a foster-mother, who provided a wet-nurse if necessary (i.e. if she had no infants of her own). There they would stay until they were weaned, and strong enough to take the next step towards adoption or a residential nursery — or even, in some cases, until they were five. This latter practice, while it sounds as if it might offer valuable continuity to the child, could in fact be quite devastating. Both child and foster-parent naturally grew attached to, and dependent on, one another, and the wrench for them both, when it came, was traumatic. Especially for the child, who thus lost a parent for the second time in a very short life.

Childcare provision came under increasing scrutiny after the Second World War, resulting in a critical shortage of foster-carers. Suitable candidates were perhaps too nervous to venture into what had become a highly regulated business. This caused problems for unmarried mothers desperate for help — and ready to pay for that help — after the birth of a child. One of them wrote to *The Times* in 1946 to explain the hidden pitfall lying in wait for an already disadvantaged single mother. She has not yet given birth to her illegitimate child. During her pregnancy, she has been able to avail herself of excellent prenatal care and clinic facilities, but can find no help at all for the first few weeks of her child's life. She knows she will have to return to work at once, and has almost reconciled herself to having the child adopted, but none of the recognized agencies will take it below the age of three months. She has tried contacting health visitors, welfare officers, the county council medical officer, and various children's aid societies, and has come to the dispiriting conclusion that it is quite impossible for her to find a foster-mother.

What is she to do? Even if she can arrange a further three months' leave of absence from work, where will she live? Friends, landladies, even the odd hotel might be willing to take on an expectant mother, but not an actual one, with a newborn baby and no father. 'Is it surprising that a woman in such circumstances is driven to 'door-step' her baby and thus provide one more unfortunate foundling?' she asks. She might even be able to keep the baby herself were she able to find someone to look after it for six months. As it is, she feels there is no alternative but to abandon it. (Ironically, if she had been lucky enough to find care, the chances are that the foster-mother would have employed another unmarried mother as a wet-nurse. This was not an uncommon arrangement.)

If a fostered baby was destined for adoption, the birth mother would be allowed in some circumstances to visit it for a limited period and at pre-arranged times until it disappeared into the embrace of its new parents, or the state. Jill handed her daughter over to foster-parents as soon as she came out of hospital after the confinement. At the end of the required six-week waiting period, she was presented with the adoption papers. These she had to take to her GP to be signed; the doctor was supposed to confirm that Jill was sufficiently sound of mind and body to take the decision herself.

In Jill's case, the doctor had her doubts. 'What do you *really* want to do?' she asked. Jill, who had felt suicidal at times since giving birth, replied, 'Keep her.' The doctor explained that she quite understood her feelings; it was not always best for girls like her to let their babies go. Besides the obvious dangers of emotional trauma, there was a more pragmatic concern in the statistical probability that unmarried mothers could very soon become pregnant again if they lost their first-born infants, to compensate in some way for the bereavement. Jill could not believe that someone in authority was giving her permission to bring up a baby without a father. Bolstered by the doctor's confidence, she found the courage to tell her parents her decision to keep her daughter in foster-care until she could afford to look after her herself, whereupon they invited them both to come home, to live together as an extended family. By this time, in the late 1960s, there were benefits available to young mothers like Jill; without these, and her parents' support, the choice of whether to keep her daughter or lose her might not have existed. It certainly did not exist for very many women in Jill's position between the 1920s and the 1970s.

Kim was only sixteen when she was sent to a mother-and-baby home at five months pregnant. When her baby was born, she cared for it for ten days, and then it was removed — wrenched from her arms in the car park of the hospital — and taken into foster-care. That same day, Kim travelled home, alone, and was forbidden thereafter to speak about the birth or to mention

237

her baby. She found out where he was, and used to visit him secretly; meanwhile her mother tried to force her to sign the necessary adoption papers. Kim refused as long as she was able, but when her mother physically stood over her until she had completed the forms, she surrendered. After all these years she still doesn't know where he is or even if he is alive or dead. Did her punishment fit the crime? She thinks not.

The social services and professional, reputable outfits like Barnardo's and the various licensed adoption agencies all aimed to provide a safe environment for their charges. But the fact that foster-care was regulated did not, unfortunately, mean that there were no villains involved in the industry. There might not have been lurid tales of baby-farms and commercial infanticide any more, but stories did emerge periodically during the 1930s and 1940s of baby trafficking. Walter and Mary Field were charged in Lincolnshire in 1932 with obtaining money by false pretences after they placed an advertisement in a Kent newspaper asking for a child to adopt. This was before private adoptions were outlawed. They asked for 'a small premium' to be paid with the child, for their trouble, and when anyone responded, spun a tale about how Mrs Field was tragically unable to have any more little darlings of her own. The mothers were assured their babies would have a very good home.

During the Fields' trial a complex scam was revealed. Several desperate mothers had handed over their illegitimate children to the couple, paying up to £8 for the privilege: quite a sum, when the average wage at the time was £15 per month. Six babies were involved in the case in all. Most of them were never seen again; either they died, or were sold on.

In 1942 a baby-farming racket was uncovered, operating on a much grander scale than the Fields' little enterprise. It supplied babies to clients for as much as £200 each. A solicitor in Yorkshire was caught charging half as much again for the infants he brokered — almost certainly all illegitimate — and you could even find a child for sale, quite openly, in eBay's great-grandfather, the unimpeachable magazine *Exchange and Mart*. These days it is not so easy to buy and sell children in private or state care — at least in the UK. But recent history has taught us how vulnerable they still are in other ways to exploitation and abuse.

Their birth-mothers were vulnerable, too. They were victimized by shame and despair. Baby Ian was put into the care of a private foster-mother who refused to look after him (once he had settled in with her) unless she could adopt him herself. Another brazenly subjected a birth-mother to extortion, refusing to give back the baby until she had been paid more money. In this case, the foster-mother had only been engaged for a week over Christmas, while the birth-mother went home to her family, who knew nothing about the baby. What a bleak Christmas Day that must have been.

*   *   *

239

Broadly speaking there were two categories of unmarried women in most mother-and-baby homes. The first comprised those who were there — as in any maternity home — simply to give birth to a baby they would subsequently keep. They might be far from home and family, for respectability's sake, and often had to pretend not to be the baby's real mother afterwards, but at least they knew the two of them would not be parted. We have all heard of the scenario whereby an illegitimate child grows up thinking its mother is its sister or aunt, and its grandparents are its mother and father. This was perhaps the most common accommodation of this particular family secret. Many mother-and-baby home residents were allowed back into the family home on these terms, and learned (with different degrees of success) to get on with life. It meant obtaining a short birth certificate, if the secret was to be kept, or hiding away the full one, but it could be done with appropriate complicity and was often surprisingly successful.

The Nobel Laureate Sir Paul Nurse only discovered his illegitimacy at the age of fifty-seven, when he was refused a Green Card to work in the United States. The authorities there would not accept his short birth certificate. No problem, thought Sir Paul — until the full version revealed his mother to be the person he had always thought of as his sister, with no name at all for his father. It was only after some careful family research that the geneticist discovered the truth (and the irony of his profession was not lost on him). His birth-mother became pregnant at seventeen; her parents sent her away to an aunt to have Paul; then her mother came to visit and pretended to be the baby's mother herself, returning home with the new-born Paul in her arms.

Sir Paul's maternal grandparents had both been illegitimate; they only confessed this when Sir Paul's daughter was asked to draw up a family tree at school (another common feature in stories of revealed illegitimacy). They must have wanted to spare their own daughter the shame they felt themselves.

Novelist Dorothy L. Sayers chose a different way. In a very businesslike manner she masked the parentage of her illegitimate son by a car salesman with whom she had a relationship in 1923 by taking two months' leave from work, booking herself into a maternity home in Bournemouth, and appealing to her cousin Ivy. She wrote Ivy a letter two days before the birth asking her to take the baby as a foster-child. His birth was kept secret from everyone else in the family; Dorothy registered the boy in her name, but asked Ivy that he be known by his natural father's surname. Then she went back to work. In 1926 Dorothy married, and took her son to live with her. He did not realize she was his mother for several years, and their relationship was never particularly close.

Women like Sarah and Victoria were able both to keep their baby and to acknowledge it as their own. For them, a stay in a mother-and-baby home or on a maternity ward should have been much the same as it was for a wife, except for the lack (in most cases) of a visiting father. In reality, however, it rarely was; because they were unmarried they were usually segregated, often patronized, and occasionally subjected to emotional cruelty, which came on top of the trauma experienced by even the most settled and conventional of mothers in childbirth. When Sarah took her daughter home, the matron's parting shot was mild, but patronizing. 'Don't do it again, dear, will you?'

The second category of unmarried mothers included all those who for various reasons planned to leave the home without their children. Their babies would either be taken away from them immediately after birth, after about ten days, or at the end of six weeks. Adoption papers were invalid if signed within six weeks; anything less than that was considered insufficient time to make such a momentous commitment. Those forty-two days constituted a cooling-off period, during which a mother initially intent on adoption, or on keeping her child, might change her mind. And sometimes, she did just that. Joyce A was comparatively all right until an inattentive nurse showed her the baby three days after he was born. After that she was unable to let him go.

The same thing happened to Betty, the housemaid who did not even realize she was pregnant (after a few imaginative cycle-rides with her young man) until a baby was born in her bed. Betty was transferred to a Salvation Army home after her confinement, and though it was never the Sally Army's policy to promote adoption, an officer did suggest to Betty that in her case it might be best, to avoid prejudice, shame, and probable destitution in the future. Betty reluctantly agreed, but on the evening before her daughter was due to leave the mother-and-baby home, she was given her for the first time, to hold and say good-bye. That was it, remembers Betty. She could not possibly part with her now; nor did she.

For Sandra the turning-point came during the adoption transfer of someone else's baby. The evening before such transfers were due to take place, the birth-mother and a chosen friend would pack the baby's box of clothes and toys; the next day all the residents of the mother-and-baby home were required to sit in the lounge with the curtains drawn. They were not allowed to look out of the windows while the hand-over was taking place. The mother would be in one of the upstairs rooms with her companion and her baby. There they would wait for the arrival of the social worker and if there was to be a direct transfer, the adoptive parents.

'It was absolutely horrendous, everyone sitting in the room hearing the girl whose baby was being adopted sobbing upstairs and knowing that our turn would come. After the people who were adopting the baby had left with it we were allowed out. We did not see the girl whose baby had been adopted again; she went straight home after it had taken place.

'During an adoption, whilst we were locked in the room, I wrote to my parents and begged them to let me keep my baby. We were all distraught and crying. My parents allowed me to keep my son and about two weeks later I came home with him.'

What devastating power lay in the hands of an unmarried mother's parents.

A change of heart over adoption — and the wherewithal to do something about it — was a luxury few unmarried mothers could afford. Nor did every mother feel it would be right to keep her child. There was a genuine and widespread conviction that children would have a better chance in life with new parents, unencumbered by the stigma and other unlovely disadvantages of illegitimacy, which might include homelessness and poverty. Plenty of people were ready to blame those single women who insisted on keeping their babies come what may. Conversely, there were plenty who blamed them for giving those babies away (though it was rarely a 'gift' of any kind) and depriving them of a birthmother's love. They couldn't win.

Susan would have done anything to keep her baby. The weeks she spent in her mother-and-baby home were passed in complete denial of what was about to happen. Her daughter was so beautiful, and Susan loved her so utterly: how could such happiness be taken away, once given? Even Matron could not quite bring herself to believe the baby was leaving. It was her job to take the little one from Susan's arms on the morning of the transfer, which she did, only to return within minutes and hand her back, asking how Susan could bear to be parted from her daughter. Susan *couldn't* bear it, and nor — in a

244

highly unprofessional (but very human) moment — could Matron. This time Susan clung on tight, and another member of the home's staff had to prise the baby from her, and remove it from the room. Susan was inconsolable.

The day of a baby's adoption never came as a complete surprise, except to people like Magdalene girl Margaret, whose twins were there one day and gone the next. Sometimes mothers were given forty-eight hours' notice, sometimes only twenty-four. But preparations had been going on ever since the baby's birth. As well as the health checks prospective adoptees were required to undergo, their mothers were asked to fill out forms detailing, if they could, the physical attributes of the father — his height, hair-colour, the colour of his eyes, his build and his interests. This was to help adoption agencies place their charges appropriately. Certain agencies asked for a letter from the mother, too, explaining something about the circumstances of the baby's birth, and her reasons for choosing adoption. 'Choosing' is an ill-advised word: her reasons, rather, for letting her baby go.

This letter would be kept on file, in case the time should ever come when the birth-mother's adult son or daughter tried to trace her. In return, she was given a photograph of the baby taken shortly before, or after, its adoption. She could decide to refuse the photo, if that made the parting any easier. Imogen accepted hers, but almost wished she had not. Instead of comforting her, it came to symbolize the enormity of her loss. 'I look at this now and see my little boy,

245

knowing that I did not give him away but rather that I was unable to keep him.'

Imogen was the deputy head teacher whom we last met with a jaundiced baby, born after a welcome period spent cocooned in the mother-and-baby home, sewing her baby's layette. She had done her Christmas shopping and commissioned a friend to post her cards at the appropriate time: the baby was due over the holiday, and no one at home knew anything about it.

After the gentle camaraderie of the home, Imogen felt lonely and abandoned on the maternity ward. She looked forward to showing off her beautiful boy to her friends when she returned, and can remember the taxi journey back from the hospital in the snow with preternatural clarity (the door flew open when it stopped and a tin of dried milk rolled out). But this was Boxing Day, and no one reacted at all. 'Christmas had defeated them and there were no glad tidings in that house.'

Imogen's next job was to contact the National Children's Adoption Association to finalize arrangements for her baby's future. Prospective parents were found for him, and after his medical, the date was confirmed. It was going to happen at the end of January. She hardly slept during those last few weeks, desperate to make the most of every minute with her child. At no stage can she remember being offered any alternative to adoption. She was alone, exhausted, and depressed after the baby's birth, too afraid to explore alternatives herself. Like everyone else at the home at that time, she felt defeated.

Imogen was interviewed twice by the adoption agency during the first month of her son's life. All the information was going in one direction, however. In those days birth-mothers were told nothing about the adoptive family. She asked that if possible, her son should be placed with someone who lived by the sea. This request was ignored. If Imogen had been able to picture her son, however vaguely, she feels her pain might have lessened a little. She felt utterly powerless, a rabbit in the headlights, about to be destroyed by a force completely beyond her control.

Now, Imogen feels the system betrayed her and her son. Her vulnerability was exploited. She has read copies of the letters exchanged between her and the agency and finds it almost impossible to comprehend them. 'My words say how grateful I was for the service they provided but I know that behind these polite expressions of thanks lay anger, disbelief and hatred for people who could engage in such an inhumane and unjust practice.' The process is kinder, more transparent and intuitive now, but that is small comfort to mothers who feel, like Imogen, that they were cheated out of their children.

It is important that we should appreciate what Imogen and her peers went through after the birth of their illegitimate babies. Jane A's experience was similarly traumatic. We have heard from her before, describing life in a mother-and-baby home where, for a while, she was the only resident. The matron there was kindly, cooking everyone a hearty breakfast on Saturdays when Betty, the cook, had her day off.

A day or two after Jane's son was born, Matron and Betty came to see her in hospital. They were allowed to visit the baby, too, in the separate nursery, and said all the right things about how fine and handsome he was. Before they left, Matron apologetically handed Jane a letter. It was a form from the adoption society, to be completed by a paediatrician confirming that the baby was fit, healthy and had no congenital abnormalities. Jane passed it on to the ward sister, who was clearly distressed that the adoption process was beginning so soon after the birth. Rather like the matron at Susan's mother-and-baby home, this sister had firm ideas of her own about the parting of a birth-mother from her child. 'Have a good long look in that crib,' she advised (unhelpfully), 'and think about it.'

Jane thought about little else. She knew the baby's father would not help to support her, and had an uneasy relationship with her own domineering and mentally unstable mother. Her instinct was to protect the child from his grandmother, rather than bring him up in the bosom of the family. 'I was too depressed and weak to do it alone . . . I felt very strongly that [my son] deserved a great deal better than I could ever provide for him. So I went along with the adoption.'

Jane was discharged from hospital ten days after the birth. She did not return to her mother-and-baby home then, but took a taxi with her mother to the town where the adoption society had its offices. There a tense-looking woman called Mrs P greeted them. They all went into a room; Jane's mother turned to Jane and said, 'Give him to me now.' Without thinking, Jane handed over her baby. He was immediately passed on to Mrs P. Before Jane had a chance to say good-bye, or even to look at him again, the woman had left the room 'as though her feet were on fire', and her boy was gone.

Five months after the birth, Jane was living at home with her parents, back at work, and life had apparently reverted to normal. She knew she had yet to sign the final consent papers in the adoption process, and was not particularly worried when they failed to arrive when expected: there had been a postal strike. They must have been held up.

One day, a visitor turned up. Jane continues the story:

'I had been home from work about half an hour, and I was starting to peel vegetables ready for the evening meal, when the knock came at the front door. I was more than a little surprised to see Mrs P there; then I thought, she must have brought the forms in person. I brought her into the living room, thankful that it was not too untidy for once. She was not smiling; she looked unhappier than ever. She had good reason.

'The adoption could not proceed, she said. The adoptive parents had returned the baby. Returned? As though he were a faulty parcel? Like you'd return a pair of shoes that didn't fit? She wasn't making any sense. I sat down, and she explained further.

'The mother, for want of a better word, had

been giving him a bath, and had noticed that he did not seem able to sit up properly. She had taken him to the doctor, and the doctor had sent him to a paediatrician. The paediatrician consulted an orthopaedic surgeon, and various X-rays and tests were taken. The result was that they found congenital curvature of the spine.

'This was shocking enough; however, Mrs P went on to explain that the parents did not feel they could continue to raise a disabled child. When they had applied to adopt the child . . . they had specified that they wanted a perfect, white, blue-eyed baby. My baby was not perfect.'

Jane's son was now in a short-term children's home in another county, awaiting her instructions. For the first time in her life, he was now solely her responsibility. Mrs P went on to explain that because of this physical 'impediment', the child would be virtually impossible to place for adoption in the future. He was now classed 'in the same category as spastics, mentally handicapped and black children'. If Jane refused to look after him, he was likely to spend his entire childhood in care.

Jane discussed the situation with her parents. Her mother refused point-blank to have anything to do with an illegitimate, handicapped grandson. Her father offered his support, but made it plain that the child could not be brought into the family home. So Jane determined to apply to social services for a flat, and to live with her son. On the following Monday morning, she received a phone call from Mrs P's assistant. The baby had been sent to temporary foster-parents over the weekend, who had fallen in love with him. They had wanted to adopt someone themselves, but the father, a prosperous local solicitor, was a year over the age limit set by the adoption society. They had asked Mrs P if Jane would countenance letting them help with the boy's treatment. Would she accept the gift of a sheepskin pram-set to make him comfortable on the many visits to hospital that inevitably lay ahead? Might she allow them to buy him one of those new folding pushchairs, so that she could get on and off buses more easily, as they knew she did not drive? They would be glad to do all this, they said, but what would make them *really* happy would be the chance to adopt her son themselves. Could Jane consider it?

She could, and that is exactly what happened.

'I opted not to go and see him, or to have a photograph. I wrote no letter to him for later in his childhood. I knew that if I was to do this, I had to do it completely. There could be no chance of changing my mind. I did not want a picture to cry over and undermine my resolve, or memories of bouncing him on my knee to torment my nights. I did not want to try to make him like me, when he found out. I did not want him to wonder what he missed.

'I hope that one day, if he is curious enough, he may come looking, so I have always made sure that the relevant people knew where I was living, and my changes of name, so that he can trace me if he wants to. I was going to trace him once, but I lost my nerve. I hope he's braver than me.'

In 2012, a few months after Jane first wrote to me, that hope was fulfilled. Jane's son *did* get in touch, and she could not be more proud of him if she tried.

9

Odd One Out: Growing Up Without Birth-parents

You have my Heart Tho wee must Part.

Now the focus shifts from single parent to illegitimate child. The unmarried mother has surrendered her baby — a decision often taken by default, it seems — and physically, they go their separate ways. After being at the centre of attention, held in the uncompromising spotlight of public disapproval and private shame, the mother leaves the stage, while her child takes on a new role as a resident in some sort of institution, an adoptee, or a migrant. Child migrants were exported in surprisingly large numbers from the seventeenth century to the 1960s; their scarcely credible stories are told in the next chapter. None of the migrants was sent abroad at birth, however. During their infancy, they shared the variable fate of all other children separated from their birth-parents. The decision to separate was never simple, certainly never easy, and rarely without some collateral damage to the parties involved.

No typical scenario results in the inevitable institutionalization or adoption of an illegitimate baby. Even so, single mothers had much in common, and some circumstances cropped up more frequently than others. The Victorian trope of the

253

domestic servant made pregnant by a member of her employer's family was repeated well into the twentieth century. She could not keep the baby unless her family (or occasionally his) agreed to take the child, or unless she could miraculously find work elsewhere with accommodation and childcare thrown in. When teenage girls and their teenage boyfriends conceived a baby, often while one or other of them was under the age of consent, or when a university student became pregnant, it was usually judged in the best interests of all concerned that their baby be taken away.

Fifty-five per cent of girls in British Catholic 'rescue' homes in the 1950s were Irish, sent over the sea, perhaps with a charitable £5 note from the local priest, to sully someone else's nest. Obviously, religion was a pressing determinant in the parting of an unmarried mother from her illegitimate child. Adultery was yet another; paradoxically, so was marriage. A woman might become pregnant to a boyfriend who decides that although he would still like to marry her, he will not do so with the embarrassing encumbrance of a bastard in tow, even if it is his bastard.

Before I started researching this book I assumed that putative fathers were probably the villains of the piece whenever a mother was compelled to hand her child over to someone else. I was so wrong: birth-fathers had no official influence at all. Before the end of the 1950s they could neither sanction nor forbid the adoption of their own children: unless they had the moral support of the birth-mother, they were helpless. It was the mother's parents, or in some cases her grandparents, who had the most strident voices of all, especially if the mother was younger than twenty-one. In fact, no mother below the age of majority was allowed to apply for an adoption order after 1933; her parents had to do it, supposedly on her behalf.

The most likely outcome for a single mother unable to marry before the 1960s was to relinquish her baby. Marriage to anyone might avoid this, not necessarily to the birth-father. If both partners were complicit, the state of wedlock was enough on its own to confer respectability on a bastard child. It cloaked all sorts of complications. But perhaps the mother was married already, to someone other than the birth-father, who was not willing to play the game of smoke and mirrors. Maybe the shadows surrounding the child's conception were too dark to ignore: that prayer-book 'Table of Affinity' laid out the terms of an incestuous relationship, of which there were more in some parts of the country than in others. (Genetic abnormalities occasioned by closely related parents are not confined to certain Asian communities. 'NFN' was an apocryphal acronym used in hospital notes to denote someone not-quite-right-in-the-head, or somehow mutant. It stood for 'normal for Norfolk'.) One of the parents might have been what was clinically termed mentally defective, or the birth-father a foreign prisoner-of-war, uniformly forbidden to marry British brides until the end of 1946.

255

Even if none of these applied, the giving up of a child could be driven by all sorts of practical and emotional responses: shame; pride; a lack of money, confidence or support; the heartfelt belief that the baby would fare better away from its natural parent(s); selfishness; cruelty; a distaste for babies in general or this one in particular. Placing a child for adoption could be a gesture of defiance by a mother pressurized by her family to keep it. It could be all about denial, or even spite. Ruth A was committed to an orphanage when her foster-parents applied to adopt her. Her birth-mother did not really want the child herself, but nor did she want anyone else to have her.

It might be that the mother tried to care for the baby on her own before getting to the stage when external agencies were involved, but found herself defeated. Jay struggled for sixteen months before allowing her son to be adopted; she was only seventeen when he was born, and lived at home with her father and two brothers, keeping house, working full-time (while the boy went to nursery) and trying to cope with the boy's respiratory problems, exacerbated by a rack of damp nappies constantly not-quite-drying indoors. She just could not manage any more.

Records of mother-and-baby homes reveal a few rare cases where a mother simply wanted rid of her child, to make life easier. Uncommon as this reaction may have been, it is one all adoptees fear when attempting to trace their natural parents. People have told me that no matter how much they know their adoptive parents wanted and loved them, and how happy they have been with them, there is always a little worm of doubt quietly shuffling deep beneath the surface. Why did my birth-parents not want me? Didn't they love me enough? What was wrong with me, that they couldn't bear to keep me? Were they glad to give me away?

★　★　★

Once they had signed the appropriate papers, most birth-mothers would not expect to see their children again. The real Philomena (played by Judi Dench in the eponymous film) had her child in a mother-and-baby home attached to a convent run by the Sisters of the Sacred Hearts of Jesus and Mary in Ireland. She cared for him for three years, until informed by the nuns that he was to be sent away to a family in America. The document she signed in 1955 to endorse his adoption still exists, witnessed by a notary public.

> I, Philomena Lee of Limerick, Ireland, aged 22 years make oath and say:
> That I am the mother of Anthony Lee who was born to me out of wedlock at Sean Ross Abbey, Roscrea, Co. Tipp., Ireland on 5th July 1952.
> That I relinquish full claim forever to my said child . . . and surrender the said child to Sister Barbara, Superioress of Sean Ross Abbey . . .
> That I further undertake never to attempt

to see, interfere with or make any claim to the said child at any future time.

With a stroke of the pen, Anthony (whose name was later changed) went from being all-in-all to his mother, to being nothing. Nothing she could acknowledge, anyway. She kept him a secret for fifty years.

Carol A had her daughter in the spring of 1960, while she was still an undergraduate. At first glance, it might appear that Carol had a lot going for her: her parents offered her a caravan in their garden in which to live with the baby if she left university, and the principal of her college suggested she board the baby out for a couple of years at a home run by a national child welfare society, while she finished her degree. Carol agreed to the latter arrangement, and got herself a resident cleaning job in a nearby hotel so that she could visit her daughter every day before term began. But as the autumn approached, Carol realized that this way of life was a compromise she was not prepared to make on behalf of her child. The home was well run, but the personnel kept changing, and every day her daughter spent there decreased her chances of being adopted by a couple in search of a baby rather than a toddler.

Carol was forced to the deeply distressing conclusion that she had made the wrong decision in keeping the baby and trying to bring her up alone. She managed to screw up the courage to admit this to the staff at the home, and to her own family, and then started the adoption process. Even so, Carol felt she could not win, and nor (except through a fortunate adoption) could her baby. She hated the thought of pretending she had no child, of masking her secret beneath a veneer of normality, but at the same time, could not bear the prospect of public shame, and was terrified of being trapped in poverty. As Carol put it herself: Hobson's choice.

In November 1960 Carol severed contact with her daughter. At least she made a decision and abided by it, however heartbreaking, which is something Sara found impossible to do. The father of Sara's illegitimate baby was married, and Sara herself was engaged to another man when it was born. Her fiancé made it clear that, while he was still willing to marry Sara (shop-soiled as she was), he could not be expected to take on a bastard as well. So an adoption was arranged through a reputable society, and went ahead in the summer of 1960 when the baby was four months old.

For the next eighteen months Sara bombarded the agency with letters and telegrams asking after the infant, and although she signed the final adoption papers, she couldn't bring herself to put them in the post. Even with a baby by her new husband on the way, she could not forget her first-born, and only returned the papers when taken to court by the adoptive parents in March 1962. She tried to attach conditions to her final consent: given that she really wanted to keep the child (she wrote), she begged that the adoptive parents would send detailed annual reports and photographs to her until it was twenty-one.

Understandably, the adoptive parents — and the law-courts — were not minded to comply. Sara's permission needed to be unconditional if it was to have any legal standing, and she had vacillated too much. The child had been with its new parents for nearly two years now, in an atmosphere of mutual love. Sara's unreasonable behaviour threatened the new family's well-being. If she could not give whole-hearted consent herself, after two years, the court would have to give it for her. The case was taken out of Sara's hands, and the adoptive parents were granted full custody. The judge acknowledged Sara's emotional dilemma, but pointed out that as she had chosen her husband over her illegitimate child, she had (and here it comes again) made her bed, and must lie in it.

It might be useful at this point to mention a few milestones in the history of adoption. The practice was not legitimized in England and Wales until 1926. It became legal in Northern Ireland in 1929 and in Scotland the following year. In 1939 adoption agencies were licensed and regulated for the first time. Ten years later, local authorities were required to supervise all adoptions, although private 'third party' arrangements — whereby a child could be passed to an intermediary who would then pass it on to adoptive parents — were still legal. They remained so until 1982. In 1950 the barrier of secrecy surrounding a child's birth and adoptive parentage was enshrined in law, and in 1958 local authorities were given the power to organize adoptions themselves. The 1976 Adoption Act confirmed the right of adoptees to access their birth records; it also required local authorities to set up various post-adoption services. And from December 2005, birth-parents have been allowed limited access to information about the children they relinquished.

Straight birth-mother to adoptive-mother adoptions involving money were outlawed by the Regulation Act of 1939, but unregulated third-party adoptions were not covered by the Act and offered considerable scope for malpractice and corruption. Some mother-and-baby homes were known to organize swift adoptions straight from the cradle with not too many questions asked, netting the staff a nice little profit. During the Second World War there were substantiated stories of babies being handed over to buyers at London's railway termini, sometimes without any paperwork at all — not even an exchange of addresses.

History was changing fast during those febrile years; perhaps that made it seem acceptable to rewrite it completely for illegitimate children. Half-foreign babies were particularly difficult to place, apparently, if their parentage was known. Maybe anonymity and obfuscation really did give them a better chance in life. After all, that is exactly what Captain Coram believed in the eighteenth century, when he re-christened foundling babies. Modern practice is that, to some extent, adoptees be kept mindful of their ethnic origins, their national heritage. It is impossible to imagine a happy medium between these two schools of thought, and equally impossible to judge which is the correct approach. The point missed by commentators in the past is that neither is right, and neither is wrong. The adoption process is not about moral housekeeping or fulfilling policy. It's about love, and you can't legislate for that.

★ ★ ★

Hardest to place of all were the illegitimate children who were not perfect, those who looked obviously foreign, who were conceived through rape or incest, or were too old to count as babies any more. The very fact that they were illegitimate could militate against them: adoptive parents preferred a wholesome little orphan, or a victim of some other tragic circumstance but with married parents. There were not many of those around, though. A survey conducted in 1926 revealed that 75 per cent of all adoptions involved illegitimate children, and couples anxious to adopt someone of their own could not afford to be too choosy as far as retrospective morality was concerned, nor too wary of 'bad blood'. The most enlightened or humane of them would not care. The sad story of Margaret, the girl raped by a shopkeeper on a day-trip from the Magdalene asylum, is leavened — redeemed, almost — by the wonderful adoptive parents found for her twin girls. They were working-class people who moved from the city to the windy fresh air of the Irish countryside to bring up their precious new daughters. As soon as the girls were old enough to understand, it was explained that they did not come from their

Mammy's tummy, but that someone very special had given them to Mammy and Dad because they could not have children of their own. So kind was that special person that she had given them not just one baby, but two.

At first, the couple had wanted a single new-born, not the pair of toddlers offered to them by the nuns. And Samantha and her sister were hardly very appealing: one of them was terrified of men and of anyone wearing glasses; they were both livid with nappy-rash and disgustingly crusty-nosed; they had not reached any of the developmental milestones they should have done, and they didn't smile very much. But Mammy and Dad were smitten. 'They just wanted to rescue us,' explains Samantha with pride, 'and that's what they did.' They were brought home on 2 December, at nine months old, and that Christmas was very special.

There was not much money around. 'But Dad just went out and bought two of everything, everything that we didn't even need, so he bought two bikes, even though we couldn't even creep yet, he bought a Wendy House, two sort of walker things — they used to have kids in walkers back then — and just two of everything he could find. And there's pictures of them in their little . . . council house which is absolutely just full of toys, toys that we were too young to play with, but he didn't have the experience to know what we'd need, he just bought everything anyway! So, forty years later, my dad just has one date in his mind when he talks about the happiest day of his life and that was the 2nd of December 1972.'

Every year, on the anniversary of the girls' homecoming, the family baked a little cake and raised a glass to the lady who had let them go. When the twins decided to trace Margaret, their parents supported them throughout the process, and cared for Margaret with kindness and compassion. 'I loved her very much,' says Samantha of her birth-mother. 'My sister loved her very much, my mother and father loved her very much and she loved us.'

They were lucky. Had they stayed in the care of the Magdalene asylum the chances are that their lives could have been as grim as Margaret's. Catholic children's homes and orphanages do appear to have been particularly brutal in visiting the sins of the parents — especially the mothers — on their unfortunate children. A certain orphanage in County Cavan in Ireland was run by the Poor Clares along the lines of an industrial school; its inmates were expected to work for their keep, and to conform completely. Residents during the 1940s and 1950s remember it as a hell-hole. 'Fear was inside of you all of the time.'

The orphanage was not some awful old Victorian pile; it had been rebuilt after a fire in 1943, in which thirty-six children had perished. They were trapped behind locked doors, and only one of them was identifiable after the event. The remains of the rest were shared out among eight coffins. The new orphanage housed 100 children (and in this case, as in most, illegitimates were classed as orphans). According to alumni, they were forced to eat potato and

264

vegetable peelings from the midden, and when one girl was sick, she was made to eat her own vomit to teach her a lesson about 'waste not, want not'. They were beaten with strips of broken orange boxes — with or without nails still attached — and humiliated beyond belief. Every week, before their bath, the girls had to stand in line in their knickers 'giggling at the girls who had big chests'; then they had to step out of their drawers and show them to the nuns before being issued with clean ones for the following week. 'We used to stand at the end of our beds holding out the knickers and shaking with fright, and then the nuns would call you a dirty thing in front of everybody. It was cruel, it really was.'

Elsewhere, the weekly ritual involved the hoisting up of knickers on a pole for everyone to see; votes would then be taken on who had the dirtiest pair. The unlucky loser would be beaten. This was in an industrial school which failed to provide lavatory paper to its inmates. Bath-night was once a fortnight, and when adolescent girls started their periods they were issued with three sanitary towels at the most; sometimes only one.

Occasionally the nuns were kind. Mother Assumpta worked in the laundry and would try to wash and dry soiled sheets in secret, so the girls would not be strapped for bedwetting. Another sister sewed little strips of lace to the hems of their utility petticoats: a scrap of beauty in an ugly world. But this was a harsh life for everyone involved. It made the girls vulnerable once they were turned out into the world as young teenagers; they knew nothing about sex or

265

the meaning of love and were exploited mercilessly. Certain local men were known to prey on newly liberated girls: 'a fellow could do what he liked with them'.

Such cruelty was not exclusive to Catholic institutions. It was relatively common practice in 1945, according to the children's welfare campaigner Lady Allen of Hurtwood, for boys to be dressed in girls' knickers when they wet the bed, as though shame could somehow mend this most persistent of problems in residential homes. Another remedy was to forbid you to drink any water, or, bizarrely, force you to wear a blanket over your head; to avoid any unsavoury fumblings in bed you had to keep your hands under your pillow or piously crossed over your chest, while restless babies' limbs were tied to their cots. Institutionalization, pointed out Lady Allen, can last for many years; long after the institution itself has been left behind.

★　★　★

Although many children's homes passively allowed individual staff members the latitude to inflict unimaginable damage on their charges, none would have considered its care regime to be actively malicious. No doubt the nuns in County Cavan and elsewhere thought too much kindness was bad for a developing soul — especially the fragile soul of a child of sin. The psychological causes of nocturnal enuresis, or bedwetting, were not widely understood before the 1950s and it must have been easy to imagine, at least for those who had no children of their own, that this was an act of petty defiance or rebellion on the child's part. Barnardo's was an organization that prided itself on its progressive outlook, however, and on its efforts to recreate families, of a sort, for its residents.

Most Barnardo's establishments were not called children's homes; they were 'villages', where perhaps 500 youngsters would be scattered around the site, ten or eleven to a cottage. Staff were assigned to each cottage, to give the children some sense of continuity and belonging. According to an internal Barnardo's document published in the early 1950s, the ideal house-mother was loyal, considerate and uncomplaining; she worked tirelessly, possessed a healthy sense of humour and was allowed to lose her temper occasionally as long as she recovered it quickly (a good example to set to the children). She never bore a grudge, and talked and listened to the children in ways they could understand. She inspired them with a love of God, respected their individuality and knew when to be cool and when to revert to 'the full warmth of her affection'. She was everything, in fact, that a real mother should be. Individual cottages had a mixed population in terms of age, and their fair share of coloured children and what were then called cripples (frequently assigned to knit liberty bodices all day, according to a former Barnardo's girl). Only the 'chronic wetbeds' had a cottage exclusively of their own, where they were apparently expected to wash their own sheets and take a cold bath each morning. Children who were 'difficult' were transferred from home to home — one particularly spirited young lady called Joyce B lived in fourteen different places during her Barnardo's career.

Not surprisingly, she remembers her shifting childhood as bleak and lonely, but there are some very cheerful memories of Barnardo's homes. They used to hold inter-village sports days, and organize treats for the children, who were allowed to keep pets and to have visitors including, under certain circumstances, their own birth-parents. In the best cottages, the house-mother would tuck her charges up at night, after a bedtime story, and kiss them on the forehead. (In the worst, she would terrorize the children with taunts about their mothers, and threaten them, when they cried, with something to cry about.) The children went to local schools; when most of them left at fourteen, apprentice-ships or positions in domestic service were arranged, and they were invited to keep in touch.

After the publication of the Curtis Report in 1946, on children deprived of a normal home life, recommendations were made that those in residential homes should be absorbed into their own communities as closely as possible. This was a noble aim, but most of the Barnardo's and other children's home alumni to whom I have spoken distinctly remember feeling different at school and elsewhere; odd ones out. Some of the most successful homes in this regard, even before the Curtis Report, were those founded by Charlotte Sharman in 1862. They were still going strong in the 1930s, with a London branch in Sydenham, a country branch in Gravesend and a seaside branch in Hastings.

The 1935 annual report for Miss Sharman's homes carries a list of gifts donated by local well-wishers during the year; not just financial gifts, but a serendipitous assortment of buns, sweets, boxes of toffees, summer frocks, gooseberries and lettuces, sixpence pocket-money for each child, iced cakes, blancmange powder, sacks of flour, a weekly supply of suet, cabbages, brushes and brooms, soap, rhubarb and vests. Sharman's children were famously healthy and happy, surrounded by love and respect, and reared with kindness and a practical eye for life beyond the home.

Coram's Foundling Hospital was similarly successful at integrating its children into local and — eventually — adult life. Residents there took part in shows and plays; parties were held with proper clowns from real circuses, and on Prize Day some major or minor royal would usually attend, with all the associated media coverage and pomp and circumstance. Each summer everyone decamped to Eastbourne or somewhere for a seaside holiday, and every so often articles appeared in the papers about Coram graduates excelling in their various careers.

Coram's was always a high-profile organization, and for most of its existence, a well-endowed one. In 1921, however, it issued its first appeal for public donations since 1739, defeated by the sheer number of war-babies left, not always metaphorically speaking, on its doorstep. So far, since

Captain Coram first opened his gates, the organization had 'maintained, educated and made into useful citizens' nearly 24,000 'unwanted children'. From 1914 to 1918 alone, over 2,000 applications were made on behalf of illegitimate babies. Coram's needed not only more money to care for them all, but more space.

In 1927, the hospital moved out of London to Redhill in Surrey, and then to Ashlyns Hall, an estate in the Chilterns near Berkhamsted, where it remained until it closed in 1954. The Foundling Museum in London has curated an oral history collection about life at Ashlyns. It was like a permanent boarding-school; children arrived there at the age of about five, after living with foster-parents. There were thirty children to a dormitory, who all had to get up and wash as soon as the seven o'clock bell rang in the morning. The girls would put on a uniform of brown serge dresses with red bands, white Dutch-style caps and holland or coarse linen aprons. The boys wore jackets and smart scarlet waistcoats with brass buttons.

One of the recommendations of the Curtis Report was to pay due regard to the psychological impact of communal childcare. It acknowledged the radical idea that children could be emotionally scarred by childhood experience; they thrived on kindness and individual attention. Coram's realized this after the Second World War, but beforehand, the regime was as strict there as in any other children's home. There was no talking at breakfast; afterwards, everyone was expected dutifully to produce a bowel movement (with two sheets of lavatory paper each) and if they could not, they were sent to Matron for some syrup of figs. They went to church twice a day — three times on Sundays — to listen to the chaplain who, in the early 1920s, was aptly named Revd Stork. They silently marched in crocodiles between lessons. There was bullying and corporal punishment, as in many schools outside in the wider world. Retrospectively, that seems cruel and inexcusable; at the time, it was a dismal fact of life.

Lunch was at noon. The food was not good, by all accounts, but margarine could be saved by the wise and used as a soothing ointment for the hands after caning, and indigestible lumps of fat could be smuggled out in one's knickers and secretly disposed of later, down the lavatory.

Playtime was outside, whatever the weather. There were sports on Thursdays, including swimming, uncompromisingly taught by the push-you-in-at-the-deep-end method. There was always a lot of music. Bedtime was at 7 p.m., after a tea of plain cake with bread and jam or treacle. There were few hugs, few words of love, and no chance — as one Coram's girl put it — to shine. Daniel was given sixpence by his foster-mother, who came to visit him soon after he had moved in. He threw it away. Unlike the young ladies at Miss Sharman's, he had no idea what a sixpence was. Alice was given a new dress and a teddy-bear when she was taken there by her birth-mother. As soon as her birth-mother left, the dress was put away for good. Beatrice remembers with icy clarity the day she realized she was illegitimate: her foster-mother had explained that Beatrice was not her little girl, but it was left to neighbours to fill in the details, just before she was consigned to Ashlyns: 'Oh, well, you see Babs, what it is, is, your mum didn't want you, so she gave you away.' On Ruth B's first day, her main concern was whether she would be allowed home for lunch. No, said her foster-mother. She must be a good girl and stay put. 'And she kissed me, and was gone.'

Unless a child was endowed with a preternaturally optimistic or unimaginative personality, any children's home was starting at a disadvantage as far as happiness was concerned, especially as children got older, went to school, and realized how different were their lives from those of 'normal' families. One man recalls that from the age of four through to twelve or thirteen, he spent the whole time waiting to go home. Perhaps today would be the day. Some girls and boys were tough enough to learn the skill of parenting themselves — being their own parents, that is — like the lad whose job it was to tell the baker, visiting in his van, what bread was needed each morning. One day, he was supposed to take a message that nothing was needed at all, thank you, but it happened to be his birthday. Instead of relaying the message, he ordered the biggest cake in the van, then carried it to a secret corner of the grounds and tucked in. He shared it with the birds: the only guests at his own little private party.

There were instances of sexual abuse of children across the spectrum of residential care, especially children with no adult connections in the outside world. Reported cases must represent a fraction of what really happened; the scale of this obscenity is still coming to light, decades later. My cousin Sue was terrified but not particularly surprised, you will remember, when the unseen whippet crept into bed beside her in her new home. Someone who was abused in the 1950s in a Welsh institution explained how the horror of what happened overshadowed his entire life. He feels dead inside, unable to form attachments or to trust anyone, guilty ('was it my fault?'), hurt, lonely, degraded and emotionally stifled. This was, and shamefully still is, the darkest secret of childcare. It did not only affect illegitimate children, of course, but because they formed the majority of residents in homes, and used to be thought inherently corrupt anyway, it is safe to assume that illegitimate children bore the brunt of the abuse.

* * *

The aim of most residential homes was to place likely children in their care with adoptive parents. Even before the 1970s, it was not always essential for there to be *two* parents. In 1915 the Women's Social and Political Union, founded by militant suffragettes Emmeline and Christabel Pankhurst, announced its intention collectively to adopt a group of war-babies and bring them up as the most politically progressive children in the land. Each would have many mothers. Catherine only had one parent: she was adopted in 1947 by the single woman she now remembers as 'the best mum in the world'. Catherine was born to a Catholic nurse from Northern Ireland, who never told her own family about the pregnancy. Her father was an RAF engineer (she only discovered this in 2001). She was born in the house of her mother's friend, a forty-two-year-old midwife, and adopted by that friend soon afterwards.

Catherine's adoptive mother was well known for being sympathetic towards couples in trouble. They would turn up on her doorstep for counselling, and she once took in the pregnant eighteen-year-old daughter of a friend until she had had her baby, which was subsequently adopted elsewhere. Catherine was in the house the day 'the snatch squad' came to take that baby away; its mother was devastated. 'She seemed to cry for at least a week, but could eventually go home with the neighbours none the wiser.' Catherine also, incidentally, remembers a rather amorous 'uncle' who ran a business from home, and whose female employees went off to have appendectomies with baffling regularity. Illicit sex was all around. Her adoptive mother never changed her name from 'Miss' to 'Mrs': she was a brave lady. Her obvious unmarried status caused embarrassment to Catherine at school, but overall the adoption was a very happy arrangement.

Catherine's was an unusual case; for the majority, a fairly rigid protocol was in place, enforced first by custom and then by law. The adoptive parents were vetted, in the case of most adoption agencies informally by volunteers, but not as rigorously as the babies were. If the child was to be adopted directly from the mother-and-baby home, its mother (if she wished to come) was accompanied to the adoption venue by a member of the agency's staff — again probably a volunteer — or by a welfare worker from the local authority. In some cases the adoptive parents would come to the home. That is when the other residents had to be locked in the lounge with the curtains drawn. Cousin Sue still feels apprehensive when she thinks about Miss Trump, the woman who came to check up on her in my aunt and uncle's home and who could have taken her back if the adoption was not considered to be a success.

Fashions in children changed over the decades. Until birth-control and legalized abortion decreased the number of adoptees available in the 1960s and 1970s, babies were traditionally more popular than toddlers or older children, and blue-eyed blonds preferable to the dark-eyed, dark-haired and dark-skinned. In 1945, immediately after the war, there was a surge in requests for baby girls — some sort of reaction, perhaps, to the violence and machismo of the war years. It did not take long for boys to come back into vogue, and soon there was a shortage of *them*. Illegitimate sons were easier for lone mothers to keep, it was thought; sensitive girls were more likely to suffer from stigmatization. Bastard daughters were damaged goods. No father equals no pedigree. It was more desirable for them to be reinvented, to start new lives with new families and new histories.

There is an element of unilateral choice in all adoptions, although less now, perhaps, than in the days when children were arrayed in residential homes like dolls in a shop-window. But choice is a dangerous thing. The birth-mother who chose to have one of her illegitimate children adopted but not the others, for example, was storing up untold problems for the future. Several of the people who helped me with this book are hurt and bewildered by the recent discovery of half or even full siblings who were unaccountably allowed to grow up with their birth-mothers. ('So why was I sent away?') Conversely, adoptive parents could choose one sibling from several in care and leave the others, thus draining away any trace of a blood relationship.

With these and other problems in mind, the policy of the NCUMC was to discourage adoption altogether. The organization believed firmly that a child's best chance in life was with its birth-mother. The Salvation Army agreed, and rarely arranged adoptions for the babies born in its homes, although it would pass them on to other agencies if necessary. Contrary to popular belief, the Salvation Army never officially encouraged single mothers to offer babies for adoption. But adoption could not be wrong *per se*, surely? Illegitimacy, when it still had any relevance to society at all, was an embarrassing and expensive problem neatly alleviated, one would have thought, by other people's childlessness.

The truth is that this solution was rarely neat. For adoptive parents, like Samantha's and her twin sister's, the day they welcomed their new children was the best day of their lives. For many of the birth-mothers involved, it was the worst. How could the two be reconciled?

Adoption was not always the answer to a child's prayers, either. There are accounts of visitors to children's homes being mobbed by young residents desperate to be chosen by a new mummy and daddy, trying to grasp the adults' hands or wrap themselves round legs. When the lights went out in the dormitory, children used to fantasize about a mother of their own: how kind she would be, how beautiful and how *married*. Remember Sue's drawings of a house with rows of flowers outside? No wonder disillusionment set in so easily. Dee cannot bring herself to call the woman who adopted her 'mother'; instead she refers to her as 'the woman who brought me up'. This woman was unbearably sanctimonious; she considered herself altogether superior to Dee's birth-mother simply because she possessed a husband. Dee disputed this; to her it was merely a matter of chance. The two women had mixed fortunes, that's all. 'Fate left her barren, and it was my bad luck to end up with her.' The adoptive mother lost no opportunity, as soon as Dee was old enough to understand, to preach about loose women (i.e. unmarried mothers). She was obviously terrified Dee would bring the same disgrace to her adoptive family as her birth-mother had to hers.

Malcolm's story is eloquent of the shame and recrimination inextricably linked to certain adoptions. He was born during the Second World War and informed at the age of three or four that his adoptive mother was not his 'real' one. Later she assured him that she would help him, if he ever wanted to trace his birth-family, but it was an empty promise.

'Of course she never did and all the things like cards and presents that I know were sent to me in my baby years were never to get to me, or saved. My birth mother kept in touch with my adoptive mother until I was about five years old, when it was agreed that it was time to break away, as I would start asking questions. I cannot remember feeling a member of the family, but more an object or trophy owned by my adoptive mother.

'I was also made aware that my birth mother and father had not been married . . . So began a story of half-truths and purposeful deceit that would follow me throughout my life. I was a classic illegitimate child from the war years, and there are many of us.'

The unhappiest adoptees, like Malcolm, appear to have had one simple thing in common. Whenever their parents introduced them to friends, they were called 'my adopted son' (or daughter). The phrase was redolent of detachment and the sort of shameful qualification no 'real' child would ever be subjected to. It emphasized over and over again that they did not truly belong.

Occasionally couples would adopt in an attempt to save a marriage failing ostensibly because of an inability to conceive. The marriage would then disintegrate anyway, leaving the child emotionally stranded. Others never told their children they were adopted, or if they did, refused to divulge any details about the birth-family. It is easy to appreciate why. Adoptive parents are hardly invulnerable. But the sure result of such artifice, such a sense of insecurity on everyone's part, was resentment, confusion and mistrust. Isobel felt so unsure of her place in the world after hearing the news of her adoption at the age of ten that she started to ask permission just to take fruit from the fruit bowl. She felt as though all her rights had been taken away. She had suddenly become a guest member of the family.

Despite these sad stories, most adoptions worked out well for the children and adoptive parents concerned — or at least no worse than any family relationship. Barry was embraced by the local community when he was adopted in Wales; even though everyone seemed to know his background, he was never teased for being a bastard, and no one considered him handicapped by his circumstances, even when his adoptive mother died when he was eleven. He blossomed in the love of an extended adoptive family; went to grammar school and then to university, and looks back with affection on a radiant childhood.

Pauline A's adoption was delayed; when she was born in 1947 she had severe rickets, and could not be released to her new parents until cured. But from the moment she went home, she could not have been more loved. 'My mother had tried for twelve years for children of her own and undergone some dreadful ordeals in an attempt to diagnose the cause of her infertility. She had originally wanted five sons . . . and she

279

desperately wanted a child. My father always said I was the best thing that ever happened to them.'

It must have been difficult not to be judgemental in the years when illegitimacy still had such toxic moral and social implications, but many remarkable adoptive parents managed it, and many wounded birth-parents were later soothed by the knowledge that their children had grown up happy and generous-spirited. Pauline is very proud of her adoptive parents. They gave her 'all the love in the world' and did everything in their power to make her life a better one: exactly what any devoted parent would wish for their child.

10

Lost Innocents: Child Migration

Rhodesia? It's the other side of Haywards Heath.

The SS *Strathaird* was stunning. She was built as a luxury cruise liner, launched in 1931, dazzlingly white and nearly 200 metres long. When David Hill sailed on her to Australia in 1959, she was a middle-aged lady, with a raddled history as a troopship behind her, but she was still magnificent. David and his friends were staggered by her size, her splendour, her sheer excess. She could carry over 1,000 passengers, in beautifully appointed cabins; she had eight decks, a swimming pool, a games-room, a library and a cinema. She swarmed with smartly dressed crew, ready to cater to your every whim, and the food was lavish, especially for children like David brought up with post-war rationing. Stepping aboard the *Strathaird* was a bit like walking into a Hollywood film, or a fairy-tale.

Just reading the menus induces indigestion. For breakfast you could choose from kedgeree, bacon and eggs, or lamb's liver with gravy and potatoes, followed by steamed peaches and toast with jam, golden syrup, honey or marmalade. A typical lunch menu at about the time David sailed boasted 'Potage Windsor' (a hearty

281

meat-and-vegetable broth); fried fillets of pomfret tartare, hamburger steak and fried egg, Malay curry and rice, creamed or Berrichonne potatoes (braised in stock) and marrow in a tomato and onion sauce; a 'cold sideboard' with roulade of veal, ham loaf or ox tongue plus a salad of lettuce, tomato, potato and capers, followed by rusk custard (custard on a crushed biscuit base, like cheesecake), Neapolitan cream ices and finally exotic cheeses, including Danish Blue, Wensleydale, Kraft and Gruyere.

A special children's menu was available for tea: a mini-banquet of creamed vegetable soup, perhaps; flaked white fish with cream sauce, Scotch (or mutton) pie, eggs to order, mashed potatoes, cold beef, pressed tongue, lettuce and beetroot salad, gooseberry pie, cream ices, pastries and cakes. A few hours later, it was the children's dinner-time: lamb cutlets and a 'Diplomat' (or upmarket bread-and-butter) pudding. On top of all this, as the ship sailed further and further east, in shimmering heat, the children enjoyed tropical fruits for the first time in their lives. What could possibly be more glamorous?

The voyage from Tilbury to Sydney lasted about six weeks, during which David and his pals must have gained a good few kilos in weight. Once seasickness was out of the way, being aboard an ocean liner was one long adventure. They watched the world going by with wonder and excitement, well-fed, and free to do whatever they wished. It would have been perfect, had they been able to share the experience with their mothers or fathers. But bizarrely, these children were unaccompanied, except for a handful of unrelated adult chaperones. They ranged from toddlers to teenagers; a few — like David — had brothers or sisters aboard, but none had a parent. They were alone, the chosen ones: child migrants on their way to a new life.

Eventually the novelty of the ship's routine began to pall. Homesickness set in, with an undefined sense of apprehension. The weather cooled as they neared the coast of Western Australia; they sickened of fresh pineapples, and it started raining. By the time they got to Sydney, winter had come. The fun was over.

A new life: that is what they had been promised. Instead, they experienced trauma on a scale that has only recently come to light. Individuals like David, indeed entire nations, are still struggling to come to terms with the consequences of child migration.

Canada declared 2010 to be the year of the Home Child — its euphemistic name for child migrants — and Ontario annually celebrates a special day in their honour on 28 September. It is all about heritage: one in ten Ontarians is descended from the children transported, or deported, from Britain to Canada between 1869 and the late 1940s. Many of these little exports were illegitimate; they were aged from six months to eighteen years, unwitting participants in a demographic experiment now regarded as one of the most shameful episodes in the history of the British Empire.

The first child migrants of all were scooped off the streets of London in the early seventeenth century and bundled to America and the West Indies to work on tobacco plantations; in 1787 British children began arriving in Australia, and later they settled in Rhodesia (now Zimbabwe), South Africa and New Zealand. The last child migrant scheme closed in 1967. That is a stretch of about 350 years, during which 'unwanted' children were disposed of to someone else's advantage, often at the irredeemable cost of their own childhood and sense of identity.

The idea behind child migration was an unsophisticated business of supply and demand. Britain had crowds of children in residential or foster-homes, particularly bastards; they were expensive to maintain and an embarrassing advertisement, if truth be told, of the degenerative character of certain sections of society. The colonies needed more people to swell the population or to do the jobs no one else wanted for the cheapest possible price. In a speech welcoming the *Strathaird* on an earlier mission to Fremantle in 1938, the Archbishop of Perth did not mince his words. Given Australia's scant population, he thought a boost from the mother-country's surplus stock was a splendid idea. It would compensate for Australia's empty cradles and empty spaces. Without this injection of new blood, he maintained, the country was dangerously exposed to 'the teeming millions of our neighbouring Asiatic races'.

The policy at present adopted of bringing out young boys and girls and training them from the beginning in agricultural and

284

domestic methods . . . has the additional advantage of acclimatizing them from the outset to Australian conditions and imbuing them with Australian sentiments and Australian ideals — the essential marks of true citizenship . . .

Three years later, in 1941, the Deputy Prime Minister of Australia drafted a speech to the Trades Union Congress arguing for another 50,000 children to be commissioned from Britain. 'The war has shown us more vividly than ever that if we are to hold this country down the years we must increase our present population by several millions,' he wrote. 'Of all immigrants, children are the most readily made into good Australians.'

The Government failed to secure the required 50,000 souls, but children continued to be exported to Australia for another quarter of a century, and as in Ontario, a significant proportion of today's Australians have the blood of British child-migrants flowing in their veins.

Not surprisingly, none of the agencies supplying children to the colonies chose to publicize the mechanistic element of their schemes. Most of them were run by religious or charitable organizations, or by individual philanthropists who regarded themselves, with varying degrees of credibility, as saviours. We have already met Annie Macpherson, escorting homeless children to foster-parents in Ontario, and the enterprising Maria Rye, who transformed London's gutter-snipes into indentured workers on Canadian farms and factories. Both were famous in their day, but the most influential players in the field of child-migration were Dr Barnardo and the Fairbridge family.

Thomas Barnardo genuinely believed that disadvantaged children in his care could benefit personally from the opportunities offered by a new life abroad. The dream scenario was that children hand-picked by Barnardo's staff as the brightest and the best available would be sponsored by the charity to travel to one of the colonies, live in a children's home there or perhaps be fostered by a family; go to the local school, or be educated at a special farm school, and then emerge as useful citizens in a new homeland. These children's unfortunate histories would be erased; they would exchange new lives for old, ready to plant a young and vigorous family tree of their own in virgin soil.

Sometimes Barnardo's transported groups of siblings together. For a while, in the late 1950s and early 1960s, it operated a 'one parent scheme' whereby children were sent out first, then a lone parent (usually the birth-mother) followed, and they settled together. There were various family schemes too, but most child migrants arrived in their designated countries alone, as far as blood relatives were concerned, cut off at the roots and discouraged or prevented from keeping in touch. Barnardo's appears to have been less culpable in this regard than other organizations where the consent of a parent or guardian was not sought, as it should have been, and where no efforts were made to keep families

286

in contact. Quite the opposite, in fact: links and lifelines were deliberately destroyed at every turn.

It was not uncommon for Barnardo's children to be sent to Fairbridge farm schools when they arrived abroad. These were founded by Kingsley Fairbridge, a native South African born in 1885 who sailed to England at the age of twenty-one and never returned to his homeland. He was an evangelist for what he termed 'Imperial unity'; for consolidating the Empire through the shifting of its populations for mutual benefit. It was his belief that the colonies should 'take something England doesn't need' — its excess children — and transmute their inherent dross into gold. He opened a series of agricultural and domestic science schools, built along the lines of Dr Barnardo's villages, where desperately homesick children were trained in the sort of skills needed locally. God-forsaken places like the veldt of Rhodesia, the backwoods of Canada or the Australian bush would be invigorated and enriched by young people of white British heritage (superseding the aboriginal population in the process), while the young people themselves would learn self-reliance and a bracing new morality from the staff who taught them at school.

Kingsley Fairbridge and his wife Ruby opened their first farm school in Pinjarra, south of Perth, in 1912. Another opened on Vancouver Island in 1935 (although Fairbridge himself had died in 1924), then one near Moolong in New South Wales in 1937, and near Bulawayo in Rhodesia in 1946. There were seven Fairbridge farm schools in all.

The Fairbridge Society continued its involvement with young people aged between thirteen and twenty-five in Britain until it merged with the Prince's Trust in 2011. Barnardo's is still very much in evidence too, and both organizations have given and still give a tremendous amount of support where that support is most needed. The period of child migration, however, was not their finest hour.

* * *

John was sent to a Barnardo's home in Barkingside, London, when he was two. He was fostered out ten months later with a family in the Cotswolds, where he stayed for the next seven years. He loved his foster-parents, whom he called father and mother, and though everyone was aware he would be recalled by Barnardo's at some stage, they all preferred not to think about that. The possibility of leaving the place he now thought of as home, the place where he had grown up, was too bewildering to contemplate.

In 1932, when John was nine, he was indeed recalled to London. His foster-mother was heartbroken, as was the boy; he was placed in a children's home in Clapham and teased and bullied unmercifully for his unfortunate surname, which was (at that time) Ramsbottom. The news that he had been selected as one of only twenty boys from the home to go to Australia was no comfort. He didn't know what or where Australia was, and didn't want to. He attempted to run away from the Barnardo's home to his Gloucestershire village, but that didn't work: he couldn't navigate his way out of London.

David Hill's story was different. He was illegitimate, volunteered as a child migrant in 1959 by a (similarly illegitimate) single mother worn down by the effort of caring for him and his two brothers. She had heard about the Fairbridge farm school scheme, thought it was a godsend, and began the application process with optimism. First, she and the boys had to be vetted, which involved a home visit from two posh-looking Fairbridge ladies. They told David and his family 'wonderful stories about Australia, and showed us brochures and photographs. The picture they painted was very attractive: we would be going to a land of milk and honey, where we could ride ponies to school and pluck abundant fruit from the trees growing by the side of the road.' It sounded irresistibly alluring.

They even promised to sponsor David's mother to follow the boys when they were settled in Australia, and assured her the family would be reunited in no time. She agreed to the proposed emigration plan, dazzled by the mirage of a new life for them all. Three weeks before embarkation she delivered her sons to a Fairbridge children's home in Knockholt, Kent. It was magnificent: large, luxurious and well-staffed. The boys did nothing but play from dawn till dusk.

Shortly after that, all the children at the home were taken up to London to be kitted out with an extravagant array of new clothes. The girls were given *two* coats, one for the rain and one for the cold; they got a sun-hat for summer and a pixie hood for the winter; a tunic, gingham dresses, a jumper and a cardigan, a skirt with a bodice, two Aertex blouses, plenty of underwear and three pairs of pyjamas, shoes, sandals, plimsolls, a swimming costume, a fully-equipped sponge-bag and a Bible. Boys got the equivalent but — strangely — no underpants.

As the date of the voyage grew closer, it was time to say farewell.

On the last Sunday before we left, Mum came to Knockholt to spend the day with us. It was one of the saddest days of my life. It was wet and miserable. We went in to the larger town of Sevenoaks, where we sat silently in a Lyons teahouse drinking tea and eating cakes before going to a cinema to see Rosalind Russell in *Auntie Mame*, which was supposed to be fun but in my eyes was a very sad movie. We hardly exchanged any words that day.

Darkness fell, and the family walked back to the home in the rain. The three boys loaded Mum up with more daffodils than she could carry, picked for her in the fields round the home, then finally said good-bye. Two days later, David and his brothers were taken to Tilbury Docks, where the *Strathaird* lay waiting for them. It was easy for children who had never seen the sea to mistake the Thames for the ocean, and its further bank for the other side of the world. Most had only the haziest idea of where they were going for what they assumed was a glorified holiday. When asked if she knew where Rhodesia was, an innocent mother answered confidently that she did indeed: it was the other side of Haywards Heath — a town just a few miles away from her home in Brighton.

Fairbridge children were chosen for their intelligence and vigour. They were supposed to have a reasonable family background. Illegitimacy could not easily be avoided, but a heritage of significant mental or moral defectiveness could. They were rejected if any close relatives had been imprisoned or suffered from tuberculosis; if their mothers had ever been in a mental hospital; if they were physically 'backward', could not read by the age of six, or habitually wet the bed. One 'very nice lad' was refused entry to British Columbia because his mother 'developed religious mania'; another, mysteriously, because he had 'glands'.

Comments from case histories in the Fairbridge archive reveal a definite type of child migrant. Serena was 'an intelligent girl — character very good. Except for sulkiness . . . ' Gracie was 'a very good little girl . . . sweet-natured — truthful and honest, healthy'. Edward's mother was 'a brick-maker; father unknown. Ability stated to be good . . . very intelligent — a sweet disposition . . . Everyone loves [him]. He is a jolly little fellow and I am sure will get on anywhere — he is such a man and never an egotist and is awfully popular.' This child was just seven years old.

Amanda was part of the first mixed party to be sent to Pinjarra, in 1921. From the sunlit uplands of adulthood she remembers the place with great affection: Mr and Mrs Fairbridge lived in a cottage in the grounds; they read the children bedtime stories, and sometimes Mr Fairbridge, or 'Daddy', took them for a ride on his horse Black Prince. In fact Amanda was so happy there that she visited on her honeymoon, and never stopped thinking of Pinjarra as home.

It is not easy to understand why. Even the official account of Pinjarra, written by Ruby Fairbridge in 1937, does not manage to make the farm school sound very comfortable. By then it had moved from its original ramshackle accommodation to a purpose-built village, surrounded by poplar trees described by Mrs Fairbridge as 'as straight and fresh as young maidens . . . or as gallant boys going forth'. The children slept in cottages — two storeys for the girls, bungalows for the boys — with bracing names like Shakespeare, Kitchener, Rhodes and Livingstone. Their days began with a breakfast at 7 a.m. of porridge or sweetcorn, and bread and jam with cocoa or tea. At 8.15 the children took part in drill, or PE, and at 9 a.m. their duties began. There was a rota, including cleaning lavatories and washing bathrooms, weeding and gardening, carpentry, driving the pony and trap to Pinjarra on errands, helping in the kitchen or the laundry, and working in the orchards.

After lunch there was an hour of story-reading, then playtime for the younger children, while the older ones got on with more work. At 3.30 p.m. the boys had 'Boxing hour' — good for discipline and dissipating aggression — followed by bathtime. Supper was at 5 p.m., followed by sports or band-practice, then bed at 6.30 p.m. It was a busy life, with not much room for formal education, but a useful one, according to Mrs Fairbridge, combining a sense of purpose with robust health and honest hard work. But as one of the residents recalled years later, unless you had a very special house-mother, there wasn't any love.

Some children did not stay in an institution at all; they went straight to foster-homes, where they took their chance and if they were lucky enjoyed a stable family life and were happy. The stories of those migrants who were unhappy, however, are still emerging day by day. They make chilling reading. An image which will always stay with me is of a six-year-old boy so lonely in this brave new world that he painstakingly sews a smile on his teddy-bear.

★　★　★

The Fairbridge Society and Barnardo's were not the only players in this business, and the memories I am about to share with you do not all involve their schemes. Alternative agencies — good, bad or ugly — included the Salvation Army, the Church Army, Middlemore children's homes, based in Birmingham, the Lady Northcote Trust, the YMCA, the Big Brother Movement (whereby young boys were mentored by older emigrants), various Catholic outfits like the Christian Brothers, and ordinary British local authorities. Naturally, different children reacted in different ways to the treatment they received, and any retrospective assessment of what happened must be coloured by individuals' personality, expectations and experiences before arriving at the home in Australia or elsewhere, and after leaving. Our response to their stories must be tempered by the changed values of our own time. We should remember that there were many adults involved in child migration who genuinely believed they were doing their best by these disadvantaged youngsters.

All that said, it is very difficult to listen to their testimony without anger, shame and — I hope — compassion.

Ruby Fairbridge recorded a day in the life of the children at Pinjarra. It sounds strict and austere, but not cruel. Here is an alternative account, written by a former child migrant in Australia. Her name is Flo, and in 1928 she is seven years old. She rises at 5.30 a.m., and after prayers is required to remove her pyjama jacket and wash in public with cold water and carbolic soap. Those with fair skin are allowed to rub cucumber peelings on their faces in an attempt to soothe the corrosive effects of sunburn. Seventeen girls share a single chamber-pot. Each makes her own bed, after turning her prickly horsehair mattress, and has her hair brushed or scraped by the girl on duty. Then it's breakfast. The porridge is beige and indigestible, and sits heavy on the stomach all morning. No one wears shoes, incidentally: all those lovely clothes bought in London were confiscated as soon as the migrants arrived at school, never to be seen again. In fact some agencies recycled them, sending them home to be issued to the next unwitting cohort of colonial pioneers. Come summer or winter, every child was barefooted.

The staff use megaphones in the canteen during meals, and preside over public thrashings. It is drilled into the children over and over again, remembers Flo, that they are second-class citizens, even here in the new world. They should not deprive 'real' (white) Australians — or New Zealanders or Canadians or Rhodesians — of work, and therefore must expect to take the most menial of jobs when they leave school. All that intelligence testing before they left was irrelevant now.

Flo does housework all morning. After lunch the girls play segregated sports, which might be hockey or swimming (with leeches). The rest of the day is spent working, punctuated by unappetizing meals based on whatever can be coaxed by the children themselves from the meagre soil.

Flo's house-mother is a mercurial character, and treacherously unpredictable. One minute she makes a fuss of Flo; the next, she will spit in her face. The store-keeper is a genial fellow who molests her, but at the time Flo interprets this as being 'kind and loving'. No one prepares her for menstruation, and when her periods begin she is issued one small towel a day, which she has to soak publicly in a bucket to clean. Worst of all, Flo's best friend commits suicide, and she is by no means the only child migrant to do so.

Boys remember labouring for hours in the glare of the sun to construct new school buildings, and being strapped or beaten for the most petty of misdemeanours. One of the priests in a Catholic home is said to have thrust sticks up the rectum of favoured boys with such vigour that the lower bowel was occasionally withdrawn with the stick. Local hospitals were allegedly called upon more than once to carry out corrective surgery of the genital area in boys and girls.

> Some of the Brothers got their kicks out of beating us and others got their kicks in other ways . . . [You] don't know what it's like to see little boys woken up in their sleep and taken from their beds. We'd hear a Brother coming — his footsteps on the wooden floor — and we'd pray he wouldn't stop beside our bed. I'd be there on a wet mattress, praying it wouldn't happen to me.

Meanwhile, family members at home were completely oblivious to what was going on. Many never heard from their children again, not knowing whether they were alive or dead, and wondering why their sons and daughters had so quickly forgotten them. Others were assured that children had been adopted by loving families and were flourishing. Letters were destroyed, false information given, birth certificates withheld and bloodlines severed, all to make life easier for other people.

No child migrant would dare complain while

he or she was still a resident. But as the first few cohorts started moving through the system and out the other end, rumours began to emerge, followed by accusations of ill-treatment and catastrophic mismanagement. In 1944 a confidential report was published by the Secretary to the High Commissioner for the UK in Australia, on the fate of the 806 boys and 368 girls sent out to Pinjarra to date. Forty-eight of the children had been repatriated (as unfit or unsuitable, despite the screening process); forty-eight had died; six were transferred to Catholic institutions. Another six were described as 'definite failures'; 825 'made good', presumably leaving Pinjarra to work, marry or both; and the remaining 241 were somewhere in between, neither disappointing enough to be sent home, nor successful enough to support themselves. In no man's land.

The inspector noticed that most of the boys he met showed no great enthusiasm for working on the land after they left the farm school, which somewhat defied the declared object of the exercise. He also questioned the level of discipline, suggesting it might be a little too harsh. Better all-round education would enable the children to follow their own inclinations, to find work that suited them. Then they would be happier. Their intellectual potential was being wasted. He considered the calibre of staff at all levels to be 'unfortunate'; better rates of pay would attract better-quality carers and managers. More women were needed on Fairbridge Society committees: there was only one in the whole of

Australia, and she was the wife of a committee chairman. There were no attempts at integration: Pinjarra was 'an English community on Australian soil', a fact which did the children no favours when they came to leave.

Confidential investigations into the after-care of child migrants noted that there was a fair amount of 'sex nastiness' among the children, but that this was 'inevitable'. One investigation in 1936 included a list of ex-Fairbridge girls requiring 'special treatment' — a euphemism for maternity care — most of whom were unmarried. A twenty-one-year-old was described as being 'virtually a prostitute'. No mention was made of 'sex nastiness' between staff and students. Most girls left the school at fourteen and were placed wherever the staff thought fit, without any consultation. Some were not even paid in their subsequent employment, just given their keep. Both girls and boys were encouraged to keep in contact with other alumni when they left, but even this was ill-advised, according to inspectors: 'There is an exaggerated family tie between Old Fairbridgians stronger in fact than that which exists between natural brothers and sisters, which draws them together and makes them seek out one another's company and which is the product of a sort of mutual self pity.' Those poor, dispossessed people: who else but themselves would understand the bitter secrets they shared?

★   ★   ★

Margaret Humphreys, a social worker from Nottingham, was the person largely responsible for publicizing the plight of the child migrant. In 1984 she started running a support group for people affected by adoption. She called it Triangle: it allowed birth-parents, adoptive parents and adult adoptees to get together and share their experiences. A couple of years later, Margaret unexpectedly received a letter from Adelaide, South Australia. It was from Madeleine, who had heard about Triangle through a friend recently returned from a visit to Nottingham.

Margaret was not quite sure what to make of Madeleine: in her letter she claimed she had been sent to Australia from a children's home in Nottingham when she was four; she had no birth certificate — was not even sure of her own name — and no idea why she had been exiled. Could Margaret help her find out? Surely Madeleine had got her wires crossed somewhere: this story couldn't be true. Margaret wrote back, asking if she was absolutely certain about what had happened. Oh yes, replied Madeleine, quite sure. 'You don't forget things like that . . . I still have nightmares. I simply want to discover my roots.'

Margaret's research led to the exposure of child migration in this country and around the Commonwealth. She discovered that Britain exported up to 150,000 children like Madeleine, the vast majority of whom grew up with no idea of who they really were. Since first hearing from Madeleine, Margaret and her team at the Child Migrants Trust have reunited thousands of families, and if it has been too late for some

— perhaps their birth-parents have died — she has at least provided them with the names, dates and faces necessary to put their lives into some sort of context. She has worked both here, on behalf of bereft birth-families, and in Australia, and it is largely thanks to her that we now appreciate the harm done in all our names, and that governments have finally been brought to account. She is the patron saint of child migrants everywhere, and a champion of natural justice.

In 1998 the British Government instituted a parliamentary enquiry into child migration. It acknowledged that some of the schemes were altruistic, but the whole movement was motivated more by economics and racism than philanthropy. The expediency of exporting unwanted children overwhelmed any sense of humanity or fellow-feeling, with the result that tens of thousands of vulnerable children were emotionally and often physically or sexually abused. They were dehumanized, and in the good old tradition of bastards throughout history (although not all of them were illegitimate) they were turned into society's scapegoats. And they were not unanimously 'unwanted', anyway. In many cases, birth-parents imagined — after being promised as much — that the sacrifice they were making in letting their children go was only a temporary one. If things did not work out they could ask for the children to be returned, and if they did work out, they could join them in a land bursting with opportunity and free of prejudice. Migration records reveal unanswered letters from birth-parents pleading with the authorities to send the children home again, because their mothers cannot bear to be without them, or never realized that emigration meant going away for ever. Their pleas were met by silence.

For its part, the Australian Government published a report in 2001 with the emotive title *Lost Innocents: Righting the Record*. It gave voice to some horrific experiences of depersonalization and brutality; it admitted that letters from home were often destroyed so that contact could never be made between birth-parents and their children, or between siblings from the same family, and that dates of birth and names were routinely changed for the same purpose. It pledged financial help in encouraging families to find each other again, in prosecuting cases of physical and sexual abuse, and in healing the wounds of the mentally damaged. Most of all, it acknowledged Australia's shame.

Prime Minister Gordon Brown extended a formal apology to child migrants everywhere in February 2010. It was an intensely emotional occasion, attended by former migrants from Australia, New Zealand, Canada, Zimbabwe and South Africa. Mr Brown spoke with humility about the pain, rejection and betrayal suffered by Britain's deported children, and acknowledged how misguided former governments were to allow it to happen, generation after generation. It was an ugly stain on our country's history.

In response, Harold Haig, a former child migrant, thanked the Prime Minister and Margaret Humphreys, whose campaign had done so much to restore that most basic of human rights denied by Britain to its exiled sons and daughters: the right to a family life. In the most moving moment of the day (and there were many), he thanked Margaret's children for sacrificing so much precious time with their own mother, so that she could help other people find theirs.

11

Mummy's Little Secret:
Staying Together

*I've known my mother all my life. I just
didn't realize who she was.*

You are illegitimate but not in care; you have not
been abandoned, sold nor given away; you are not
available for adoption and you are not an emi-
grant. Therefore you must be one of the lucky
ones. You must be staying with your birth-family.
That means you have been accepted, that blood
really is thicker than water and that you are
where you belong.

Well, maybe; maybe not. It could also mean
that you are at the centre of a bewildering
network of secrets and lies; at the mercy of
hidden family agendas; just as unsure about who
you are and how you fit in as any of the children
we have met so far.

Even that most traditional of solutions to
the problem of illegitimacy — keeping it in the
family — had its drawbacks. It was unusual to
attempt it without pretending the baby in question belonged to someone else, or its mother was
really its sister, or its parents were in fact married
but the father had died or disappeared or something. Complete honesty required a degree of
defiance, courage or obstinacy on the part of the

unmarried mother's (or father's) parents in an age when social deviance of any kind invited relentless gossip. Welcoming an apparently wayward daughter and her child into the bosom of the family, expecting everyone to accept the situation without demur, was a brave — perhaps naive — thing to do. But the alternative was hardly straightforward, even if it did spare blushes. Disguising the child's true relationship required virtuosic levels of obfuscation and denial, especially if the child itself was to be duped along with everyone else.

Felicity's story proves just how complicated it could be to keep the facts hidden. Masquerade was supposed to make illegitimacy disappear, to hide it in plain sight; in Felicity's case, it muddied the waters so much that the family is still trying to discern the truth through all the murk. Felicity is in her mid-eighties, and only found out that she was illegitimate a few years ago. She has been piecing her history together, fragment by fragment, ever since. Her mother, Maggie, married a Catholic in 1919. The husband abandoned Maggie and their young son soon afterwards, and in 1928 Maggie met someone else, a commercial traveller from the other end of the country, and conceived twins. When panicked attempts at abortion failed, she was persuaded by her family to chase the man down and invite him to sort out the problem, somehow, himself. So, heavily pregnant, Maggie made the arduous journey to his place of work by the seaside, where shortly after her arrival, she gave birth.

Felicity is uncertain what happened next: presumably, one of the twins died. She has a photograph of her birth-parents sitting on a beach and holding a baby she assumes to be herself. She knows her mother left without her while she was still a baby. Her half-brother was at a Catholic boarding-school by now, and to pay his fees, Maggie needed to return to work as soon as she could. Unable to get a divorce from her husband, she set up home with Mr Commercial Traveller in London while Felicity spent the first five years of her life secreted somewhere far away. She has no memory of where that might have been, or in what circumstances.

Eventually, Felicity was redeemed and brought to London to live with her father's unmarried sister and paternal grandfather. She remembers her father visiting occasionally, but never her mother. After two years of this, she moved in with her parents at the age of seven. Her half-brother had left school by now (which would surely have been necessary earlier if his mother's secret had got out), so Maggie was free to leave work and look after Felicity.

The girl was desperately unhappy, and tried to escape from her parents and return to her aunt and grandfather's house, where she sensed she had been loved. The atmosphere at home was awful; Mr Commercial Traveller resented Maggie's close relationship with her son (who lived with them after leaving school) and constant rows resulted in the young man finally being banished to Maggie's sister's, a mile or so away.

Felicity was frightened of her father, who was considerably older than her mother and had strict Victorian views on the control of children, involving corporal punishment and the rigid maintenance of a stiff upper lip. Felicity had much to cope with: she missed weeks of primary school through contracting pneumonia two years in a row; she spent a long, lonely convalescence in a sanatorium, and when she returned, was frequently dispatched to amuse herself in the local park. Playing on the swings one day she managed to fracture her skull, which led to more time away from school, and further isolation.

She passed her 11+ and looked forward to grammar school, but in 1939 her half-brother was killed in an accident on army manoeuvres, which changed everything. Felicity remembers Maggie embracing her and saying, 'Now you are all I've got.' Felicity felt glad he was dead, because now she would have an exclusive mother of her own. They became closer than they had ever been, renewing her father's jealousy.

When she was nineteen, Felicity was asked to Paris with a girlfriend and her family, and excitedly applied for her first passport. To her astonishment, on her birth certificate she found not her father's name, but the name of Maggie's first husband. What did this mean? Maggie uncomfortably explained that she must have got flustered because Felicity had arrived in such a hurry, and only slipped up with the name because she couldn't think straight at the time. Felicity's father had to travel to the place of registration to sign an affidavit that *he* was her real parent, but the name on the certificate remains unchanged to this day. Once a birth is registered, it's registered, and that's that. Only an adoption order will supersede the original document.

Felicity married in her twenties, and though her possessive father refused to give his approval or his blessing — predicting a brief and disastrous marriage — the couple have now been together for over sixty years. What Felicity did not realize until recently is that her parents' wedding was only two years before hers. Maggie's first husband had eventually obtained a dispensation to marry again, which freed Maggie to do the same.

Felicity's parents never told her any of this. When she was in her seventies, an elderly aunt broke silence and revealed to her that not only was she illegitimate, but she had spent the first five years of her life hidden away from her family; her parents had lived 'in sin' for much of their lives, and she herself had been shielded — or barred — from the truth by concerted complicity. The happiness of her own married life outweighs the unhappiness of her youth, she says, but she cannot help feeling restless and confused by it all.

It did not have to be like this, of course. Nancy A's parents got together in the 1930s after her mother was widowed and her father had abandoned an unhappy marriage. They had five children together, all of whom knew that they were bastards: their school-friends kindly informed them of the fact, without prejudice. In fact the only prejudice Nancy can remember came from the local ladies of the Methodist Church 'who looked down on us from a great height'. There were no secrets; the family worked hard, struggled sometimes but stayed together, and ultimately did well. 'I wouldn't marry you if you were the last man on earth', Nancy's mum used to say to her dad. Nancy has no doubt she meant it, but it raised a smile.

There are other single parents in this book who cared little what society thought of them. Heidi was the woman who kept falling over molehills and consigning child after illegitimate child to the care of Suzanna, her eldest daughter (and then to Suzanna's sister when Suzanna left home). She was brazen, but at least she kept her family together. Mistresses of married men did the best they could, accepting the limitations of their circumstances but often choosing to bring up their children with as close a relationship as possible with the birth-father. Countless single mothers returned home from mother-and-baby units to a close and loving family, where their children flourished in the knowledge that they were wanted, much loved and a source of great pride.

As the free-spirited sixties began to offer alternatives to conventional morality, characters like Margot began to catch the attention of social commentators. Margot did not particularly want a husband; only a baby. In 1967 she was a successful artist in her early forties who publicly stated her intention to have a child, 'anybody's child', before it was too late. It might not be an uncommon ambition nowadays, but in the 1960s it was shocking for a single woman to articulate the need for a baby, and her determination to conceive. Margot had the money, the time and the desire to be a mother; she just lacked the necessary mechanics. She was trying to find an obliging father, but it was difficult.

One journalist, reporting Margot's mission, believed the problem Margot shared with other solvent, independent and mature women was caused by the conflicting expectations of a newly permissive society.

This is a little-known aspect of our free-living, free-loving society — the women who begin as gay 'bachelor girls' and later find themselves condemned to childlessness because they practised contraception all too well. Unmarried motherhood in these circumstances can be a last, desperate plunge by a woman for whom sexual emancipation turned sour.

Even though she is an artist, there is no suggestion that Margot is a hippy; if she were, according to the popular press, she would hardly have needed to worry about finding a partner. In communes, hippies shared motherhood and fatherhood around, just like wacky baccy and brown rice. Illegitimacy was the norm for them, and therefore irrelevant. For a while, permissiveness ran parallel with conventionality, and it was not until the 1980s, when the term 'illegitimate' was itself made illegitimate, that single-parent families who did not even have the decency to hide their shame were widely accepted with equanimity.

Natalie was an eighteen-year-old student when she conceived her son in 1967, the same year the papers were discussing the likes of Margot. Natalie's widowed mother supported her, but forbade a hasty shotgun marriage to the baby's father, who was only nineteen. Natalie lived with her mother, who cared for the baby while Natalie worked, and though she and her boyfriend split up a year or so later, Natalie was content. She could not envisage marrying (in common with many single mothers reluctant to impose an 'unnatural' father on their child, or vice-versa), but when her son was six, his father got in touch again out of the blue, and three months later, they were wed. When Natalie contacted me, they were about to celebrate their ruby wedding. That is about as neat a solution to illegitimacy as you might find.

The majority of single mothers went on to fall in love with partners other than their child's father, even before the 1970s, when divorce carried almost as marked a stigma as illegitimacy. That much is obvious. It is intriguing how many of them resisted the possibility of constructing a new family unit, however. Celia had Nick in 1944. His father was a soldier who showed no interest in the child, so Celia was left to care for Nick on her own. She put him in a local nursery while she worked for their keep, and when one of the nursery staff offered to adopt him, she refused adamantly. She also refused to marry, just in case her husband might not want the child. This meant a harder life for them both, materially, but it did leave Celia in control.

Perhaps Celia had read this letter, submitted to the problem page of a national newspaper at about the same time as Nick was born.

Do you think it possible for a man — just an average fellow with feelings — to love a child that isn't his own, but given to his wife by another man, a kind of man who isn't a really decent type? Some people think it is inhuman for me — I am the former man — to want the child sent away. Yet I know in time the child would lead a pretty rough life, especially when children of my own would come along. Don't you think it always best to have the child sent away?

The printed answer can be summarized as 'don't be judgemental', which is far easier said than done. The members of the Legitimation League, who believed in 'wedlock without the lock' and hailed as their heroine the feisty Miss Edith Lanchester, locked up by her father for refusing to marry her lover: they weren't judgemental. The trouble is that most people thought their campaign for soluble partnerships rather than marriage was loopy. Eccentrics whose behaviour was somehow condoned by celebrity were not judgemental either. Or, rather, they believed themselves to be beyond judgement. That is why all sorts of fancy aristocrats, intellectuals and artists were forgiven, more or less, for having and keeping their illegitimate children. They were not like the rest of us, so could only be expected to behave differently.

The National Council for the Unmarried Mother and her Child tried always to be open-minded, along with the Salvation Army and Barnardo's. The NCUMC's very first mission statement in 1918 declared an intention to provide single mothers with the physical and emotional support necessary to bring up their (blameless) children in an unapologetic and encouraging way. Increasingly, as time went on, this meant providing hostels and bedsits where childcare was provided either in-house or nearby, and priming the neighbours with judicious propaganda so that as few of them as possible complained. The question of where to live played a critical part in any decision about whether or not it was practical for an unmarried mother to keep her child. In 1964 the NCUMC published a pamphlet describing an ideal housing scheme. It consisted of a group of flats run by housing associations or local authorities, divided into bedsits for wage-earning mothers over the age of seventeen; there would be an on-site creche and a voluntary organizing committee whose members would take it in turns to collect the rent and liaise with the landlords.

Being a remarkably proactive outfit, the NCUMC soon had such a scheme up and running in north London. Ten single-parent families lived in a large white house called 'Hopedene', which had been partitioned into self-contained flatlets with a council-run nursery on the ground floor. This provided a home, full-time childcare, and a ready-made community. Barnardo's opened similar schemes around the country, all heavily oversubscribed. Very gradually, the possibility of finding accommodation like this metamorphosed into an expectation, particularly if the local authority was involved. The year 1967 was designated Human Rights Year; the fight for women's rights was still in full swing; the right to birth-control and abortion was hotly debated, and articles began to emerge in the press about the entitlements of single parents.

'The Right of a Woman to her Own Child', runs a headline on a woman's page that same year. The following feature is on the newly formed 'Mothers in Action' group, the first self-help organization run by, and for the benefit of, single mothers. Its current focus, according to the journalist, is the Maintenance Orders Bill lumbering its way through parliament, which will (if passed) increase the maximum affiliation payment to £5 per week from £2 10s. They are demanding more help with the day-to-day inconveniences of single parenthood, too: child-care in the school holidays, for example; grants towards higher education (for the mothers rather than their children), and equal rights with legitimate children for bastards whose mothers or fathers die intestate. At the minute (in 1967) if a parent dies without making a will, his or her illegitimate child cannot inherit. And if the illegitimate child dies with an estate but no will, its parent, similarly, gets nothing.

The Mothers in Action are all young; their chairman is only nineteen. There is a touching mixture of defiance and vulnerability about their stories. Some of them got pregnant deliberately,

313

believing it their right (that word again) to have a child. I wanted one, so I had one. But others, including the group's secretary — fastidiously noted by the reporter as *Miss* Barbara Ford — saw themselves as victims, due some sort of compensation. 'Nobody with our low incomes would choose to have a baby. They were definitely all accidents,' says Barbara. 'This is not part of the permissive society, it's dealing with the results of that society,' she continues, and recalling *The Millstone*, Margaret Drabble's novel of unmarried parenthood, makes a depressing statement. 'Of course we love our children, but they're millstones round our necks.'

Every parent knows that looking after children of any age can be a worrisome, tedious and lonely business. The responsibility feels overwhelming at times. Sharing the negative moments with family or friends helps, and the Mothers in Action had each other, just as the residents in 'Hopedene' and elsewhere did. But single parenthood is particularly isolating, and one senses an air of resentment in articles like this, that no one told these blithe young women just how hard it would be. The permissive society noisily beat the drum for free love and extravagant sex and following your instincts and choosing your destiny; when you indulged yourself and were faced with the consequences, it sneered at you.

★ ★ ★

It is difficult to grasp just how much prejudice was directed at unmarried mothers and their

314

children in the past. You have to imagine it whispering away in the background of this entire book, louder in some places than others, louder at some times than others, but always there. The Windrush generation of immigrants to Britain from the Caribbean were used to notices on landlords' doors stating 'No Blacks, No Irish, No Dogs'. The signs might as well have read 'No Whores, No Bastards' too. Any whiff of immorality brought a neighbourhood down. Having a single mother next door cheapened the area, unless you lived in the back streets of Tiger Bay or somewhere (cheap as dirt already) or a fashionably Bohemian quarter of London, where no one cared. Nice children did not play with bastards. Respectable housewives did not consort with tarts.

Jill was desperate for a home of her own, even though her parents were willing to take her in with her daughter. The baby's adoptive parents had been all lined up, but just as the hand-over was about to take place at six weeks old, Jill found she could not go through with it. She made new plans. The intention was to spend a maximum of six months in the family home, living on benefits (this was 1968), before finding a flat, a nursery place, and a job. Jill felt the benefit system was demeaning. Every so often she was required to attend the local Social Security office 'when they would grill me for details of the father'. Officers staged home visits too; when a female came she would usually make a fuss and coo over Jill's daughter, but the male officer would simply demand to know where the baby was. It was obvious he was only there to check that Jill was not trying to diddle the state by falsely claiming to be responsible for a child.

A council nursery place materialized first, and was offered to Jill on the condition that she worked full-time. But it took a whole three years to find somewhere to live. Because she was living in her parents' house she was not given any sort of priority, and private landlords seemed not to want to touch her with a barge-pole.

Finally she found a one-bedroom flat in a basement, but the landlord only agreed to let Jill and her daughter live there if it was rented by her father, even though she was over twenty-one. The flat was so damp Jill once had to wear wellington boots in the kitchen, but she was not able to move into a two-bedroom property until her daughter was thirteen.

The ever-resourceful NCUMC suggested a strategy to combat this deeply entrenched distrust of single mothers. Ever since it was founded, society had accepted the war widow and her children with equanimity: she was a single mother too, but her story was more about honour than dishonour. While not quite admitting that it might be a good idea for unmarried mothers to pretend their fictitious husbands had also been killed (a common enough tactic), the NCUMC advised them to apply for the sort of job traditionally occupied by the indigent widows of Britain's fallen heroes in both wars: as live-in home-helps, perhaps, or housekeepers. This is an extract from a 1950s publicity piece for the Council:

[T]here must be households in which the unmarried mother of the better type and her child could be welcomed, and even become assets. Households with young children of their own, for example, where there is either no man, or the man is a great deal away — a husband in the Services, perhaps, or in the Merchant Navy. There, the child becomes one of a proper family, while the fact of having another woman in the home means that the housewife has someone to baby-sit and help with chores, besides contributing to the budget. Possibly the notion persists that a girl who has 'gone wrong' must be coarse and domestically a slut. But the council would take care to ensure that anyone recommended as a house-sharer is also a desirable companion.

Many unmarried mothers were only able to keep their children with them because of jobs exactly like this one. If they could not or would not accept help from their own parents, the obvious solution was to find work with accommodation and the possibility of childcare. Jenny grew up in a 'toddlers' home' where her mother was on the staff. Sandra's mum found a position as nanny, where she could look after Sandra at the same time as her professional charges. It was a bittersweet time: when Sandra learned to talk, her first word was 'Dad-Dad'; she had heard the other children saying it, but sadly didn't realize what a 'Dad-Dad' was.

Victoria's family would have helped her if

necessary, but when she had her daughter in 1965 she was determined to manage on her own. She did agree to change her name to that of the baby's father (and the baby) by deed poll, and wore a wedding-ring; otherwise she aimed to be entirely independent. She had trained as a midwife, but found it almost impossible to return to such a demanding career immediately after the birth, so replied to a classified ad for a 'domestic'. Her arrival sounds like something out of *Jane Eyre*.

'Tracked down through *The Lady* magazine, we went to housekeep for a divorced, middle-aged businessman whose two children were at boarding school, but expected home for the holidays. He was a kind, somewhat remote man, fed up of returning home after dark to subsist on a boiled egg. The house was large and rambling and we arrived to find that we had been allocated a cold, unwelcoming wing bedroom, where the bed had not even been made . . .

'I hadn't bargained for my employer's wife. Somehow I had received the impression that she was living in London. Not a bit of it. She inhabited a flat above his office in the nearby town. Maybe she became jealous, because she started visiting the house and criticising my arrangements. Eventually I answered back, rather roundly [*not* very *Jane Eyre*] after which I was sacked for being rude.'

The next stop for Victoria and her daughter was a mother-and-baby home, where she was appointed deputy matron; eventually she found a cottage to rent from another single parent and was able to return, part-time, to nursing. Not everyone had the luxury of a job, however. Christine's mother was too busy at home to find work outside. Christine was born in 1945, the eldest of six illegitimate children, none of whom was ever told who its father was. Christine does not even know how many — if any — of her siblings is a full-blood brother or sister. She remembers their neighbours falling into two distinct camps: the embarrassingly kind, who showered the family with sad smiles and cast-offs; and the stand-offish, who forbade their children to play with Christine because she 'didn't have a dad'.

It is the poverty that Christine remembers more than the prejudice. Poverty was hardly the exclusive province of single-parent families, but Christine feels the two were inextricably intertwined, and that the family's lack of funds was exacerbated by the shame and false pride surrounding her illegitimacy. Children at her primary school were asked to bring in sixpence to contribute to certificates for the annual sports day. When Christine told her teacher that her mother hadn't given her the money, he made her stand on a chair for the rest of the lesson as an example of someone who chose not to contribute to the school community. Another, more sensitive teacher found her on a wet day trying to dry her sodden socks on a radiator. Instead of scolding her, he kept her back after the lesson and helped to cut some cardboard insoles to put inside her useless shoes.

When a Christmas trip was organized to a

local theatre, the cost was a mighty three shillings. Christine did not even bother asking her mother for it this time. She used her own savings, carefully mustered from hard-won 'pennies for the Guy'. When her mother found out, she blamed Christine for selfishly having spent the money on herself instead of on Christmas presents for other people.

At least (we can say, to comfort ourselves) these children were wanted. They may have been temporary 'mistakes', but their mothers, or occasionally fathers, or even more rarely *both*, could not let them go once they had arrived. Patricia's father was a Canadian soldier who tried to send for the girl when he got back to Canada, but her mother would have none of it. She cocooned Patricia in the heart of her family — three uncles, two aunts, and one set of grandparents — and Patricia was the apple of all their eyes, the centre of their lives. No one was going to take her away — especially not to Canada, which was (according to her grandfather) altogether too cold for any child. A more extreme example of emotional tug-of-war involved an English widow living in the United States around the time of the First World War. Very unusually at that time, she had two illegitimate children by a black father, a married bricklayer twenty years her senior, who had known her late husband.

The first child was born after the father had visited the newly widowed woman to console her, and to help with odd jobs around the home. She conceived the second when he comforted her over the shame of bearing a half-caste bastard. When he realized that the younger one was on the way, the father made a bargain with her. He offered to take the baby for $100 and induce his (black) wife to adopt it as a foundling. He duly appeared at the door with a blanket soon after the birth, but the widow could not bring herself to hand over the baby, even to its father, whom she loved.

The father tried again — and again — and after a few more strange disappearances and reappearances with an empty blanket and a dismal expression, his wife grew suspicious. She tracked the widow down, and generously began visiting her, realizing that she had two illegitimate children, but not, at this stage, that they were her own husband's. When this eventually became clear, she volunteered to take both children into her home, to live with her and their father. For some reason the widow agreed, thus losing her lover and two of her children at a stroke.

★   ★   ★

Keeping an illegitimate child in the family was rarely achieved without compromise. Countless shotgun weddings attest to this. Jean was told by her parents that she could only hold on to her baby if she agreed to marry the family lodger, twenty-two years her senior. He had nothing to do with the baby at all, but was happy to fall in with the plan. Perhaps he was paid by Jean's parents to do so: stranger things have happened. Another young mother was allowed to bring her son back from the mother-and-baby home, but not to the house where she and her parents had lived before. Her father resigned his ultra-respectable job in the police force first, and moved the family to another part of the country, so that no one would know their shameful secret. Everyone *did* know, of course, or guessed, and 'cut' their new neighbours whenever they were out with the baby. This young mother must have found the responsibility of shouldering her whole family's disillusionment hard to bear.

Evelyn was kept a virtual prisoner in her own home after she had her baby in 1961. Her parents treated her horribly, and it makes her angry now that mothers who let their illegitimate children go for adoption are so often cast as victims. 'No one was forced to give their baby up. This is a story put about by mothers who opted for an easy life . . . ' She hates 'those sanctimonious programmes' where the mother sobs because she lost her child at birth. She didn't always have to, insists Evelyn, embittered by the cruelty of her own parents and her struggle to bring up the child.

There must have been times when Evelyn questioned her determination to keep the baby. She was not alone in this. It can't be easy to admit it, but sometimes mothers do voice regrets, and feel resentment against those 'do-gooders' (like the NCUMC) who encouraged them to steer away from adoption.

If I hadn't kept the child I'd have been all right. I could have gone off somewhere, found a decent job in a factory and made a go of things. It was the worst decision of my life. People tell you to keep your baby — I'd have a thing or two to say to them if I had the nerve.

Often it was the child who suffered most in the emotional fallout. In the time-honoured tradition of fairy-stories all over the world, the wicked stepmother or stepfather figures heavily in tales of family woe. Perhaps the birth-parents were forced to marry by their own parents; then the relationship broke down, there was a divorce (or just a separation) and another partner arrived. He or she either wanted to clear the nest before moving in, or resented the child and picked on it mercilessly. A bastard was easier to victimize than the legitimate child of a former marriage, being perceived as morally tainted and inherently inferior in all sorts of ways. Bullying step-parents — or insecure ones — found them gratifyingly easy prey. I cannot bring myself to relate all the awful histories I have heard on this subject. Ella's story can speak for the others, who all — still — need sympathy, understanding and in a number of cases, professional help to come to terms with the way they were treated decades ago by their nearest and, supposedly, their dearest.

'My birth in 1932 took place in a home for unmarried mothers. My mother was thirty-five years old, penniless, and had previously been in service to 'the Gentry'. I was fostered by a couple with a twelve-year-old son. I was loved and happy. All this changed when mum became pregnant with twin girls and she married a herdsman. One twin was stillborn and the other lived for only a few weeks. My half-sister was born in 1937, was adored by both parents and spoilt. I returned to live with them when I was five years old, after much upset with my foster-family.

'My stepfather hated me and never failed to take his thick leather-buckled trouser belt and strike me if I displeased him or I upset Dorothy, my sister. Mother was afraid of him and went by the belief that a man was never wrong, ever, solely because he was a man. Ernest, my step-father, died in 1939. When mother said, 'I now have to wear black,' I answered quite unkindly, 'Good.' Neighbours said if he hadn't died, it would have been me.

'Mother remained depressed for years, and went out to work cleaning in the evenings. We children were looked after by an over-religious neighbour, who also took me to Sunday-school on Sunday mornings, the 11 a.m. church service and Sunday-school again in the afternoons, but not so my sister. Mum lived only to go to church in the evening, and her promise to Ernest to look after Dorothy never wavered.

'Life was better when we had London evacuees billeted with us. I was not so discriminated against. When Dorothy's grand-father and her blood relatives visited us, I was always told before they arrived that they were 'nothing to do with you', and I had to stand behind my sister. One of the aunts who lived in Surrey used to invite me to go to stay with her, which I did. She treated me with love!

'My godmother's son once called at my home with my birthday present — a large tin of Blue-Bird assorted toffees — and collected me to spend the weekend at his parents' home. Upon my return, I dashed to my tin of sweets to find just one toffee in it! Mother and Dorothy had eaten the lot with mum saying to me, 'You can't have everything . . . '

'I was quite bright at school and became head girl, but due to financial problems I was unable to attend high school despite passing all the necessary exams and mother sent me to work at fourteen in a factory time-and-wages office. I earned £1 1s a week and I was given my own ration-book and told to look after myself. I had to cook and clean for us three after work and at weekends, whilst Dorothy sat in the bedroom doing her homework. She attended high school but did not achieve good grades at all and went on to teachers' training college. Mother worked herself to the bone to pay for her . . .

'When, at fifteen years, I asked mum who my father was, she replied, 'It's nothing to do with you,' and refused to tell me. It was believed that I could have been conceived when mother was in service to the titled household she worked for.'

Ella concludes her story with a simple sentence: 'It's been difficult to write this.'

It is difficult to read, too; so are the memories illegitimate people have shared of sexual abuse, neglect, physical and emotional deprivation and the deliberate, damaging withholding of identity. All these things can overshadow an entire lifetime, and leach a dark stain of guilt into the fabric of the family for generations.

To try to avoid the stigma and practical problems associated with bastardy, it was natural to pretend that everything at home was normal. A little complicated, perhaps, but absolutely normal. This involved a conspiracy of silence or artifice. The most common scenario was the one already mentioned, whereby a child was brought up in ignorance of the fact that its mother was really the person it thought of as its sister or an aunt. The dissimulation could last well into adulthood, only to be revealed when a full birth certificate was required for something or an indiscreet relative said too much. The current passion for genealogy and the filling-in of gaps on the family tree has betrayed many a secret like this, surprisingly close to home.

I know several people — I'm sure everyone does — who are trying to unravel the tangled skeins of family relationships by way of painstaking research into records and census forms. Illegitimate sons and daughters have a harder task than most, baffled by the impossible assertions of their birth-mothers or fathers, by the blatant changing of dates and places, or by the intransigence of those keepers of the family secret who are still alive. Until relatively recently, whenever someone registered the death of a parent it was common for the registrar to enquire politely whether they would like to be acknowledged on the certificate as 'son' or 'daughter', or merely as 'informant'. The latter would mask the true relationship to future researchers. Wrong names were habitually volunteered for birth or marriage certificates, lies were written on to the fly-leaves of family Bibles, and fictions created and perpetuated to deny the truth. There is so much more to family history than meets the eye.

The shock of realizing you are not who you thought you were — as far as illegitimacy is concerned — can be accommodated in time, though not without a certain stirring of the deepest emotions we possess. But Frances, for example, never got over it. When her sister died in 1969, her widowed brother-in-law revealed that she had not been her sister at all, but her mother. Frances was born when she was eighteen, and was slotted in as the youngest of several siblings, none of whom knew that they were really Frances's aunts and uncles rather than brothers and sisters.

Frances was fifty when the secret was spilled, and the news appalled her. She had always been brought up to believe that illegitimacy was a terrible sin (a defence mechanism common among families harbouring their own illegitimate child) and that it carried the worst possible stigma. She had felt especially close to that particular 'sister' and was stunned at being deceived by her all her life.

The effects of the masquerade were, and are, profound. Frances had a half-sister from her mother's marriage who died at eighteen months, of whom Frances never really took much notice. Frances's children had a granny they were never able to acknowledge as such. Frances spent the rest of her life, after discovering the secret, convinced that she was somehow fraudulent, not good enough for her husband or her children, her grandchildren or her great-grandchildren. Her daughter says she was never the same again.

Charlotte was always aware of what she calls a question-mark over her childhood, but did not discover why until she was twelve. She found a bundle of letters squirrelled away in an old suitcase, telling the story of her mother's stay in a maternity home, her own birth, and the identity (with a photograph) of her father. He was *obviously* her father: she looked far more like him than like the man who was married to her mother.

In an inversion of the usual pattern, Charlotte never told her mother that she had discovered the family secret — that she *was* the family secret. She knew her mother was easily upset, especially when discussing her childhood, and hated it when she was mysteriously forbidden to play with certain children by their mothers, or stared at in the street. Now, of course, it was a mystery no longer: Charlotte knew herself to be illegitimate. She quietly replaced the letters, put the suitcase back in the bedroom cupboard in which she had found it (not wanting to admit to having been snooping), and waited.

When Charlotte was sixteen, she and her mother were out shopping when someone approached them and started chatting. Charlotte's mother looked agitated, and introduced him to Charlotte as 'my friend from some time ago'. Charlotte knew exactly who he was: she recognized the man in the photograph. This 'friend' was her father. A week or so later, Charlotte's mother told her the truth — or edited highlights of it — which Charlotte greeted with suitable shock. Because her mother was so obviously upset, Charlotte never asked any further questions.

Her mother died of cancer. She confessed to Charlotte that the disease was her punishment. Apparently no one in the family had ever met Charlotte's birth-father, and after the initial hoo-ha, he was never mentioned. When her adoptive father died (having formally adopted Charlotte when he married her mother) she found nothing in his papers but her adoption order. The suitcase in the cupboard was empty.

Charlotte only found the courage to tell her own husband about her illegitimacy shortly before their wedding; she told her children when they were grown up, and still finds it hard to contemplate. 'These memories lie deep,' she told me, 'but never forgotten.'

         *   *   *

If Charlotte's mother had chosen not to get married, she could have adopted Charlotte herself. It seems a bizarre notion, for a birth-mother to adopt her own child, but for many years this was the only way a single parent could erase legally (if not culturally) the stigma of illegitimacy. Adoption conferred irrevocable rights, including the right to inherit. Instead of a birth certificate with a dismissive line in the 'Name of Father' space, the child was given a perfectly legitimate adoption order to produce without embarrassment whenever the occasion arose. Adoption offered legal endorsement to those independent women determined to raise a child on their own. It also completely shut the birth-father out of anything to do with his child unless the mother desired contact. This last point was unsuccessfully contested by a number of birth-fathers in court during the 1960s, and is probably what stopped the NCUMC from wholeheartedly advocating sole-parent adoption to its female clients, although it did recommend it as a way of avoiding many of the pitfalls of illegitimacy. The process worked both ways, of course: birth-fathers could adopt on their own, as well as birth-mothers. However, it was exceptional for them to do so. Obviously society was not quite ready to eliminate birth-mothers from the business of bringing up a child. That would be unnatural.

A fervid supporter of single-parent adoption was one Montague Chandler, who found himself in the High Court in London in 1967, accusing his birth-mother of breach of promise. She was unmarried when he was born, a seventeen-year-old dressmaker who could not cope with the prospect of bringing up a child. Montague was sent to a children's home and then migrated to Canada at the age of nine. When he became an adult at twenty-one, he was given his family history. Curious about his roots, he returned to England in 1933 and managed to trace his maternal grandfather. Grandpa greeted Montague with the news that his mother had died, but soon after this revelation, on a trip to a Lyons tea room in London, Grandpa orchestrated a meeting with a smartly dressed woman who approached their table and announced that Montague was her son. She wasn't dead, but a different person from the girl who had given him birth, with a new, untainted life. He remembered their rather surreal conversation perfectly. It was succinct: 'Monty, I am very pleased to see you,' she said. 'I am very happily married. Will you promise never to come near me?'

The reward for keeping himself secret, according to Monty, was the promise of a £36,000 legacy on his mother's death. The average wage at the time was about £188 per annum, so this was an unimaginably vast amount of money. Monty agreed, and duly disappeared. In 1964 his mother died — and left him nothing. Her secret was a double-bluff. Because he was illegitimate, he had no right to make a claim, hence the court case. The matter was eventually settled ex gratia, but Monty only ever received £250. In consequence, he vowed to devote his energies to a crusade to prevent other illegitimate children falling into the same trap as he had done.

Poor Monty seems to have had a rough deal all round. His story sounds like the product of a popular murder-mystery-writer's imagination — except that the mother wasn't murdered in the end — and there is no trace of his crusade. But two years after the case was brought, in 1969, the Family Law Reform Act finally allowed illegitimate children to inherit from intestate birth-parents. Little by little, the bastard was being rehabilitated into society. It's a pity it came too late for Monty.

12

Bad Blood: Attitudes to Single Parents

*I've had to live with it all my life. It just
smacks my face all the time.*

The quotation above is from Jessie, aged eighty,
being interviewed in the 1970s. She had two
illegitimate sons while she was a mill-worker in
West Yorkshire; one born in 1913 and the other
five years later, just before the Armistice. Even
though both the boys were gathered into her
numerous family — she kept her blood under
the same roof, as the saying goes — she never
forgot the shame of their illegitimacy. Her voice
on the tape is soft: 'I can't get the words out,' she
apologizes. 'Maybe that's why I've been ill all my
life.' The knowledge that she was the mother of
bastards weighed her down. Occasionally she
forgot it, but it hit her again and again, and it
confused her. 'People think you're bad if you've
had illegitimate children, but I wasn't.' Yet how
can she have been otherwise, according to the
mores of her time, to fall so far, and *twice?* In the
fifth century BC the tragedian Euripides wrote:

> How true it is that noble children spring
> from noble sires
> And evil blood engenders but its like.

332

Two-and-a-half thousand years later people were still talking about the concept of bad blood, of there being an inherent defect in the moral and mental faculties of bastards and their mothers. According to a pamphlet published in 1895, 'The children of immoral parents are no less to be shunned and suspected than the children of diseased, deranged, drunken or low-caste parents.' Jessie certainly believed it.

Had she been allowed to, Jessie might have accepted what she perceived to be her guilt, accommodated it somehow, and moved on. The problem was that for many single parents like her, illegitimacy was not a private matter. They were surrounded by God's police, self-appointed: people who considered it their duty to make sure transgressors never forgot their mistakes, and never ceased paying for them. The wages of sin is shame and no one should be allowed to default.

I have already written about society's attitude to illegitimacy, and about the legal status of bastards. This chapter concerns the *personal* experiences of unmarried parents: how they were treated by friends or family as individuals, and how they treated themselves. The discrimination encountered by many of them beggars belief. On a practical level, it could range from being spat at in the street and verbally abused, to abandonment by the family or committal to a mental institution. An Irish girl sent to a Magdalene home on giving birth in 1940 was returned to her father once the child had been adopted. He refused to take her in: 'You've disgraced us,' he shrieked at her. 'You're not right in the head. You can't be right in your head and bring a child into this world, and you deserve punishment.'

Sarah, another young mother, had all the support she needed from her family when she brought her daughter back from the mother-and-baby home in 1963. She was a confident young woman who defiantly refused to be victimized. Yet even she was cowed by some of the prejudice she met in the course of trying to bring up her daughter independently. Her first job after the birth was in a civil service post. It was in the town where she had gone to grammar school, so inevitably the secret got out. After that, the atmosphere at work was intolerable. The men in the office were particularly judgemental. Her next employers, in London, forbade women of childbearing age to apply for the six-month stint abroad to which all their male counterparts were entitled. What were the bosses afraid of? That their female employees would immediately lose their heads and messily fall pregnant? Sarah did not feel herself to be in a strong enough position to argue that one. But she did resign her post, and went into primary-school teaching instead.

Soon she was earning enough to think of renting a little flat for herself and her daughter. On one memorable visit to an estate agent, an old gentleman bumbled out of the office and, after Sarah explained that she was a single parent, asked what she did for a living. 'I'm a teacher,' she told him. 'And what *else* do you do for a living?' he leered. Sarah left. When she was eventually able to find a place of her own, she went along to the local electrical shop to hire a television. The TV man asked outright if she was married, and when she informed him that she was not, told her to go elsewhere. This was in the early 1970s.

Rather than grinding her down like Jessie, Sarah found attitudes like this flicked switches in her that have powered the rest of her life. Bravado is a transferable skill, and in a world of nudges and winks and cheap jibes, what fails to floor you can indeed make you stronger. It is peculiarly insulting to have your sexual habits called into question, however. About a year after her daughter was born in 1968, Jill was invited to the pub for a drink by a mum at nursery. When they got there, it became obvious that the mum was meeting a boyfriend, and had arranged for Jill — her cover — to be driven home by another man. That was fine, and Jill arranged to see him again for a drink. This time, on the way home he unexpectedly drove to an industrial estate and raped Jill. She was naturally terrified, believing that he would kill her if she resisted and fearing she would never see her daughter again.

When the man realized how upset she was, he apologized to Jill and explained that he had thought it would be all right, since she already had a baby. What she still finds difficult to understand is that when they got back to her parents' house after this episode, he asked to see her again — and she almost agreed. That's how lonely she was, and how sorely lacking in self-esteem. She was worried that she might be pregnant again and would have to take him to court. She could not possibly afford to bring up two children on her own, and was well aware that no one would believe it was rape. Given the reported reaction of the judge in a case involving a single mother in the 1930s — that 'such women are filled with animal passion' — she was probably right.

Members of one's own family could be just as cruel as outsiders, if not more so. In the worst cases, single parents found themselves playing piggy-in-the-middle, trapped between the twin resentments of their parents and their children. Unmarried mothers anxious to shut a door on the past were told they must keep the baby as a punishment, so that every day, as life got harder and harder, they would be reminded of how wicked they had been. It was the job of everyone else in the family to make sure life *did* get harder and harder. So they were not allowed out, relegated to being skivvies, emotionally and perhaps physically abused, or laden with all the family's flotsam of discontent and bitterness. If ordered to send the baby for adoption against their wishes or their instincts, they were taunted about it for years. Their siblings blamed them for tainting their own reputation by association. Martha says her sister still refuses to speak to her, decades later, because of the shame when Martha brought her bastard baby home. Unmarried mothers were trouble; they disrupted family relationships and embedded a fat, dirty, unbidden secret into everyone's lives.

Their children were embarrassed by them, or blamed them for what one illegitimate adult called 'a life full of tensions and cross purposes'.

Em did not love her mother, who blamed Em for spoiling her life. It was as though Em had chosen to be born illegitimately out of spite, and her mother never forgave her. The accusations were mutual: Em always felt her illegitimacy to be a curse deliberately called upon her by her mother. 'At seventy years of age I live with the stigma of illegitimacy. I divorced over twenty years ago. I met an Italian man when working in Italy. My divorce was no problem for him to deal with, nor was the fact I had three adult children. When I said I was illegitimate he was horrified and the romance was immediately severed. I live with my illegitimacy because I have to.'

Alison is the young woman who was date-raped and gave birth to twins, one stillborn and one who died at a few days old. When she eventually summoned the courage to tell the sons and daughter of her subsequent marriage about their illegitimate half-brothers, the daughter and elder son were full of sympathy and sadness for her. The younger son's reaction was devastating. He told his mother she 'must have been a right slag'.

Unmarried mothers were held responsible for uprooting the family tree and poisoning the bloodline. Punishment for this had few limits. In the most extreme circumstances, they lost their lives for it. Atavistic husbands killed their adulterous wives when they discovered they were pregnant by someone else. As any trawl through court records will show, this scenario was common during the years covered by this book, and it can still happen today. Some outcasts

committed suicide when faced with the uncompromising reality of trying to bring up an
illegitimate child with no financial or emotional
support.

One elaborately tragic story I came across
smacks of Thomas Hardy at his gloomiest: it
involves a young nurse called Winifred Rumble
and Gerald Hartnell, a married post office
engineer twenty years her senior. One day in
1928 Gerald's wife received a letter from an
unknown correspondent. Being a dutiful wife,
she handed it to her husband unopened. He read
it, then left the house, ominously taking with him
the revolver he kept in a wardrobe drawer. His
wife had been under the impression that the two
of them were blissfully happy together, until she
discovered what the letter said. It was from a
character called Mr Clow, who was owed money
by Winifred Rumble. Clow's vengeance for
non-payment of debt was to betray the secret of
Winifred's four-year affair with Mr Hartnell.
Clow had once been Nurse Rumble's lover
himself, and may or may not have been the
father of her illegitimate child. It is not clear
whether Hartnell knew she had had a child at all,
and if so, whether he assumed it to be his. The
precise motive for what happened next remains
uncertain.

When Hartnell's secret was revealed by Clow
in the letter, the engineer went straight to Nurse
Rumble's house and shot her, before turning his
gun on himself. Everything came out in court:
the secret love-child, the passionate letters
Hartnell wrote to Winifred, her belief that

Hartnell was divorced and planned to marry her the following year, and her parents' complete ignorance of what had been going on in her turbulent life. The only person left untouched by the proceedings was the child. Hardy would have thought of some suitably fateful twist to the tale; in reality, it had probably been adopted long ago, and its past buried in nice, safe anonymity.

We have no way of knowing whether Nurse Rumble ever felt contrite about her illegitimate child. Whether she should have done is another question. There is evidence that she tried to get several different putative fathers to cough up affiliation payments for it, including Mr Clow, and that she lived in fear of the birth being discovered by her apparently respectable family. Perhaps she felt more fear than guilt. It was guilt that drove many birth-parents to punish themselves for their 'mistakes'. Even if other people in their lives were forgiving, they found it impossible to forgive themselves. Nellie lived in a retirement home, and was regularly visited by a woman who was obviously fond of her. But Nellie could not confess to the other residents that this woman was in fact her illegitimate daughter: as well as being scared of disapproval, she felt she did not deserve the pleasure and pride that acknowledgement would bring. Joe had two illegitimate sons in her youth, yet feels she has never been a proper mum. They were both adopted and now I get the impression that Joe forfeited her ability to love and be loved when they went. Another woman was so afraid of her son's father, and so despairing of her reliance on him, that she took their child to the police and begged them to give him to Barnardo's, so that she could go and drown herself in peace.

All this is depressing stuff, but it is important to realize how grim the reality of illegitimacy could be for birth-parents. Some mothers and fathers forbade themselves from having more children, even legitimate ones. Others transferred their sense of guilt to their children (while never really losing it themselves). 'It's made me very hard,' I was told by a married lady who had had a child out of wedlock. 'I don't seem to have any feelings.'

A peculiar corner of hell is reserved for those mothers whose illegitimate children are disabled in some way, possibly because of the botched attempts at abortion made during pregnancy. Their upbringing becomes even more closely associated with penance, and their difficulties a constant reminder of what a disapproving lawyer in the Rumble — Hartnell case called 'unbridled illicit intercourse'. There is, as ever, another side to the story. Sarah's experiences moulded her into the feminist she is today. Feisty Heidi never apologized to or for her several illegitimate children, nor ever blamed herself. You might remember Maud, the suffragist who moved in with Fred, built up a business with him, had children by him but chose not to marry him: she lived life on her own terms, was confident enough not to care what others thought, and was happy.

Douglas's mother was a mistress of reinvention. She gave birth to him shortly after the

Second World War, and though Douglas's father was available for maintenance payments, she chose to cope alone. The father was already married with legitimate children of his own; she did not want to deprive them in any way — or perhaps she was too proud. She moved in with her parents while training to become a teacher; changed her name to the one Douglas shared with his father, and launched herself on a distinguished career (culminating in a headship) as a thoroughly respectable widow. She would never have succeeded professionally had the truth come out, and Douglas himself was only told of his illegitimacy on his engagement. He admires his mother; she was intelligent, beautiful and formidable. She knew her own worth, and never felt herself compromised in any way; nor did Douglas, who grew up secure and confident of his place in the world. If feminism means self-determination, then his mother was surely a feminist.

Ingrid's reaction to her dysfunctional childhood is a little surprising. She also maintains that her mother was a feminist, who made a political statement through suffering. Ingrid was born in 1941 after a liaison between her mother and a Canadian soldier in the Medical Corps. He was eighteen, five years younger than Ingrid's mother. Though he offered to get married, his mother in Canada and the army padre dissuaded him, and he disappeared from Ingrid's life for over forty years. In 1945 her mother married a widower, and they had a daughter together. Ingrid was treated atrociously by her stepfather.

He abused her 'in every possible way', so that she used to stay out at night-time and hide in the wash-house (with her feet in a copper kettle to keep them warm) or in the woodshed, rather than come home.

Her mother scolded Ingrid for her sullen silences and for appearing to resent the marriage so much — until she found out about the abuse. Then, remembers Ingrid, she disappeared to the allotment and 'dug and dug for days' so that no one would see how distressed she was. 'She could see then why I had such a chip on my shoulder but I question whether she did anything about it. I fear not.'

Ingrid has blocked out much of her childhood, and went on to become an inspirational mother herself. If her illegitimacy cheapened her somehow, that does not worry her now. In fact she sees her mother's 'woundedness', occasioned by Ingrid's illegitimacy, as something of a virtue, and her determination to hang on to her daughter, come what may, as a sacrifice to the feminist cause. Whether or not she inherited it from her mother, Ingrid has a generous spirit.

So does John, a former child migrant. John has no recollection of his birth-mother; he was a Barnardo's boy, fostered by a family in the Cotswolds before being sent to a Fairbridge farm school in Australia at nine years old. Shortly before his sixteenth birthday, he came in from working in the fields to find a letter on his bed. It had an English postmark, and turned out to be from the person he learned to call his 'maternal mother'. John was staggered to think that not only was his birth-mother still alive, but that she obviously knew where he was, and wanted to make contact with him. Why had she not been in touch before? Why had she relinquished him in the first place? He went to the principal of the school for advice, and was warned to keep his distance. Maybe his mother wanted money out of him, now that he was almost an adult.

After some thought, John wrote back to his mother, and then received from her another, far longer letter telling the tale of their joint history. She was working as a waitress when she met her first boyfriend at the age of twenty in 1914. He was serving in France, but they planned to marry on his next leave. He proved unfaithful to her, however, and married someone else. She found comfort in the arms of an older, more sophisticated gentleman, who she discovered — too late — was already married. By now she was expecting a baby; even though the father offered to pay maintenance, he could not marry her, so she and her illegitimate daughter returned home to live with her parents.

It was not long before she met another man, an accountant, who fathered John. He disappeared as soon as the pregnancy was announced. The next suitor said he wanted to marry John's mother, and moved in with her. But he turned out to be a scoundrel. He stole money from her parents, and after the police were called, he too disappeared. Shortly afterwards, John's younger sister arrived.

So here was a young, unmarried woman with three children by three different partners, only one of whom was maintained by its father. She could not cope. She decided to place John with private foster-parents on the condition that she could see him every night and weekend. This arrangement came to an end when it was discovered John's foster-father was beating him. Now John's maternal grandmother assumed charge, whisking the boy away from his foster-home and into the institutional arms of Dr Barnardo. 'I had not a say in the matter,' his mother assured John, insisting that he and his sisters were 'pure — free from all complaint and disease; you were never tried to be got rid of'. She asked for John's forgiveness, and a photograph of himself.

Young John wept for his mother's wretched life, and tried to save enough money to sail back to England and visit her. By the time he was able to accomplish this, she had died. John had his own brush with death during the Second World War; he was hit by a mortar bomb, and while he lay wounded in the mud, it was not his maternal mother's face that came to him, but that of his beloved Cotswold foster-mother, Rosa. He pitied his birth-mother, but he loved the woman who gave him a childhood.

It does not seem to have occurred to John to blame his mother in any way. To him, she was not feckless, just ill-used. Charles was another child migrant, dispatched to Australia in 1947. He felt the same.

When I was young I used to feel <u>bugger</u> my mother, she dumped me, I don't want to know her. But she must have felt so guilty when she had me. She was unmarried, a Catholic in Northern Ireland, she must have been under terrible pressure. I should think, from what I now know of my gran, that she said to her, 'You won't enter my house again ever if you keep the babe.'

Charles used to fantasize about the moment of reunion with his birth-mother. He would find her house, open the front door, and call, 'I'm home, Mother, I'm back!' One can imagine her humming at the sink, then turning to greet him with the sunshine streaming through the window behind her and lighting up her hair like a halo. Everything would be happy ever after, the past forgotten.

In reality, Charles — like John — was too late to meet his mother in person. She had been dead six years by the time he traced her. He bought a headstone for her grave and grieved for her, his private dream intact.

One of the criticisms levelled at Lettice Fisher when she founded the National Council for the Unmarried Mother and her Child immediately after the First World War was that she was too soft. She was told that her approach to illegitimacy was more sentimental than practical, and was more likely to encourage libertinism than to arrest it. 'You all have large hearts,' commented a cynical delegate at an Infant Welfare conference addressed by Mrs Fisher in 1919, 'but I question whether you have good brains.' Compassion was the cornerstone of the NCUMC's philosophy, however; without that, their work would have no value. The Council was founded to make life better for illegitimate children and their parents, not to cleanse them from modern society, nor to punish them for their nonconformity. It was unique in its treatment of the 'problem' of bastards, even compared with organizations like the Salvation Army and Barnardo's, in that it did not regard them as a problem at all. The problem was society's.

It is hard to imagine the NCUMC keeping records like the Fairbridge Society's, for example, where the mothers of illegitimate children were routinely described as depraved, rapacious, 'a bad character' or 'a bad lot'. The NCUMC aimed to support without patronage or censure, and they were not entirely alone. In April 1918, an inquest was held into the death of Lily Mulholland, a soldier's wife who had gassed herself. Her husband was on active service in France and had heard about her illegitimate baby. He threatened divorce proceedings, and a day or two before Lily died, she received a letter from the Army Paymaster, stopping her allowance. That letter was the catalyst for suicide, claimed the jury, and the Army needed to change both its practice and its attitude.

So did the Ministry of Health, according to the President of the Local Government Board that same year: with an astonishingly progressive outlook, he called for maternity and child welfare schemes to be made equally accessible to single and married mothers. He also wanted local authorities empowered to award grants to unmarried patients in mother-and-baby homes. This wish did not come to full fruition until the workhouses closed some thirty years later.

Members of the nursing profession had similar concerns about discrimination against illegitimate children and their mothers. From the evidence offered to me, it appears obstetric staff were as likely to be snooty as sympathetic, but the midwife who delivered Annie's baby deserves a cheer. Annie was a mill-worker in West Yorkshire, like Jessie, but when she conceived her illegitimate baby Annie was a widow, aged forty-three and with almost grown-up children. She was a big woman, able to deny the pregnancy (to herself as much as to others) by hiding the bump under the expansive apron she wore for work. When she went into labour she was on a tram. She managed to stagger home from the tram-stop and send her shocked fifteen-year-old daughter Blanche for the midwife. In came the rest of the family from work — including eldest son Sidney, who promptly announced with disgust that he was moving out. There was mayhem: shouting, groaning, recriminations and bluster, until the midwife silenced the lot of them with a good, sound telling-off. Pull yourselves together, she snapped. Never mind the whys and wherefores: you need to return some of the support Annie has given you all over the years. Stand firm, rally round, and get on with family life. So they did. Annie might have been unchaste, unwise or unlucky, but there was nothing wicked about her. She was still our Annie.

If a family closed ranks around an illegitimate child, it was for one of two reasons. Either it signalled an exercise in mass denial involving the sort of cover-stories we have already heard about, or it meant that everything was going to be all right. As all right as the circumstances allowed, anyway. Patricia was illegitimate; the father played no immediate part in her upbringing but her mother's family surrounded her with love and pride, as did the families of thousands of beloved little bastards. It is notable — but probably unsurprising — that those are the people who have asked me to use their own first names in this book. 'I'm honest,' Patricia told me, 'and my mother was always honest.' Her life had, and has, nothing to do with pretence, so she has nothing to be afraid of; no secrets to betray. Victoria feels similarly positive — although she did ask me to change her name, to protect other people. The last word, for now, is hers.

'Although life as a single parent was never exactly straightforward or easy, I realized a long time ago that I might subconsciously have been wanting a child — I certainly wanted a partner; that having one forced me to stop being a rolling stone and to settle down to make a life for my daughter and me; and although I would like to have married, I might have made an unhappy marriage and many married people are lonely or unhappy. Life is a bed of roses for very few people; we all struggle through it the best way we can and being single has its advantages:

348

independence, the ability to follow a career of my choosing, the ability to undertake adventurous travel and so on. I love my daughter and grandson profoundly; they are by far the most important people in my life.

'Who knows how my life would have turned out if I had not had a child? As it is, I feel enormously enriched.'

13

Shame and Pride: Reflections

Never mind blood versus water, nature versus nurture and all that guff. All I care about is love.

Victoria and her daughter are, and always were, part of each other's lives. For birth-parents and their children separated by adoption, migration or other long-term arrangements, that shared history does not exist. The lack of it can overshadow everything, especially in an age like ours, obsessed with ancestry and finding one's roots. A television advertisement for a well-known genealogy website has a queue of people dressed in various period costumes waiting to shake hands with a delighted young fellow in modern dress. They are all past members of the man's family, and all so *interesting:* medieval knights, Regency dandies, Victorian inventors, First World War nurses. The implication is that together, they have made him who he is. Everyone has someone to be proud of in their past. But if you are not possessed of the simplest of tools to search for that past — the true name of your birth-mother or birth-father — where does that leave you? If you were a single parent whose only perceived contribution to the family tree was the rotten fruit of illegitimacy, your sense of shame could betray any legacy of pride.

Historically the odds were stacked against such birth-parents and their illegitimate children ever being reunited and reconciled, especially if those children were born when adoption records were habitually destroyed after years; when there was no obligation to pass on any family details to former child-migrants, or when separated parent and child had neither the right nor the means to contact one another. Registered organizations like the late, lamented NORCAP (the National Organisation for Counselling Adoptees and Parents), Family Care (now known as Birthlink, Scotland) or the Natural Parents' Network, designed to help facilitate or support searches between birth-parents and their children, have only existed since the 1980s. Before the 1975 Children Act was passed, adult adoptees had no access to their original birth certificates and the right of a birth-parent to contact adult birth-children, provided those children have assented to being traced, was not enshrined in law until 2002. Before all that, there was only obscurity at worst and at best, a bewildering and dispiriting obstacle-course involving a confused mesh of red-tape, hidden trap-doors and utter inscrutability.

Whenever anyone was kind enough to respond to my request for help in researching this book, I sent them a questionnaire. As well as the usual queries about when and where and how, I asked what each respondent felt most proud of in their lives, and what caused them the most regret. For some, the fact that they found the courage to search for their birth-parents (usually their mother), or their lost child, was their proudest achievement, particularly if the search proved successful. For others, it was the fact that they never felt the need to search. They had learned how to be content without reference to their closest relative, and had come to the conclusion that blood is not thicker than water after all.

Douglas is aware that he shares his surname with his birth-father: his mother told him so. He also, as he grew up, learned the odd detail about his birth-father's legitimate family, including on one occasion the fact that a half-sibling was currently at university. When Douglas went to a conference hosted by the same university, he was astonished to realize that the room in which he was staying (during the university holidays) belonged in term-time to that very half-sibling. But he calmly did nothing about it. It remained a coincidence, rather than the catalyst for exploring a whole new area of his life. A former foundling at Coram's hospital put it like this: I've firmly shut that door. There is no need to open it again.

When listing their regrets, many parents wrote bitterly about being parted from their illegitimate babies, about the awful impotency of not knowing whether they were happy, and being ashamed of lacking the confidence to attempt contact. Almost everyone mentioned the obduracy of social attitudes in the past; how damaging maintaining an illusion of respectability could be, and how lives were corroded by secrets. They wonder at their acceptance of what adults said to them without question. In those days, before the invention of teenagers, you tended to do what you were told by your parents, even if that meant losing your child, their grandchild. Why didn't I stand up for myself? Why did I acquiesce? What would have happened had I kept my child, had I stayed with my mother, or knew who my father was? These are questions asked again and again by people still trying to come to terms with events which happened decades ago, when the social landscape was very different.

It sounds crass to say that the need to answer questions drives our preoccupation with family history; of course it does. But for everyone involved in illegitimacy, those questions assume an urgency altogether lacking for those of us simply curious about that particular part of the past belonging uniquely to us. Never mind finding out about long-lost great-uncles and cousins twice-removed; what if I have a full or half-sibling I know nothing about? Are my parents still alive? Is my child?

The fact that you do not have any idea about your medical history goes beyond embarrassment or regret. So does the possibility of unwitting incest — remote, but demonstrably present. I found a joke about that, written in 1921. A young Scottish lad was courting, and asked his father for permission to get wed. 'Father, I want to marry Janet McTavish.' 'Dinna do that, laddie,' answered his father. 'Ye canna, she's your sister.' Undaunted, he waited a few months, and then returned to his father. 'Father,

I want to marry Mary Findlay.' 'Ye canna, laddie; she's your sister.' The process was repeated once or twice, the boy always receiving the same answer. At last, he went to his mother. 'Mother', he said, 'I canna get wed, for Father says every lass in the village is my sister.' 'Nay. Laddie, dinna fret. He's not your father.'

It's funny, but also rather plausible, not just in Scotland — primitive and distant to this particular comedian — but anywhere.

Laura was very hesitant about searching for her birth-mother. She did not realize she was adopted until the age of about seven. She and her parents were visiting one of her aunts in the town about three miles away from Laura's village — the town where she understood she had been born. Laura went out to play with some local children in the street while the adults had their chat indoors. When she annoyed one of them, they started jeering at her: 'Well, you're adopted, so there!'

Laura was astounded, and ran inside to ask her parents if this was true. They were evasive. 'You are our little girl,' said Dad with a smile, while Mum asked, 'Would it matter if you were adopted?' The subject was never discussed again, but Laura saw her adoption certificate a few years later, so she knew then that it was true. When she started getting serious about the young man she would later marry, she felt it her duty to inform him of the shameful news (adoption being so often assumed to be the natural corollary to illegitimacy) but he replied that he already knew: his mother had told him. It seemed *everyone* knew but Laura, making her even more ashamed. If the subject of adoption came up amongst friends after that, she always kept quiet and changed the subject as soon as she could.

Laura told her own children when they were in their early teens. 'I made this big announcement (along with the usual tears),' she remembers. 'They just looked at me and said, 'What difference does that make?' A great relief . . . ' Her daughter Katy was keen to try to construct a family tree, but for years Laura would not let her, out of loyalty to her adoptive family. Only when her parents and aunts had died did she agree to Katy beginning the search. To Laura's amazement, she discovered that she was indeed born in the town close to the village where she grew up — she had always thought adoptions happened far away from the adoptee's birthplace — and that she was indeed illegitimate. Her mother, Brenda, had somehow managed to keep the birth entirely concealed from the rest of the family. None of them had any idea of Laura's existence when Katy eventually made contact.

In 2000, when Laura was in her mid-sixties, she met members of her birth-family for the first time. 'The emotions I went through that evening were truly off the scale! When my cousin wanted to show me a photograph of my birth-mother I had to ask her to let me prepare myself before I looked . . . I laughed at something and my cousin and aunt looked at each other and said it sounded exactly like Brenda. I said I had

355

documents to prove I was who I said I was. But they said they did not need them.

'I missed meeting Brenda by three years. I later met my half-sister and another aunt. My sister did not give our mother a very glowing report. From what she told me, Brenda always seemed to be very hard on her. Brenda also had a son, who seemed to be her favourite. I don't know if she would have agreed to meet me, but rejection is something I have feared all along and felt I couldn't take.'

It was not all about loyalty to her adoptive parents, then: in common with almost every illegitimate person who has been adopted, Laura was terrified of finding the person to whom she biologically belonged, only to be rejected by them again, this time with full knowledge and consent. In her case, she was lucky: she found her blood-relatives without having to run that risk.

For William, the need to know who his birth-mother was outweighed anything else; he spent over twenty years searching for her before successfully tracking her down, and like Laura, did not feel able to begin his quest until his adoptive parents had died. Johnny is still searching, contacting anyone he comes across with the same surname as his, even though it's his adopted surname, in case they can give him any clues about who he really is. He even went to the funeral of someone he did not know, just because of a shared name and the vague chance of a link to the past. *His* past.

* ★ ★

A fear of rejection is not unique to illegitimate children seeking their birth-parents. It works the other way round. Sensitive parents aching to contact the babies they relinquished are frightened of being blamed for a decision which in many cases was not really theirs; of being thought selfish, flighty or cruel. They worry their children will doubt their motives for wanting to get in touch by assuming it's more a selfish, conscience-salving exercise than anything to do with love. They are hesitant to crash into a carefully constructed new life as though they had some special claim to their birth-children, even though they have had nothing to do with bringing them up. They were not there for their infants, so why should they expect those infants, now grown up, to be there for them?

Hannah expresses these dilemmas beautifully. She had her son in 1963 by someone in the public eye whose mistress she had been for over a year. As soon as it became obvious that she was pregnant, and the press started sniffing around the story, he went back to his wife and Hannah was left to cope alone. He 'turned rather nasty' when the suggestion of financial support was made, and in the end Hannah and her parents decided on adoption. She wanted what she called a 'proper' home for her boy, with a mummy, a daddy and perhaps some brothers and sisters. The private agency she used assured her that the new parents would be able to afford a good education, which Hannah could not. Her gift to him was a life without her.

'After he was born, I did not see him; I knew that if I saw him, I would hold him, and if I held him I'd never let him go. Now, I would love to see him, just once, just for a few minutes. I understand that the adoption was a successful, happy one, and I do not wish to intrude in his life; I do not want to try to be his 'mother' (the woman who adopted him, who sat up at night with him when he was ill, who worried about any problems he had — she is his 'real' mother, I feel . . .). I do not even want to try to be his friend. I would just like to see him for — as I've said — a few minutes.'

Some years ago Hannah contacted her son through a professional intermediary, who talked to him and explained Hannah's wish to see him. He refused. 'I think with today's attitudes and the near normality of unmarried women having and keeping babies, he does not understand that nearly fifty years ago, although I was very willing to keep him, it was very much in his best interests that I chose to let him be adopted. I certainly did not take the decision lightly, and I certainly did not simply 'give him away'.'

Denise and Cliff's experience was different. Their son was born out of wedlock, and placed for adoption for much the same reasons as Hannah's. Denise and Cliff subsequently married, however, and now have three more children. Ten or fifteen years ago, they made the decision to find out what had happened to their first-born, and began a search on their own, which fairly quickly fizzled out due to lack of money and expertise. Then Cliff went to NORCAP, who acted as intermediaries; NORCAP located the son, and sent him a letter from Denise and Cliff, who at this stage did not know where he lived.

Their son replied, but declined to give an address. He did give permission for Denise and Cliff to correspond with him through NORCAP, and the next time he replied, the address was there at the top of his letter. Soon afterwards they met, and now Denise, recently widowed, has a warm and loving relationship with him and with her grandchildren. There is just one thing, however: the son's adoptive parents do not yet know about the contact. Neither Denise nor her son want them to feel they have somehow been supplanted in his affections. They haven't; the relationship Denise shares with her 'new' birth-family runs on parallel lines. She is not trying to be his mum, she insists. Like Hannah, she does not feel she has the right.

I have come across many sensitive stories like Hannah's and Denise's, of searches ending in reconciliation (or not); Kate's is more unusual. She was traced by her daughter, who lived on the other side of the world, in the best spirit of the television programmes *Surprise, Surprise* or *Long Lost Family*. Kate did not immediately agree to this reunion; for one thing, she had not yet told her other children that they had an older half-sister, and even though this was in the mid 1990s, she still feared the stigma that had been so prevalent thirty years before, when her daughter was born. She would have to tell all her friends, explain the circumstances, dig up the past and revisit the anguish of having lost her daughter all over again. The girl was still a family secret, Kate having promised her own mother — who was still alive — to keep it so. She says her emotions got the better of her, though; she never forgot the joy of caring for her baby during the first twelve weeks of her life (her birth-father was Asian, which in those days meant the infant took longer to place for adoption), and Kate wanted to rekindle that same feeling.

Kate and her daughter met a few times before Kate was invited overseas to stay. Their first encounters were fine, but the few weeks they spent in the same house did not go well. Kate found her daughter's emotions difficult to read; the two of them did not connect as Kate had hoped they might. And Kate found herself longing for her baby again; not for this detached, unknown adult, but for the same little person she had been when she and Kate were self-contained and all-in-all to one another.

When Kate found the courage to tell her friends about having been a single mother, they were surprisingly supportive and non-judgemental. She had counselling after returning to the UK, and now feels she understands herself and her daughter much better. She forgives herself for being persuaded by her own mother to relinquish the child. No one ever explained that there might be an alternative to adoption, and she truly believed that it would offer her daughter as good a chance of normal life as possible. Kate is now involved with a network helping other natural parents, like her, to come successfully to terms with their past. Sometimes that means meeting their birth-children, sometimes not. She feels more relaxed, now that she doesn't need to guard the secret any more.

The greatest breakthrough for Kate was acknowledging that it was not her secret, anyway: it was her mother's, for whom it was absolutely paramount that no one should ever know what had happened. Malcolm came up against the same uncompromising denial when he tried to find his birth-mother: first he traced her legitimate children, his half-siblings, but they absolutely forbade him to contact their mother, for shame. Even now, in the second decade of the twenty-first century, they cannot stand the thought of having a bastard for a brother. That is a pity: I had more responses from birth-parents and children happily reunited than from those for whom attempts to close the circle were not a success. People speak of the sense of relief, closure, confidence and peace of mind they find through forgiveness (which is what birth-parents generally seek) and absolution (which, similarly, birth-children are pleased to give). Nevertheless, it is important to realize the long shadow cast by an illegitimate birth. Some of those involved inhabit it still.

* * *

After her best-selling novel *Oranges Are Not the Only Fruit*, the author Jeanette Winterson wrote a memoir. *Why Be Happy When You Could Be Normal?* is the real-life story behind the

Oranges . . . book, describing Jeanette's search for her birth-parents. That search nearly destroyed her, she claims, both physically and emotionally. Before the mid 1970s, adoptions were based on closed records and anonymity was guaranteed to all concerned. Jeanette was adopted in 1960. She found what she thought were her parents' names on a piece of paper in a drawer in her adoptive home, but they did not match the names on her birth certificate. There followed a quest of Byzantine complexity, through all the obfuscation and misinformation of the system responsible for placing her with Mr and Mrs Winterson, before she was able to discover where she came from and who she had once been.

Jeanette found that her mother was a machinist in a factory, aged seventeen, when she gave birth. Jeanette's father had wanted to keep the baby, but this was impossible. 'My mother tried to throw me clear of her own wreckage and I landed in a place as unlikely as any she could have imagined for me.' You need to read *Oranges* . . . to appreciate just how unlikely that place was.

She did eventually trace her mother, Ann, whose first contact in response to Jeanette was a text to 'My darling girl'. They met, and immediately Ann wanted to mother Jeanette; to take her over. By their third meeting, Jeanette was shouting recriminations at Ann, and she admits at the close of the book that she has 'no idea what happens next'. It is fascinating to learn that Jeanette herself doesn't keep records of things. She burns the notes of work-in-progress when she has finished with them, and destroys diaries. It is as though her own chaotic past has made her distrustful of history itself. On the other hand Suzanna, whose mother Heidi produced a family of illegitimate half-siblings, is enchanted by genealogy. She is the faithful archivist of several generations' letters and photographs, and knows everyone's perch on the family tree. It might be a bit of a hybrid tree, but in Suzanna's care it still stands proud and upright.

Different as they are, it is tempting to ascribe both Jeanette's and Suzanna's attitudes to their own illegitimacy. Each has a heightened awareness of the part played by the past in making them who they are. There do seem to be certain characteristics shared by children born out of wedlock. Several have told me that they still feel as though they are carrying the guilt of their birth; of making their parents' lives so difficult and causing so much trouble. It does not matter how enlightened we consider ourselves now, how tolerant our society claims to be: illegitimacy can still be a live problem for the generation which was born, or gave birth, before the 1970s. 'I am so ashamed of being illegitimate myself — I am in my sixties now — that I have never had any kind of social life, or friends ever at all, in case it should be revealed by chance.' That comment was made in the 1980s, and if it is shocking to think it might have been true then, how much more shocking it is to realize that today, thirty years later, most of the people whose stories make up this book — well over 100 of them — required me to keep their names a secret, either to shield other members of their families, or themselves.

My cousin Sue reckons that her illegitimacy, and the consequent hushing-up of her past, informed her decision not to have children. She was reluctant to leave an uncertain legacy of flesh and blood to the world, since she didn't really know who she was. I have mentioned Joyce B before: she was the troublesome child who got through a total of fourteen children's homes. She did have children, but only illegitimate ones.

I don't believe in marriage. It's all the bother of getting a divorce and separation and all . . . I think there's more respect with people that are living together. I mean, they have their rows, but they seem closer together and more attached to the kids than they do when they get married. People, if they're pregnant, say they're getting married for the sake of the kids. That kid suffers more than if they didn't get married. They only get married to give the kid a name, but the kid has a name anyway.

For Adele, parenthood brought new understanding. Through the instinctive love she felt for her own child, as a single mother able to keep and care for it, she was better able to appreciate what her mother — forced to give her up — had felt for her. Yet Em feels she has no emotional bond with her children at all. Is that, as she suggests, due to her illegitimacy? Who knows.

Understandably, there is a lot of anger gusting around the subject of bastardy, even now. I use the word advisedly: those who choose to call themselves 'bastards' are usually the ones who find the stigma of illegitimacy hardest to bear. One man sent me a succinct message in answer to a general appeal for contributions: 'Parents not married, still don't know who my father is. Social services saw fit to dump me on a poor mentally ill couple who lived in extreme poverty. I am still suffering the consequences as I had to give up a good job to look after them.' And that's it. Many former child-migrants are beyond furious at the way they and their birth-parents were treated. 'What the hell [were they] playing at? I feel savage about it,' spits Charles. In the space for 'What do you regret most?' on my questionnaire, Alan simply writes, 'One loss of a childhood.'

Mike had a wonderful childhood. He has an enviably sunny personality anyway, but it cannot have been an unendingly cheerful business growing up separated from his birth-family in a succession of children's homes during the late 1940s and early 1950s. He suspects he might be half-Italian — he certainly looks it, with dark eyes and black curls — but has no knowledge of his ancestry. He only knows that he was born on a farm in Devon in 1944, then sent to Barnardo's while still an infant, first in Derbyshire and then Shropshire.

Despite memories of having soap put in his mouth when he said rude words, and being stood on top of a fragile-looking glass cover over a vertiginous stairwell for punishment, Mike says he loved being a Barnardo's boy. There was a massive garden at the Shropshire home, and no end of children to play with. But when he was seven, a taxi arrived out of the blue and took him away. They dressed him up for the journey (though failed to tell him where or why he was going) and he can imagine how he looked: an utterly bewildered little boy in horrible old NHS glasses, with wonky teeth and wearing a silly little tweed jacket — no doubt a serial hand-me-down.

Meanwhile, in a Buckinghamshire village, a couple prepared to meet their new son. Mike's mother-to-be was a remarkably strong character: she had married in 1936, and wanted children, but an accident on a motorcycle she was driving meant she was unable to conceive. During the war she and her husband looked after a couple of evacuees, one of whom had so loved the experience of being with them in the soft-lined countryside of the Home Counties that he stayed close by ever after. Following this happy episode, the couple decided to adopt. Mike's progressive mother asked for a black child, but instead she got him. Why he was chosen, from a children's home right across the country, no one knows. It is not as though Shropshire was anywhere near Mike's birthplace, so there could not have been any thought of avoiding other members of the birth-family in moving him so far away.

Whatever the reason, Mike — now a grandfather — is very grateful. His only regret in life is that his adoptive parents were not his real ones. Their love for one another was deep and mutual; Mike is one of the best-known and best-loved characters in the village. He gives talks on local history, after a career spent as an agricultural engineer. He never wanted to work anywhere but on a farm, and was intrigued to learn that he had been born on one. If anyone embodies a sense of community and deep-rootedness, it is Mike.

I suspect he is the sort of person who would make the best of any circumstance, but it is striking that in his story of illegitimacy and separation, everything seems to have worked in his favour. His was a best-case scenario. Other generous souls admit that their experience as an illegitimate child has made them extra-empathetic, good observers, non-judgemental, quick to look for the silver lining, resilient and proud. Like Mike, they consider themselves to be lucky.

The legacy for single mothers can be similarly positive, especially if they were able to keep their babies, or have managed to find them again and enjoy a redemptive relationship. The needs of single fathers are as frequently ignored in this aspect of the illegitimacy story as in so many others, incidentally. Gary Coles, in his book *The Invisible Men of Adoption*, found that most illegitimate adult adoptees professed themselves to be indifferent to their birth-fathers; to have little interest in tracing them and little understanding of any emotional damage they might have sustained. Gary, the father of an illegitimate child himself, maintains that far from being callous or uninterested, sensitive birth-fathers feel horribly guilty, or are angry. From their point of view, it is often the girl's parents who deserve much of the blame (although this wasn't so in Gary's case); even if a birth-father's family have offered to support a young couple, or the child without its mother, her parents ride roughshod over their plans and would rather have the little bastard adopted than relinquish it to the man who spoiled their daughter.

I must say that my contributors were not as defensive as Gary's appear to have been: many said they loved their fathers, even though they never knew them (maybe it's their *idea* of a father they love), and a few — like Lesley and Ingrid — define themselves to a certain extent by who their fathers were. Lesley's was a South African soldier, and her visit to his homeland late in life helped her to feel complete. Ingrid's was a Canadian, and she is delighted by the spiritual congruity of her own daughter's newly acquired Canadian citizenship. It is what her father wanted for *her*, Ingrid insists, and feels like a gift to him.

Perhaps the most widely-held and lasting legacy of giving birth out of wedlock is an inability to talk about it. Such deep and guilty secrets are hard to betray, even after a generation or two and to those who love you best. As in the case of Laura with her children, once people do find the courage for revelations, those listening tend to wonder what all the fuss is about. In fact many of us find it rather intriguing to think we might have a family member born on the wrong

368

side of the blanket. While this attitude may be refreshing and liberating, it can also seem paradoxically harsh. It begs the question of what all that suffering was for. If it doesn't really matter to people now whether you are born in or out of wedlock — in fact when the probability is that your parents *won't* be married — then how could it possibly have mattered so much then, just a few decades ago?

Comparatively few adoptions in Britain these days are occasioned solely by illegitimacy. In 1968, 12,993 bastard babies were adopted. This was supposedly the zenith of the permissive age, when public morality and pragmatism had not quite caught up with the sexual revolution in practice. Twenty-five years later, when those 1968 babies were having children themselves, the figure had dropped to 4,072. The availability of contraception and abortion played their part in this drastic fall in numbers, of course, but so did the growing liberality (or laxity, depending on your point of view) of society's attitude to marriage, divorce, and illegitimacy. Pauline A told me that she regretted her mother had to witness the moral code to which she adhered being completely destroyed in her own lifetime. This devalued everything she held dear. It also made nonsense of the sacrifices single mothers and their children had to bear.

On a more practical level, Stephanie implies that had her son's birth not been concealed, he would never have been adopted. An aunt told Stephanie years afterwards that if only she had known, she would have helped birth-mother and child to stay together. Stephanie envies today's young women, to whom it does not even occur to be ashamed of having a child out of wedlock. Mo is glad in some ways that times have changed, but cannot help feeling that they might have changed a little too much. Evelyn simply thanks God that illegitimacy just doesn't matter any more.

I wonder if that is really the case. True, there isn't even a word for illegitimacy in this context now, and it would be hard (I hope) for anyone to argue that a child should be defined by the behaviour of its parents. One can skirt round the concept, talking about children born outside marriage, 'non-marital' children, or biological ones, but there is no semantic equivalent, in its purest form, of the word bastard. Yet illegitimacy still matters in Ireland and to certain ethnic and religious minorities in British society. The problems of sponging single mums and feckless single dads are perennially discussed in Parliament and the press. The difference today is that outside those minorities, society does not generally regard this problem as a moral one. It remains an economic concern, as it has been ever since the Poor Laws of the sixteenth century, and challenges public health, given the prevalence of STDs. But it is impolite and politically incorrect to impugn someone else's morality.

The trouble is that you cannot conveniently legislate for emotions. Modern children, whose fathers are not present in their lives, can feel rejection just as sorely as any of my fatherless bastards do. We hear of married women giving birth to other men's children and so splitting families apart in clouds of betrayed trust and recrimination. There is still a sense of 'otherness' among many adopted people — children and adults — and it can take courage not to conform by having a child in your later years through IVF and without a partner, or as a same-sex parent. Society is evolving, I suppose. The worry of those who criticized the work of the National Council for the Unmarried Mother and her Child back in the 1950s and 1960s was that society would evolve ignobly, to accommodate its lowest common denominator.

* * *

One definition of stigma is 'a token of infamy or subjection', another is 'a mark of disgrace', and there can be no stigma, no infamy or disgrace, without an assumption of guilt. I began *In the Family Way* with a story about my mother, Helen, and did not imagine that I would have much occasion to mention her again, certainly not in connection with guilt. She was not illegitimate herself, nor did she have any illegitimate children. On the contrary, she did all she could to eradicate the stigma through her social work, and by bestowing one of those progressive short birth certificates on my elder sister in a spirit of solidarity with single mothers. But very recently, while visiting another cousin (not Sue, this time), I learned something about Helen which shocked me, and made me realize that she has played a far more significant part in this book than I had appreciated. It also illustrates just how fickle the concept of guilt can be.

Before returning to Helen, we should catch up with some of the other people who have figured in this book. As well as being the guardian of part of her family's history — or as much of it as can be acknowledged, given the varied parentage of her siblings — Suzanna is still a matriarchal figure, at the heart of a numerous family which gives her despair and delight in equal measure. Her defiant mother Heidi was thrown out of the Mothers' Union when her colourful history became known, so livened up the less censorious Women's Institute instead, and eventually, having reinvented herself as a respectable lady, she became a pillar of the local church establishment. She told Suzanna she blamed the local doctor for her numerous family, as he had refused to prescribe her contraceptives. When she died, there was a huge funeral. Her rather dubious parting gift to the children was an unevenly distributed legacy (most going to the boys) and a letter for everyone informing them that she was a carrier of a rare genetic disease. And still, Suzanna remembers her with admiration, and feels grateful to have been given life by such a free spirit.

Jill is the young woman who decided to keep her baby, but who struggled to find somewhere for them to live, because her parents were willing to accommodate her, even though she was determined to be independent of them. She is the one who was raped by an acquaintance giving her a lift home one night; he said he thought it would be OK because she already had an illegitimate child. Her daughter has been a constant joy.

'When she was little she had a close relationship with my mum but sadly Mum died when she was just seven. However, she then became very close to my dad who worshipped her. She did well at school, got a degree and then a Masters . . . She later gained a postgraduate degree in social work, and worked with vulnerable adults. She seems extremely well-balanced, has been with the same partner since she was nineteen and I have two lovely grandchildren. She assures me laughingly that the only thing she missed as a child was not being able to play one parent off against the other. What I said went! As for me, I eventually got married for the first time at sixty!'

Alison's twins were conceived after a date-rape. She is married now, to all appearances a normal wife and mother with children and grandchildren. Despite the love and support of a 'wonderful daughter' the grief persists, with the guilt she felt not just at being pregnant, but at viewing her unborn sons as 'an alien force' growing within her. She tells only a select few about her past — 'although I'm getting better' — and still fears judgement. She told me she was going to pass the letter she wrote to me about her experiences to the rest of the family, to give them deeper insight into what she — and so many others like her — went through. Her account was one of the most courageous I read, and included a series of poems and reflections written at the time of her sons' birth. After a visit to their grave, five weeks after they were born, she wrote this: 'I will live, and I will know joy and happiness, because they died. Thank you, my children. I <u>shall</u> live.'

Elisabeth, who had to endure botched attempts by her family to abort her illegitimate baby, is not quite ready yet — some fifty years after the event — to tell her other children about the half-sister who was born in Scandinavia. 'I don't think I'll ever make a decision. There has been so much water under the bridge. The subject is so huge and I don't know whether they would understand even though I am very close to all of them.' I wish her well.

Sarah smiles when she tells me of the looks she still gets, sometimes, when she reveals that her daughter was born while she was an unmarried teenager. Despite the imprecations of the local estate agent and the TV hire man, who considered her too morally corrupt to be a client of theirs, Sarah prospered. So did her elder daughter, who got a degree from Cambridge and is now at the top of her chosen profession. Sarah doesn't know whether her daughter has a relationship with her birth-father; that's not Sarah's business. She made sure it would be possible for the girl to do so, and left it at that. Like Ingrid, Sarah credits her feminism to her experience of illegitimacy. She has had to fight to succeed all her life, and despises what she calls the 'man-made values' which made so many innocent people suffer. By this she means the same sort of values still liable to elicit a fruity response from some of her more unenlightened (and usually male) acquaintances. She chose what values to pass to her daughter, and they were all to do with strength and integrity, not shame.

Imogen's son was born in the same mother-and-baby home as Sarah's daughter, though not at the same time, and the two women did not meet until years later. Sarah was able to keep her baby; Imogen, sadly, was not. She has been searching for him all her adult life. Every day, since she relinquished him in the early 1960s, she has thought about him and longed for information on his welfare. Her search for him through official channels was obstructed at every turn until the Adoption and Children Bill — for which she openly campaigned — was passed in 2002. That meant she was entitled to certain information from the local authorities, but beforehand, there was nothing to go on at all. During what she calls 'the unhappy years' she joined NORCAP and the Natural Parents' Network, which meant she had a better chance of being found, should her son wish to seek her. These organizations offered her moral support, but neither (at that stage) could help her look for him.

A letter in a NORCAP news-sheet reported one day that a natural parent had managed to trace her child with the help of a professional agent, so Imogen tried that. She engaged a NORCAP researcher. His work, together with the cost of obtaining copies of 298 'possible' birth certificates, came to £3,500. The one valuable piece of information he unearthed was a list of children known to NORCAP whose adoption had been arranged — like her son's — through the High Court. It was this that led, eventually, to success.

Now she had a name, Imogen remembered what Matron had said all those years ago when the baby was taken away: that the new father belonged to the profession Matron admired 'not the most, but the next most'. Imogen inferred that he must be not a clergyman, in that case, but a doctor. This knowledge helped identify her son further. Imogen was able painstakingly to begin to piece together his life-story. She discovered where he had lived at first, then where he lived next, and finally where he lived now. NORCAP offered to broker contact, but when Imogen wrote to her son, he declined to reply. She is still writing twice yearly; he remains silent.

Nothing was straightforward for Imogen. She says she would have found it so easy to take a baby from a pram in the bleak, desolate weeks after he went. Five years after he was born, a close family member adopted a son, and quite coincidentally picked for him the same name as Imogen had chosen for her boy. She wrote an article about her experiences in 1999, and when certain friends and relations read it, they agonized her by asking why ever she didn't tell them at the time. They assured her that they could have helped, if only they had known. The most heartbreaking thing Imogen told me is that even now, she still cannot bring herself to cradle a baby in her arms, and when she takes a bundle of linen from the airing cupboard and it's warm and heavy, she thinks of her boy, and the last time she held him.

The stigma of illegitimacy is as relevant to Imogen now as it ever was. Beneath the gradual enlightenment in social attitudes and the progress in provision for single parents and their children during the half-century covered by this book, there runs an undercurrent of shame. That undercurrent is given impetus by the secrets still being revealed, year by year, about illegitimacy. They might be private secrets, like Elisabeth's, told to families who are shocked, sad, excited or unsurprised. They might be public ones, like those festering away behind the squalid walls of certain children's homes or Magdalene laundries. They might even be national ones, masked by grandiose terms like Child Migration or Imperial Unity. Common to them all is the exploitation of the most vulnerable of people: the illegitimate child.

They share something else, too. This is what the recent discovery about my mother, Helen, has taught me: all these secrets could have been kept in part, at least, because of love as well as shame. Maybe the parents of the girl who fell pregnant couldn't bear anyone to know because they feared for the girl's future. They wanted to protect her. Maybe the single mother couldn't tell her subsequent children about their unknown sibling because she was afraid of rocking their foundations and making them unhappy. It is difficult to rationalize in terms of love the carer who abuses his or her charges in a children's home, or the nun who is brutally cruel to the unmarried mother in her custody, but perhaps those who committed the children or the young women in the first place might have done so because they genuinely believed it would be in their best interests.

Recent history suggests that there is no one as contemptible as the thief who stole children from their beds in Britain and sold them, essentially, to the colonies. The scandal of child migration has driven governments to unprecedented acts of public apology, and made us all uncomfortably aware of what terrible things can be done in the spotless name of philanthropy. But even this awful episode was tempered with love. This is not the sickly pronouncement of some ghastly cross between Pollyanna and a bleeding-heart liberal; I know it to be true.

I mentioned having learned something about Helen lately which shocked me. A month after they met in Cambridge, punting in opposite directions, she and my father Neil married. Soon after that Neil was posted to India for two years, and Helen — not yet twenty-one — went out to work for the first and last time. She trained in social work, and joined a team of professionals whose job it was to place children in local authority care, and then to arrange adoptions. She did not talk much about her job in later life; I know it was upsetting, and that some of the children she dealt with were terribly distressed. Her favourite trick to calm down hysterical toddlers was to shout above the screams, 'I know a dog with three legs!' It almost always worked: with mouths still open and tearful eyes grown wide, the children would be stunned into silence and fascinated by the story Helen would then proceed to tell about her beloved Staffordshire bull terrier, Biddy.

Upsetting it may have been, but Helen would not have carried on with the work had she not also found it satisfying. She had a strong social conscience, and was gratified to feel that she was playing some part in making life better by rescuing children from disadvantage. She never mentioned the mothers involved or, indeed, the fathers: the parents from whom these infants were being rescued. In those days, the late 1940s, it was all about looking ahead, not back.

A few weeks ago — as I write — my sister and I met up with a cousin who knew Helen before we did. Because this cousin worked in a similar field, she and Helen used to chat about work. At the end of the 1980s news began to filter into the public arena about the reality of child migration. She never mentioned it to us, her daughters, but according to our cousin, Helen was mortified. As a compassionate woman, of course she would be distressed: we all were. But apparently it was more than that. Helen felt guilty. Back in the dingy, austere years following the war, the promise of a new life in the sun for her wretched 'unwanted' children was hard to resist. She helped send some of those children away. Maybe she was duped by the authorities too. She obviously thought she was helping them by getting them out of England, to be transplanted in more fertile, generous soil. But it was now becoming increasingly obvious to her that instead of being an agent for good, she had helped condemn those children to greater misery than ever. Her pride turned to shame.

That must have been hard to take. The history of bastardy is ugly. Its obvious victims are the stigmatized parent and child, but spare a thought for others caught up in society's efforts to cope with it. The revolutionary change in attitude towards illegitimacy since the late 1960s should not obscure the fact that before then, it mattered more than almost any other social problem you can think of. Its implications governed people's lives, and in some cases, still does.

When the McAleese Report into Ireland's Magdalene homes published its findings in the Irish Parliament in 2013, Margaret's daughter Samantha was there. She had testified in support of her mother, along with many other courageous women committed to a Magdalene home themselves, or related to someone who was. Samantha is aware that governmental apologies can be regarded as slightly venial, as exercises in public relations, but she sensed that the Taoiseach's remorse was genuine and heartfelt. It meant so much, she says, that someone assumed responsibility for what happened, said sorry, and took the secret away. The witnesses who were ashamed to be seen going into the building to give testimony, for fear of being recognized as 'Maggies', walked out of it, after the apology, hand-in-hand with unbowed heads.

I wish the same sense of release, even pride, to all those who have contributed to this book. And in the words of one of them — Jo's daughter — who was illegitimate and does not judge: 'Thank you, Mum.'

We do hope that you have enjoyed reading this large print book.

Did you know that all of our titles are available for purchase?

We publish a wide range of high quality large print books including:
Romances, Mysteries, Classics
General Fiction
Non Fiction and Westerns

Special interest titles available in large print are:
The Little Oxford Dictionary
Music Book
Song Book
Hymn Book
Service Book

Also available from us courtesy of Oxford University Press:
Young Readers' Dictionary
(large print edition)
Young Readers' Thesaurus
(large print edition)

For further information or a free brochure, please contact us at:
Ulverscroft Large Print Books Ltd.,
The Green, Bradgate Road, Anstey,
Leicester, LE7 7FU, England.
Tel: (00 44) 0116 236 4325
Fax: (00 44) 0116 234 0205

Other titles published by Ulverscroft:

YOUNG WINSTONE

Ray Winstone and Ben Thompson

Ray Winstone's amazing talent for bringing out the humanity buried inside his often brutal screen characters — violent offender in *Scum*, wife-beater in *Nil by Mouth*, retired blagger in *Sexy Beast* — has made him one of the most charismatic actors of his generation. But how do these uncompromising and often haunting performances square with his off-duty reputation as the ultimate salt-of-the-earth diamond geezer? The answer lies in the East End of his youth: the home of gangsters, bank robbers, Bobby Moore, and family and friends who looked out for each other . . .

NOT MY FATHER'S SON

Alan Cumming

Alan Cumming's father was the dark, enigmatic heart of Cumming family life — a man who meted out violence with frightening ease. But he was not the only mystery. Alan's maternal grandfather, Tommy Darling, had disappeared to the Far East after the Second World War. When Alan's mother was thirteen, the family was informed that he had died in an accidental shooting. Curious to explore this second mystery, Alan committed to filming an episode of the BBC's *Who Do You Think You Are?*. Then out of the blue his father, whom neither he nor his brother had spoken to for more than a decade, called. He had a secret to share — one that would shock his sons to the very core, and set in motion a journey that would change Alan's life forever.